TRIBAL DEVELOPMENT SCHEMES AND PROGRAMMES

Retrospect and Prospect

ABOUT COUNCIL OF ANALYTICAL TRIBAL STUDIES (COATS) KORAPUT, ODISHA

COATS is a premier Research-*cum*-Academic Institute in the field of Tribal Studies. It is affiliated to Berhampur University, Odisha. COATS is a Registered Body under Societies Registration Act of 1860 bearing Registration No. 712/82 of 1991-92. It is situated in Koraput town in the district of Koraput, Odisha which is the heart of central tribal belt of the country.

COATS mainly aims at acquainting and educating the students, scholars and development workers about the tribal life, culture and development programmes. Presently, it imparts M.A. and M.Phil. courses in 'Tribal Studies' and its academic staff guide research scholars who are doing research leading to M.Phil. and Ph.D. degrees in tribal affairs. The Institute also undertakes District Planning and other evaluation studies entrusted by Central and State Governments. It organizes seminars, workshops and training programmes from time to time.

About the Author

Nandi KishorTandi (1965) completed his Post Graduate Degree in History in 1993 from GangadharMeher College, Sambalpur. He joined as a Welfare Extension Officer in the ST & SC Development Deptt. in 1994 and got an opportunity to serve the ST & SC downtrodden people of Odisha. He completed his M.Phil Degree in Tribal Studies from Council of Analytical Tribal Studies (COATS), Koraput in 2006 and completed his Ph.D Degree under the Joint-guidance of Dr. P.C. Mohapatro, Director, COATS, and Dr.Arunendra Nanda, Sn. Lecturer in History, Aeronautics College, Sunabeda, Koraput in 2017. At present he is the District Welfare Officer (DWO) of Nuapada District, Odisha.

TRIBAL DEVELOPMENT SCHEMES AND PROGRAMMES
Retrospect and Prospect

Nandi Kishor Tandi

Published for

COUNCIL OF ANALYTICAL TRIBAL STUDIES (COATS)
KORAPUT

By

CONCEPT PUBLISHING COMPANY PVT. LTD.
NEW DELHI - 110 059

ISBN: 978-93-5594-536-5

First Published 2023

Published and Printed by

Concept Since 1974 **Concept Publishing Company Pvt. Ltd.**
A/15-16, Commercial Block, Mohan Garden
New Delhi-110059 (India)
T : +91-11-41101460
E: publishing@conceptpub.com, W: www.conceptpub.com

Cataloging in Publication--Courtesy: D.K. Agencies (P) Ltd. <docinfo@dkagencies.com>

Tandi, Nandi Kishor, 1965- **author.**
Tribal development schemes and programmes : retrospect and prospect / Nandi Kishor Tandi.
pages cm
Study conducted in Koraput and Malkangiri districts of Odisha, India.
Includes bibliographical references and index.
ISBN 9789355945365

1. Koraput (India : District)--Scheduled tribes--Government policy. 2. Malkangiri (India : District)--Scheduled tribes--Government policy. 3. Koraput (India : District)--Scheduled tribes--Economic conditions. 4. Malkangiri (India : District)--Scheduled tribes--Economic conditions. 5. Koraput (India : District)--Scheduled tribes--Social conditions. 6. Malkangiri (India : District)--Scheduled tribes--Social conditions. 7. Rural development projects--India--Koraput (District) 8. Rural development projects--India--Malkangiri (District) I. Council of Analytical Tribal Studies (India) II. Title.

LCC GN635.I4T36 2023 | DDC 307.772095413 23

Foreword

Tribes constitute a significant percentage of Koraput region consisting of Koraput, Rayagada, Malkangiri and Nawarangpur districts. As per 2011 Census tribal population constitute more than 54 per cent of the total population of Koraput region.

The present study on Tribal Development Schemes and Programms: Retrospect and Prospect is a case study of Koraput Region. The scholar has selected two districts, four blocks and 24 villages in the multistage sampling process for a detailed study on the subject.

Ten important schemes and programmes have been selected for a detailed analysis. The limitations in the implementation of these programmes have been spelt out by the scholar. He has also provided viable suggestions for the successful implementation of the programmes.

As a Field Officer working in Koraput district for more than a decade, he has been able to pinpoint the limitations and suggest viable measures.

In addition to his field experience he has referred to almost all-important reports on tribal issues.

I hope the study will be useful for the government officials for formulation of development projects and successful implementation of the schemes and programmes.

(P.C. Mohapatro)
Director, COATS

Books from Council of Analytical Tribal Studies (COATS), Koraput, Odisha

Sl.No.	Title of the Book	Editors/Authors/Publishers
1.	Forest Management in Tribal Areas	P.M. Mohapatro & P.C. Mohapatro (Ed.) Concept Publishing Company (P) Ltd., New Delhi (1997)
2.	AmoGaon O AmoSasan (Odia)	J. Samal & N.N. Pradhan (Ed.) Hindustan Offset Printers, Jeypore, Koraput (2002)
3.	Dongar Katha (in Odia)	J. Samal Hindustan Offset Printers, Jeypore, Koraput (2002)
4.	Organisation and Management of Tribal Markets	K.K. Behera Independent Publishing Company, Delhi (2003)
5.	Tribes of Koraput	K.K. Mohanti P.C. Mohapatro & J. Samal Hindustan Offset Printers, Jeypore, Koraput (2006)
6.	Sustainable Development in Bonda Hills	P.M. Mohapatro K.K. Mohanti & P.C. Mohapatro Perfect Print and Graphics, Bhubaneswar (2009)
7.	Didayi — The Primitive Tribe	Gopinath Pradhan Hindustan Offset Printers, Jeypore, Koraput (2009)
8.	Law Preventing Land Alienation by Scheduled Caste and Scheduled Tribe	Jagannath Shroff Concept Publishing Company (P) Ltd., New Delhi (2013)
9.	Participatory and Sustainable Development among the Didayi	P.M. Mohapatro K.K. Mohanti & P.C. Mohapatro (Ed.) Concept Publishing Company (P) Ltd., New Delhi (2014)
10.	Shifting Cultivation in India — A Tribal Livelihood Alternative	N.K. Rath Concept Publishing Company (P) Ltd., New Delhi (2015)
11.	Watershed Management — Effective Tool for Sustainable Livelihood	A.K. Mohanty Concept Publishing Company (P) Ltd., New Delhi (2017)
12.	Tribal Folklore — A Study on Kuvis (Kandhas) of Koraput	Jagannath Rath Concept Publishing Company (P) Ltd., New Delhi (2019)
13.	Tribe, Poverty and Exploitation — Kandhas of Koraput District in Odisha	Jagannath Rath Concept Publishing Company (P) Ltd., New Delhi (2022)

Preface

As a field Officer in the S.C. & S.T. Development Department of Government of Odisha, I developed a keen interest to take up some research studies on the tribal development schemes and programmes. During my service period in Koraput district I completed my M.Phil. degree and started working for my Ph.D. degree in the Council of Analytical Tribal Studies (COATS) a premier Research-Cum-Academic Institution at Koraput. I received my Ph.D. degree from COATS which is affiliated with Berhampur University.

I am grateful to Prof. P.C. Mohapatro, Director, COATS who has supervised my dissertations both at my M.Phil. and Ph.D. degree. He has provided me all the important reports related to tribal problems and tribal development.

I am thankful to Prof. J. Samal for his affectionate behaviour and guidance during my research period.

I am grateful to the Principal Secretary of S.C. & S.T. Development Department of Govt. of Odisha for granting permission to take up the research work leading to my Ph.D. degree.

I am grateful to my parents who have encouraged me during my research period.

I am thankful to all the members of the staff of COATS for their cooperation in providing me necessary facilities during my research period.

I extend my heartfelt thanks to Concept Publishing Company Pvt. Ltd. for publishing this work within a short period of time.

Nandi Kishor Tandi

Acknowledgements

I gratefully acknowledge my indebtedness and deep sense of gratitude to my esteemed guide Dr. Prophullo Chandro Mohapatro, Director, COATS, Koraput and for his scholarly guidance, constructive suggestions, advice, constant encouragement and inspiration that enabled me to accomplish this endeavour. I also express my gratitude to my co-guide Dr. Arunendra Nanda, Lecturer in History, Aeronautic College, Sunabeda, for his scholarly guidance, valuble suggestions, constructive encouragement and enough inspiration to complete the thesis.

With profound honour I express my deep sense of gratitude to Dr. Jagabandhu Samal, Professor in Tribal Studies, COATS, Koraput for his helpful guidance, constructive suggestions and deep sense of eternal inspiration with encouragement for its completion.

I am also expressing my deep sense of appreciation to Sri Ashok Kumar Nanda, Sri Laxmi Narayan Padhi and Sri Gopinath Pradhan for their unhesitating help.

I acknowledge my deep sense of gratitude to my esteemed authority Dr. Gopinath Mahanty, IAS, Director ST& SC Development Department, Bhubaneswar, Odisha, who kindly granted permission to me to do Ph.D. work and encouraged me to complete this thesis.

I am also indebted to all staff of the different educational, institutions financing and programme implementing agencies as well as the respondents of the study areas for providing necessary information during my fieldwork.

I am immensely thankful to Dr. Nityananda Pradhan, Professor & Head, Department of Extension Education, North East Regional Institute of Education (NERIE), NCERT, Umiam, Shillong, Meghalaya, India for his inspiration.

I express my whole hearted sense of gratitude to my parents whose inspiration and blessings helped me to complete this book.

I am thankful for the assistance and sacrifice of my wife who has typed the work neatly. Without her help this book would not have got the final shape. I express my sincere thanks to her.

Nandi Kishor Tandi

Contents

List of Maps, Tables and Photographs

Maps

Tables

Photographs

Abbreviations

AAY	:	Antyodaya Anna Yojana
ANM		Auxiliary Nurse Midwife
APL	:	Above Poverty Line
AS		Ashram School
ATDC	:	Academi of Tribal Dialect and Culture
BBSR	:	Bhubaneswar
BC	:	Before Christ
BDA	:	Bonda Development Agency
BPL	:	Below Poverty Line
CAPART	:	Council for Advancement of People's Action and Rural Technology
CDPO	:	Child Development Project Officer
CHC	:	Community Health Centre
CMAS	:	Chasi Muliya Adivasi Sangha
COATS	:	Council of Analytical Tribal Studies
DDA	:	Didayi Development Agency
DKDA	:	Dongariakandha Development Agency
DPEP		District Primary Education Programme
DRDA	:	District Rural Development Agency
DTDP	:	Dispersed Tribal Development Programme
DWCRA	:	Development of Women and Children in Rural Areas
EAS	:	Employment Assurance Scheme
EFP	:	Emargency Feeding Programmes
EGS	:	Employment Guarantee Scheme
EMRS	:	Ekalabya Model Residential School
FAO	:	Food and Agriculture Organisation
FLR	:	Female Literacy Rate
GDP	:	Gross Domestic Product
GGHS	:	Government Girls High School
GP	:	Gram Panchyat

HH	:	Household
HQ	:	Head Quarters
IAY	:	Indira Awaas Yojana
ICDS	:	Intigrated Child Development Scheme
IGS	:	Income Generation Scheme
IRDP	:	Integrated Rural Development Programme
ITDA	:	Integrated Tribal Development Agency
IWDP	:	Integrated Waste-land Development Project
JGSY	:	Jawahar Grama Samriddhi Yojana
JRY	:	Jawahar Rojgar Yojana
KS	:	Kanyashram School
LAMP	:	Large Sized Multipurpose Cooperative Society
LI Points	:	Lift Irrigation Points
LSDA	:	Lanjia Soura Development Agency
MADA	:	Modified Area Development Approach
MBPY	:	Madhu Babu Pension Yojana
MDM	:	Mid-day-meals
MFP	:	Minor Forest Produce
MGNOAP	:	Mahatma Gandhi National Oldage Pension
NFBS	:	National Family Benifit Scheme
NFFWP	:	National Food For Work Programme
NGO	:	Non Governmental Organisation
NIRD	:	National Institute of Rural Development
NMBS	:	National Maternity Benefit Scheme
NREGS	:	National Rural Employment Guarantee Scheme
NREP	:	National Rural Employment Programme
NSSO	:	National Sample Survey Organisation
ODP	:	Odisha Disability Pension
OSFDC		Odisha Scheduled Caste Finance Development Co-operation
OTELP	:	Orissa Tribal Empowerment Livelihood Programme
PBDA	:	Poudi Bhuyan Development Agency
PC	:	Percentage
PDS	:	Public Distribution System
PESA Act	:	Provisions of the Panchayats (Extension to the Scheduled Areas) Act
PHC	:	Public Health Centre
PIA	:	Programme Implementing Agency
PMS	:	Pre-Matric Scholarship
PRI	:	Panchayati Raj Institution

PSH	:	Primary School Hostel
PSM	:	Panchayat Samiti Member
PTG	:	Primitive Tribal Group
RLEGP	:	Rural Labour Employment Guarantee Programme
RS	:	Residential School
SC	:	Scheduled Castes
SCA	:	Special Central Assistant
SCSTRTI	:	Scheduled Castes and Schduled Tribes Research and Trining Institute
SGRY	:	Sampurna Grameena Rojgar Yojana
SGSY	:	Sampurna Gramya Swarozgar Yojana
SHG	:	Self Help Group
SMPT	:	Special Multipurpose Tribal Development Block
SOAP	:	State Oldage Pension
SS		Seva Sharam
ST	:	Scheduled Tribes
TD	:	Tribal Development
TD Blocks	:	Tribal Development Blocks
TRYSEM	:	Training of Rural Youth for Self Employment
TSA	:	Tribal Sub-plan Approach
TSP	:	Tribal Sub-Plan
UGPHC	:	Up-Graded Primary Health Centre
UNDP	:	United Nations Development Programme
UNICEF	:	United Nations International Children's (Emergency) Fund
WHS	:	Water Harvesting Structure
WP	:	Widow Pension
ZP	:	Zilla Parishad
ZPM	:	Zilla Parishad Member

1
Introduction

1. Introduction

Tribes are an integral part of Indian Civilization. Their cultural integrity in diversities of their languages and physical characteristics is unique. They possess a very rich cultural heritage which has survived through the ages. The first Prime Minister of India, Pandit Jawaharlal Nehru while addressing a conference in 1952, had said "I am not at all sure which way of living is better, ours or theirs. But in some ways I am quite certain, theirs is better. A great deal of things can be learnt from their culture" (R.C. Verman, 1995). These words are highly relevant in the present scenario for proper appreciation of their culture and values. In order to preserve their cultural integrity and inner values they have developed some habit of quiet withdrawal. This habit is often misinterpreted for isolation or aloofness which is not correct. Tribals are notable for their adaptation in their physical environment. They have a symbiotic relation with the natural setting having unique love for their homeland, its forest, hills, rivers, caves, springs etc. It is very difficult to understand their love for their home land which amount to mystical identification with nature. The tribals are peace loving and their feelings are naturalistic. The love of nature and the solidarity find expression in various forms of arts, dance and rituals; they have natural gifts of various handicrafts, hunting skills and martial arts. The ancient and medieval sources of information including the Vedic and Epics literature mentioned various tribes were homogeneous and self-contained unit without any hierarchical discrimination. Each tribe enjoyed equal status, with the growing need of protection; each tribe was organized under their chief. The most capable person of their society is being selected as the chief by the members of the concerned communities. Gradually, the chief started wielding power over his people and assumed certain privileges for himself. Each tribe has its own system of administration. There was decentralization of authority among the tribes. The traditional tribal institutions were vested with legislative, judicial and executive powers. At present, the term tribe according to writers, generally means an ethnic group, geographically isolated or semi-isolated, identified with one particular territory and having distinct social, economic and cultural traditions and practices. In the Indian context, the term has undergone further change, particularly in post-independence period.

Tribes are called variously in different countries. For instance, in the United States of America they are known as "Red Indians", in Australia, as "Aborigines", in the European countries "GYPSYS", in the African and Asian countries known as Tribes. India has the second largest concentration of tribal population after that of African continent. The Indian tribes are the autochthonous people of the land who are believed to be the earliest settlers in Indian peninsula. In India they are generally called "Adivasis" implying original inhabitants. However, under the Constitution of India, people belonging to various tribes have been specified as "Scheduled Tribe". The tribes live in the forest, hills and natural isolated regions known by different names meaning either the people of forest and hill or the original inhabitants and so on. The popular names are Vanyajati (castes of forest), Vanvasi (inhabitants of forest), Pahari (hill dwellers), Adimjati (original community or primitive people), Adivasi (First settlers), Janajati (Folk people), Anusuchit Janajati (Scheduled Tribes) and so on. Among all these terms, Adivasi is used most extensively. Scheduled Tribe is the constitutional name, covering all tribes. Scheduled Tribes have been specified in all states and union territories except the states of Haryana, Punjab and Union Territories of Chandigarh, Delhi and Pondichery. In terms of the Constitution, Constitutional safeguards are applicable to only those Tribes who have been specified as Scheduled Tribes under the Presidential orders issued from time to time since 1950.

From time immemorial, the tribal people like to settle themselves in the dense forest and highland area of the country. The forest provides them food and shelter, they collect fruits, roots, tubers, leaves fibers herbs, honey, and wax etc. Besides these, the forest provides them the housing materials like timbers, bamboos and other many housing materials as well as grazing facilities to their domestic animals. According to the 2011 Census, the Tribal population of the State is 95.91 lakh which account for 22.85 per cent of the state population and 9.20 per cent of the tribal population of the country. There are as many as 62 Tribal communities including 13 primitive tribal groups in the **State of Orissa**. About 44.12 per cent of the State's geographical area is covered under Tribal Sub-Plan Area. In term of the tribal population, Odisha ranks third tribal concentrated state in the country. There are about 461 principal tribal groups concentrated in different parts of the country. Out of these 62 ethnic groups are found in the

State of Orissa. The tribal population is predominantly rural. As per 2011 Census, 93.79 per cent of tribal population are dwelling in rural areas. The population density per sq.km is also low and it varies from place to place like 91 in Kandhamal district, 106 in Malkangiri and Debagarh districts, 217 in Keonjhar and 214 in Sundargarh districts in 2011 Census. Besides, the forest products the tribal people depend on Agriculture, hardly 6.21 per cent of tribals are urban based as against 26.80 per cent of total population of the State. According to 2001 Census, the Tribals with their traditional skills and practices are very much acquainted with the shifting cultivation system. Frequent deforestation since pre-independence deprived the tribal people to get sufficient resources for their day to day life. On the other hand, the tribal people were deprived from the forest and forest products due to the adoption of different Forest Acts and policies during the British period.

1.1 Definition of Tribe

W.J. Perry defines "tribe as a group speaking a common dialect inhabiting a common territory." (Bhowmik, L.K. 1971)

D.N. Majumdar defines a "tribe as a collection of families or groups of families bearing a common name, members of which occupy the same territory, speak the same language and observe certain taboos reading marriage, profession or occupation and have developed a well-assessed system of reciprocity and mutuality of obligation." (Majumdar, B.N. 1980)

Dr. Revers defines a "tribe a social group of a simple kind, the members of which speak a common dialect and act together for such common purpose as welfare."

The Imperial Gazetteer had defined a "tribe as a collection of families bearing a common name, speaking a common dialect, occupying or professing to occupy a common territory and which is not usually endogamous, though originally it might have been."

Kamala Devi Chattopadhyaya defines a "tribe as social group usually with a definite area, dialect, cultural homogeneity, and unifying social organization. It can include several sub-groups."

1.2 Tribal Conditions in pre-Independence Era

The tribal people living in the remote hills and forests for many centuries led a life of their own and struggled for their existence. Generally, uninfluenced by the main currents of developments outside, it was with the entry of the missionaries into these areas that the officers of the administration started paying some attention to them. But this contact was only superficial and prompted them to come to some equally superficial and conclusions. The foremost of which was to isolate these people from the rest of their countrymen and separate the tribal areas from the purview of the normal administration. The people in the plains were either too subdued or too ignorant to mind what happened. If the administration contributed to the difficulties of the tribal people by its policy of isolation, the people of the plains added to the problem by their conscious and unconscious neglect.

The British policy of isolating the tribes resulted in exploitation. The technique was simple. Zamindars, landlords, money-lenders and contractors exploited the tribal to the maximum. The programme of conservation and preservation of forests resulted in a progressive encroachment on the rights enjoyed by the tribal for centuries past in respect of the use of fuel and timber, exploitation of minor forest produce and hunting. The impact of this was felt by the tribals who could not take kindly to this policy of intrusion which shook their last foothold of sustenance. The British could not control the Zamindars and Jagirdars in the management of their private forests which in turn intensified the suspicion in the tribal mind. The coming in of the contractor, who carried away the profit of forest produce, resulted in sordid exploitation. It was not unnatural that these incursions into tribal rights over forest resulted in sporadic relationship which eventually led to a dislocation of the tribal economy and consequent frustration in the Tribal mind, yet in the name of safeguarding them from the possible consequences of incursions of non-tribal they were cut from the main currents of Indian social and economic life. What the tribal people needed was not isolation but planned contact on the basis of a positive policy of economic progress. Even the tribal people were not adequately represented in the legislatures and local bodies. (Dheber Commission Report, 1961).

1.3 Colonial Economic Policies

In the colonial economic policy, the tribals were badly affected. The Forest Act of 1855, 1865, and 1878 paved the way for the regulation of rights and restriction of privileges of forest dwellers over forest land and forest product. Finally, they were deprived from the forest right and faced serious problems. The low price of raw materials on which the economy of most Third World countries depend and the refusal of the rich countries to fix their floor price. Protectionism and the bias against any processed product coming from the Third World by taxing them and allowing in only raw materials. The tribals were exploited by middlemen, contractors and landlords.

1.4 Shifting Cultivation

The shifting cultivation is an important source of livelihood of the tribal people. Around twenty per cent tribal population are depending on shifting cultivation. In this system, cultivation is made for two to three years consecutively and the land is left fallow for a period of 6 to 20 years. But over the years increase in tribal population and shortage of land this podu cycle period has been reduced to 2 to 3 years and in some case one year. The income from the shifting cultivation has reduced. As a matter of fact, the economic condition of the tribal people depending upon the shifting cultivation became deplorable. The shifting cultivation systems resulted in deforestation, soil erosion, diminished rainfall, silting up of the rivers, reservoirs and deterioration of the climatic condition of a region. The promulgation of stringent forest law completely banned the shifting cultivation in the new area, so it has created tremendous problems of food insecurity to the tribal and their standard of living become very deplorable.

1.5 Socio-cultural Dimensions of Tribal Problems

The Scheduled Tribe is distinct ethnic group without any stigma of unsociability or hierarchical inferiority. Some Indian writers have not only denied an independent social status to the tribal but have described them as "Backward Hindu." This amount to assimilation of tribals into dominant Hindu society. Such an approach will lead to extinction of tribal culture, religious belief, traditions, lifestyle and obliterate all distinctions between castes and tribes. The tribals are very much agitated over such an approach. They are fully aware of the plight of the untouchable even though unsociability has been abolished and would not like to become one of them. Pandit Nehru, the first Prime Minister of India was opposed to imposition of any things on the tribal.

The wasteful customs, marriage, death and religious ceremonies further aggravated their deficit nature of economy and compelled them to borrow. The implementations of commercial vending of liquor in Tribal areas have started impoverishing the tribal population, making them victims of indebtedness and exploitation.

1.6 Land Alienation Among the Tribals

The land alienation of tribal is an important one among the tribal problems. The cause for and the process involved in the alienation of tribal land point out in every graphic manner the disequilibria in the power balance in operation between the socially, educationally and politically powerful landlord and the powerless tribals. Mostly, the money-lenders, landlords, village Sahukars, liquor vendors have played vital role to make the tribal became landless labour by giving their crops in part or whole to the creditor by selling it to them at the low rate. This is mainly due to loopholes of existing law the tribal land continued to alienate in favour of non-tribals. In the wake of development process, a large chunk of fertile tribal land has been acquired by the Government for industrial, irrigation, power, mining and other projects. In this way, the displaced tribals were hit hard by the withdrawal provision. The process was further facilitated by the bureaucracy at the time of the land settlement which took place in 1968-69. The settlement officers ruled in most cases in favour of the outsiders, as the tribals were unaware of the manipulative tactics employed by the Sundhies. Consequently large tract of land belonging to the tribal were transferred to the non-tribals and the original owner cultivators of the area were rendered landless .

1.7 Indebtedness

Indebtedness is another major problem among the tribals. The subsistence type of agriculture on which they mainly depend and the absence of any viable subsidiary employment opportunities makes the tribal economy perpetually a deficit one. Their wasteful custom of marriage, death and religious ceremonies further aggravates their deficit nature of economy. The initiation of commercial vending of liquor in tribal areas have started impoverishing the tribal population, making them victims of indebtedness and exploitation .Orissa money-lender regulation, 1967 (Regulation 2 of 1968) was in operation since 15th November, 1968 with a view to regulating and monitoring money-lending activities of the Scheduled Areas of the state. The state government has enacted the Orissa Debt Relief Act, 1980 which have been in force since 13th March, 1981, with a view to providing relief to small farmers, rural artisans and agricultural labourers to wean the tribes from indebtedness. Any debt incurred by a Scheduled Tribe before the commencement of the Act including the amount of interest were waived.

1.8 Bonded Labour System

Indebtedness has led to degenerated system of labour known as bonded labour which is locally known as "Goti or Halia". This is a system where the labourer has to work for the land owner, money-lender or his master. In view of interest on the loan taken by him or the loan received by his forefathers or both. This system has been prevalent in the state since time immemorial and a poor tribal becomes often its victim. As the tribals are uneducated and most probably illiterate they are ignorant about the proper account, so when they were taking the loan from the Zamindar and village Sahukar, it was easy to cheat the tribal, the system is the result of indebtedness which has been prevailing for a long period among certain economically exploited and weaker sections of the society. Gandhi Peace Foundation, which had conducted a survey in 1978-79 in the ten states of Andhra Pradesh, Bihar, Gujarat, Karnataka, Madhya Pradesh, Maharastra, Orissa, Rajasthan, Tamil Nadu and Uttar Pradesh have estimated the number of bonded labours at 26.17 lakh (R.C. Verman). However, according to the government sources, the total number of bonded labour, identified by the end of March 1988 was about 2.36 lakh, out of which 2.02 lakh have been rehabilitated. (Report of the Commissioner for Scheduled Caste and Scheduled Tribe 27th Report, Part-I, 1979-80). Article 23 of the Constitution prohibits beggar, traffic in human beings and forced labour. This expression has wide implications and includes not only prohibition of slavery but also traffic in human beings for immoral and other purposes. With the enactment of Bonded Labour System (Abolition) Act, 1976, the bonded labour system has been abolished in the country.

1.9 Displacement

The most significant problems of the tribal people is the displacement which led to forced or voluntary eviction of them from their land and natural habitat and subsequently rehabilitation has been a serious problem, that remains to be addressed by the Government of Orissa. In between 1951 to 1990, nearly three lakh eighty thousand people have been displaced as a consequence of seventy major and medium irrigation projects (Walter Fernandes & Md. Asif). As a matter of fact, the major percentage of the tribal people faced the socio-economic and environmental problems which led them into impoverishment.

The Balimela Dam Project in the tribal concentrated zone in Koraput region was started in the year 1962-63 which affected 91 villages, thus evicting 1200 families (Alternate government source 2000 families) in the process 17,180 ha. of land had been acquired by this project (Walter Fernandes & Md. Asif : 1997). As per the document of the Government of Orissa, the Upper Kolab multipurpose project in Koraput district submerged 11,350 Ha. of land. 3179 families were displaced of which 1421 families (44.7%) were Scheduled Tribes, 442 Scheduled Caste (13.9%) and 1316 other castes. Further due to establishment of the Nalco Company at Damanjodi under the Koraput district, 1076 Scheduled Tribe, 234 Scheduled Caste and 1058 other caste people were displaced (Walter Fernandes and Mohammed Asif : 1997).

Like the dam project and Nalco Company many people were displaced for the establishment of the Aero-Engine Factory in the Koraput district.

The construction of Telingiri Dam Project at Ranigada under Jeypore panchayat samiti of the Koraput district in the year 2002 has projected to complete the project work in the year 2010-11 covering 500 ha. for its reservoir. For which 8 villages from Jeypore Block and Koraput Block have been affected and 566 families will be displaced (Telingiri Project, Jeypore).

1.10 Impact on Tribal Women

In the tribal society the tribal women play a key role for day-to-day management of their family. She performs different activities of her family towards cooking food, collecting minor forest produce, fire wood and selling the same in the nearby markets and purchase necessary materials of her family. So the woman is more responsible than the male in the tribal family.

Due to the displacement while all the tribals suffer, women are the worst victims of the present pattern of development in general and that of deforestation and displacement in particular. In the traditional division of work it is the women's role to make provision for basic necessities, like food, fuel and water. Among the tribals food was obtained mainly from the forests which are close to their villages. Hence, the economic demands of shifting cultivation and collecting fire wood did not clash with the other household duties of the women. With deforestation the distance of forest from the villages has increased. This has established the close social and economic relationship between the tribal women and the forest. Because of the greater distance of the forest and the paucity of resources, the woman has to work more for less food.

1.11 Forest Policy and Deprivation of Forest Right

The traditional symbiotic relationship between tribal and forest has been completely shattered due to drastic policy changes, their traditional forestry right have been reduced to mere concession. Due to incomplete survey and settlement operations and records of rights, lands traditionally held and cultivated by the tribals have been claimed as forest land under the new forest policy. Consequently, a large number of tribals occupying forest lands have been turned into encroachers on their own land. The traditional protectors of the forests have been branded as the destroyers of the forest.

Before entry of the British in India, there was only regulation by custom of the people's right over forest and forest product. The tribal people had complete freedom to enjoy forest wealth. But after the advent of British, the British rulers issued a number of memorandums regulating the movement of forest dwellers. The Forest Acts of 1855, 1865, 1878 etc. paved the way for the regulation of rights and privileges of forest dwellers over forest land and forest produce. 37.36 per cent of the total geographical area of the state being covered under forests, which is an important aspect of the tribal economy. The forest provides food and shelter during the need of the tribals. They collect the fruits, roots, tubers, leaves, fibers, herbs, honey, wax, host and animals for maintaining their livelihood. Besides these, the forest provides them the housing materials like, timber, bamboo and other housing materials. The forest not only provides them the above materials but also provides grazing facilities for their cattle and different medicinal herbs for treatment of their different diseases. But due to the adoption of forest policy by the British Government, the tribal people were deprived from the forest product and gradually their socio-economic condition and standard of living became very deplorable.

1.12 Migration of Tribal Labour

The migration of tribal labour is also significant problem among the tribals. This has assumed serious proportion. Several factors like erosion of the resource base, alienation of land, restrictions of rights over forest produce and lack of employment opportunities in the areas of their domicile have forced the tribals to seek jobs outside the region especially in the enterprises employing unskilled labourers, like brick kilns, agriculture and excavation work. In the wake of development activities, a large number of industrial, mining, irrigation, power and other projects, are coming up in the tribal areas but the tribals have not been benefited by the new opportunities mainly because of the lack of required skills, training and other wherewithal to participate in the new ventures. Their unpreparedness to face the socio-economic and cultural impact of the process of the industrialization has also been partly responsible for their migration to other areas. Besides large scale displacement of the tribals from their lands have forced them to migrate in search of employment. But in the process they are badly exploited by their employers and even the public functionaries coming in contact with them. They are not paid even the minimum wages and are forced to work against their will even though they are not physically fit due to illness or other reasons. If they show any slackness, they are physically assaulted.

1.13 Health Problems

The monographs left by administrators and anthropologists reveal that the tribal people generally led a healthy life though some of them suffered from manifold diseases like malaria, scabies, leprosy, tuberculosis, venereal diseases and black water fever. The incidence of malaria is high in almost all the tribal areas. It is stated by many authorities that the spread of venereal diseases and tuberculosis in the tribal areas was the result of outsiders entering them.

In order to cure the diseases they mostly depend on their traditional priests and medicine men. They also used herbal remedies. Except for a few sporadic efforts by the Government and Christian missionaries, no organized endeavour seem to have been made before independence to provide medical services in tribal areas (Dheber Commission Report : 1960-61).

The health problems of the tribal people are another important factor. The major difficulties are that, they do not go to hospitals or use modern medicine. They prefer to go to their own traditional medicine man. Secondly, the conception of disease in tribal society is that, it is caused by hostile spirit or due to breach of any taboo, what is spiritually caused must be spiritually cured. So they want to use their own traditional medicine and *guni garadi*. On the other hand no medical team and doctor can visit their village easily by crossing the impassable road. The tribal people also are unable to cross the impassable road along with the patient. So they are facing many difficulties regarding their health problems in spite of sincere efforts made by government to open PHCs and CHCs as well the ANM centres in the tribal area. The male health worker, female health worker and the Anganwadi workers are frequently visiting the villages, immunization and vaccination programmes are being taken up continuously. Still the tribal people are depending upon their own traditional medicine man.

1.14 Drinking Water

Availability of drinking water facilities among the tribals is another important problem since long. Supply of drinking water has always been a serious problem in the difficult terrain of the tribal areas. This has been one of the reasons for spread of intestinal diseases. Most of the tribal villages in the hilly areas generally use the spring based water available in their locality or open well. Due to lack of favourable communication no machines are being send to the hilly area villages to dig the tube well. So due to non-availability of tube well water, the people use the spring, river and open well's water for their drinking and other purposes.

1.15 Consumption of Liquor

Consumption of liquor is very common in a tribal society. It is closely linked with all the religious and cultural festivals of tribals. From the birth till death, in every festival liquor constitute an important item. The children and women also take liquor during observation of some religious and cultural festivals. So long as they were preferring their liquor from Mahua flower, they were able to manage without any difficulty. But with the introduction of wine vending by outsiders, they started borrowing money and suffered from a deficit economy. Due to their wasteful customs of marriage, death and religious ceremonies, which are generally beyond their means further aggravated the deficit nature of their economy and compelled them to borrow (P.C. Mohapatro, 1987 : 175). Indebtedness has led to a degraded system of labour known as bonded labour and ultimately led to alienation of land from tribals to non-tribals.

1.16 Endangering of intellectual Right

The traditional knowledge of the tribal on the forest eco-system is very deep. They know the intricacies of the relationship among the living components of environment. In this process, the tibals have developed invaluable indigenous knowledge, which has passed from generation to generation through the medium of oral tradition. Folklore and folk tales which find a place in various life cycle events including treatment of diseases. Though the tribals depend on the biological resources, their life style and livelihood is very much shaped by these resources. Thus, their survival and subsistence is closely linked to conservation and utilization of these resources. However, they do not have any codified text of rights to accredit their legitimate ownership (P.C. Mohapatro, 2009 : 36).

1.17 Ineffective Implementation of PESA Act, 1996

The 73rd and 74th Constitutional Amendments of 1993 followed by the Panchayat extension to scheduled area through the panchayat (Panchayat Extension to Scheduled Areas) PESA Act, 1996 are landmark achievements in the process of decentralization of power and authority to panchayats and Gram Sabha. In addition the Government of Orissa recently have transferred power of more than eighteen departments of the State Government to the different tiers of the Panchayati Raj Institutions. These include some specific aspects of departments like Agriculture, Cooperation, School and Mass Education, Food Supply and Consumer Welfare, Scheduled Caste and Scheduled Tribe Development Department, Health & Family Welfare, Women & Child Development Department, Fishery and Animal Resources Department, Rural Development, Panchayati Raj and Water Resource. However, the State Government has to take appropriate measures to transfer the other powers in the list of panchayat bodies as per the guideline of the Constitutional Amendment to enable the tribals to have say in their own affair.

Active participation of people in the process of planning and development of their own problems will go a long way for accelerating the process of economic development in the tribal areas. The concept of Gram Sabha has to be made a reality in the village level. Though the PRI members have been elected from the tribal communities still they are not properly exercising their power and position. Somewhere it is seemed that the tribal PRI Members are completely ignorant about the PESA Act, 1996 and became puppets in the hands of block officials and PEOs as well as other PRI members.

1.18 Educational Problems

Education is the key catalyst for the development of human resources. Lack of education is largely responsible for the exploitation and pitiable plight of the tribals. Thus, Education is the pivot on which their success depends, which disseminates knowledge, knowledge gives inner strength which is very essential for the tribals to attain freedom from exploitation and poverty. Due to ignorance arising out of illiteracy, the tribals have not been able to take advantage of new economic opportunities. Low progress of literacy is an another major problems of the tribals in Koraput region. Following are some of the important reasons for the low progress of education and literacy: (a) Poverty of the parents, (b) Inadequate educational institution and supporting services, (c) Absenteeism of students and teachers, (d) Problems of medium of instruction, (e) Insufficient teaching staffs in the educational institution, and (f) Lack of sufficient reading and writing materials and communication facilities.

1.19 Unemployment

The Scheduled Tribe population is predominantly rural, as per the 2011 Census—93.7 per cent of tribal population live in rural areas as against 85 per cent per cent in respect of general population. As per the 2011 Census, 80 per cent of workers among Scheduled Tribe population of the state depend on agriculture either as cultivators or agricultural labours. Displacement or forced/voluntary eviction of tribals from their land and the tribal land alienation are the main factors to create unemployment among the tribal people. Large scale land alienation from tribal to non-tribals has taken place during the British rule. Indebtedness, *benami* transactions and tempering of records by influential landlords are some of the important reasons for such land alienation. As a matter of fact, many tribals lost their landed property and became unemployed. The collection of minor forest produce was an important part of the tribal livelihood. Before entering the British in the India, the tribal people had complete freedom over the forest to enjoy forest wealth. The tribal people were collecting the fruits, roots, tubers, leaves, fibres, herbs, honey, wax, and animals for maintaining their livelihood. But the British rulers had issued a number of memorandums regulating the movement of forest dwellers. The Forest Acts of 1855, 1865, and 1878 paved the way for the regulation of rights and privileges of forest dwellers over forest land and products. This resulted in restriction of forest rights and loss of livelihood of the tribals.

1.20 Communicational Difficulties

Generally, the tribals are dwelling in the hilly and forest area, where there are no communication facilities with outside world. The significance of the conspicuousness, lack of means of communications in the tribal areas needs to be emphasized. Few of the tribal areas of the country are approachable by rail-line or all weather roads. The roads are often bad and unusable during the rains. For which tribal areas of the country are completely isolated from outside world for long periods on account of rains and floods. The absence of permanent and easy means of communication and transport tend to limit the economic horizons for the tribals. The lack of good communication system led the tribals into the various problems, during the health hazard or epidemic, the tribal people dwelling in the impassable areas face difficulties to get the required treatment during the need. Further they are deprived from the education, sanitation and different economic activities.

1.21 Unfavourable Markets and Money Economy

The tribals of the different areas of the country depend upon the marketing facilities, for sale and purchase of their different forest products. But due to lack of communication and market facilities the village mahajan-cum-middleman and petty traders are the main purchaser of their agricultural and forest produces. The lack of marketing facilities due to the inadequate communication and transportation facilities tend to compel them to sale their products at a very low price, very often at a throw away price and purchase their necessities at an exorbitant price. Their transactions are confined to their immediate vicinity and characterized by the compulsions of speedy disposal and their lack of bargaining capacity. The co-operative structure including the LAMPS in tribal areas has failed to extricate them from this pathetic dependence on village mahajans and petty traders. Taking the advantage of lack of communication and marketing facilities, the village mahajan and petty traders are exploiting the tribals.

1.22 Backdrop of Koraput Region

Koraput region, a part of Dandakaranya, described in the holy epic *Ramayana* has a hoary past and rich cultural heritage. History records that this area was known as "Trikalinga' which formed part of the empires of Satavahanas, Vakatakas, Nalas, Marathas, Eastern Gangas, Chalukyas, Somavamsis, Gangas, Kalachuris, Chindikanagas, Matsya dynasty, Silavamsis and lastly the Surya Vamsis (Solar dynasty). The 32-steps throne (Battisa Simhasana) at Nandapur is ascribed to the Sila dynasty rulers who with their power and pelf emulated the glory of the famous king of Ujjain. The Matsya and Sila dynasties merged into one in the early 15th century and the monarchs were acting as the 'Chief Feudal Lords' of the Southern dominions of the Gajapati kings of Kalinga (Orissa). As many as 25 rulers belong to the Solar race ruled over Jeypore estate (Koraput District) from 1443 A.D. to 28.12.1952. Then the estate vested in the State Government under the provisions of the Orissa Estates Abolition Act on 29.12.1952, the Jeypore estate was taken over by the Government. Ten 'Anchals' were formed for managing the affairs of the vested estate and regular Ryotwari system of administration, which was introduced with effect from 14.11.1957. (The old Koraput district comprising 17 Tahsils, six Sub-Divisions and 42 Blocks, split up into four new districts, namely Koraput, Malkangiri, Nabarangpur and Rayagada on 2nd October, 1992). It may be mentioned here that Koraput district is declared as a 'Scheduled Area' under the paragraph 6 of the Fifth Schedule to the Constitution of India. Koraput district (the former Jeypore Estate), separated out of Vizagapatnam district under the erstwhile Madras Presidency, was included in the state of Orissa in pursuance of the notification No.18, dated 1.4.1936 of the Government of Orissa. The district was further divided into four districts, viz. Koraput, Malkangiri, Nabarangpur and Rayagada with effect from 2nd October, 1992 *vide* notification No. 49137/R of Revenue and Excise Department, Government of Orissa, Bhubaneswar.

The green meadows, dams, reservoirs, rapids and falls, the high ranges of mountains, elevating ghat roads spirally ascending lofty hills and descending steep valleys, and many sophisticated railway tunnels of this area has its own appeal to the visitors. The environment with its mystery and enchantment as well as landscape with peaks as high as 5486 feet in the undulating terrain of a peculiar geographical setting identified these lands as nature-lover's paradise. The aboriginals, the prime inhabitants of this area of antiquity, termed as 'Adivasis', the first settlers of this region. Their culture and religion revolve round the forests, hills, mountains, rivers and lands, which they deem it as nature's gift to them. It may be pertinent to mention that 'Bonda', one of the tribes living in Khairaput area, is recognized as the pioneer of rice producers in the world. In fact, the history of the tribals *vis-à-vis* Koraput territory is synonymous. The tribals played a significant role in the freedom struggle during 1942, where many lost their lives.

1.23 Composition and Demography of Tribes in Koraput Region

Koraput region is mainly inhabited by tribal population. Out of 461 tribal communities in India (Singh, 1994:2) 62 are found in Odisha. In Koraput region more or less 61 tribes are found except Mankirdia tribe in 2001 Census. However, Koraput Region is the home land of eighteen tribal communities. They are Bhattora, Bhumia, Bonda, Dharua, Didayi, Gadba, Gond, Holva, Jatapu, Kandha, Kanda-dora, Kotia, Koya, Omanatya, Parenga, Poroja, Pentia and Saura (Mohanti *et al.*, 2006). As per the 2011 Census, the total population of Koraput region is 41,81,696. Its district break up is 13,79,647,613,192, 12,20,946 and 9,67,911 for Koraput, Malkangiri, Nabarangpur, and Rayagada districts respectively. As per 2011 Census, 54.41 per cent of the total population of the undivided Koraput district were tribals. If we add the Scheduled Caste population to it then 69.99 per cent would belong to backward population. In 2011 Census, there has been a increase the percentage of both Scheduled Tribe & Scheduled Caste population in Koraput region from 69.30 per cent in 1991 Census to 69.99 per cent. Another feature of the region is that nearly 88.78 per cent of the people live in the village area. Hence, the region is rural in character.

Out of 62 different Scheduled Tribe communities, 13 are belonging to primitive tribal groups. The Tribal communities show a great variety of interesting features, in their social structures, cultural patterns, economic pursuits, belief systems, art and dance forms and magico-religious practices. They are fond of primitive hunting, food gathering and shifting cultivation practices. The primitive tribal groups are Bonda, Didayi, Dongria Kondh, Lanjia Soura, Soura, Kutia Kandha, Juanga, Lodha, Hill Kharia, Mankirdia, Paudi Bhuyan, Chukutia, Bhunjia and Birhor. In the undivided Koraput district Dongria Kandha and Lanjia Soura are in Rayagada, Bonda and Didayee are inhabited in Malkangiri area.

A realistic approach aiming at all-round development of the primitive groups living in 17 micro project areas was taken during the Fifth Plan period, this effort is continuing till today.

1.24 Tribal Economy of the Koraput Region

The economy of the tribes in this region is mainly characterized by three different ecological settings. The hills having some forest cover where the tribal practice mainly shifting cultivation of the slash and burn type (Podu) and adopt terraced cultivation in suitable places. Secondly, the hills that have almost denuded of forest cover where tribals cultivate such hills and foothill lands with whatever soil cover is left and thirdly the plateau and plains where settled agriculture is practiced. In addition to agriculture and collection of forest produce, the tribals depend upon agricultural and non-agricultural wage labour where such opportunities are available. Besides these, horticultural and animal husbandry practices are also followed by them.

1.25 Agriculture

The tribal people mainly depend upon the agriculture, and it is the prime source of economy of Koraput district, Paddy is the major crop among the other crops. In addition to paddy ragi is the another important crop in tribal economy. The yield rate of HYV of paddy has been increased to 23.71 qtl. per ha. during 2011-12 (Economic Survey, Orissa, 2012-13) . The total area under paddy cultivation is 99,133 ha. (2011-12) having the production of 23,50,934 qtls. with a yield rate of 23.71 qtls. per hectare. The other crops include wheat, maize, green gram, black gram, horse gram, niger, groundnut, mustard, potatoes, brinjal, cabbage, sugarcane etc. The upper Kolab multipurpose dam project has an important role in the economic development in the Koraput region.

A number of cash crops have been introduced in Koraput district to improve the lot of the tribals. To wean away the tribals from Podu cultivation and to improve their socio-economic condition, the district administration in consultation with the Coffee Board decided to carry out coffee plantation over 1000 ha. in the district. Coffee plantation have been taken up at Koraput, Similiguda, Nandpur, Pottangi, Dasamantpur, Lamtaput and Laxmipur Block, likewise the cotton cultivation has been introduced at Naryan patna and Bandhugan Block, Tobacco cultivation which is a profitable Cash Crop has been taken up at Nandpur Narayanpatna, Laxmipur, Bandhugaon, Jeypore, Borigumma, Kotpad, Kundra and Baipariguda. The people are getting more profit from the medicinal plant Pipia cultivation in the Lamtaput Block.

1.26 Horticulture

The Dongria Kondhs of the Niyamgiri hills under Bissamcuttack Tahsil of Rayagada district are expert horticulturists. They grow various types of fruits, like mango, banana, jackfruit, pineapple, orange etc. in the hills for which the natural environment is quite suitable. They also grow turmeric, chillies and garlic in the hill slopes in addition to other food crops. The cool climate inside the hill ranges and the beautiful horticultural gardens by the side of the hill streams and some waterfalls are the natural sceneries which attract the tourists in large numbers.

1.27 Forest Collections

The tribal economy mostly revolves round the forest. Forest is inseparable economically, ecologically and socio-culturally from tribal life. Tribals depend upon forest for employment, food, fodder, fuel wood, housing materials, medicines and recreation. It is because of low quality of agricultural land mainly due to undulating landscape, its productivity is low. Inadequate availability of suitable cultivable land in the hands of tribal, traditional agricultural technology, scarce water resources for irrigation and above all, low income or poverty of the tribal. Hence, the tribal generally supplement their income as well as food requirements through forest collection. Important minor forest produce which they collect in different areas and in different seasons include, Tamarind, Myrobalen, Adda leaves, Sabai Grass, Beedi leaves, Sal seeds, Resin, Lac, Soap nuts, Reeds, Canes, Honey, Arrow-root, Mahul flower, and seeds, Cleaning nut, Wax, Horn, Skin, Nux-vomica, Kusum seeds, Brooms, Silk Cotton, Kath and Medicinal herbs. They also collect fuel wood, wood for agricultural implements, Charcoal, Bamboo and other food articles, like various types of root (Kanda) fruit, flowers, leaves and seeds. After keeping the required products for self-consumption, they sell the surplus to earn some cash income.

1.28 Animal Husbandry

The tribals of the region keep and rear several animals and birds. This sector of animal husbandry as a source of income and employment has not gained much importance. Bullocks, cows and buffaloes are mostly used as drought animals and used in agriculture. Many of the tribal groups do not milk their cows. They still believe that the milk of the cow is solely meant for her calf and hence, milking a cow is sin. The tribals keep birds and hens, eggs of the hens are found sometimes sold in the local weekly markets. Pigs, goats, and sheep are reared by the tribals, but their utility in socio-religious rituals and festivity is more than that of commercial consideration.

1.29 Trade and Commerce

Trading is not common among the tribals. Trading in the tribal country is generally done by outsiders and also by Scheduled Castes such as the Dom and other caste, such as Sundhi and Kumuti. The tribal people are commercially dominated by the outsider. However, the tribals collect different forest products such as fruits, roots, tubers, leaves, fibres, herbs, honey, wax, animals and the housing materials, like timber, bamboo, fire wood etc. from the forest and sale in the nearby market and town. Besides these, tribal people cultivate oil seeds and green vegetable near the river, spring and sale in the market with other agricultural products.

1.30 Importance of the Study

A number of developmental schemes and programmes have been adopted for Tribal development during the last eleven Five Year Plans. A number of programmes have been formulated and implemented for elimination of various methods of tribal exploitation and improving their condition of life. Different income generating schemes and projects have also been implemented for the economical development of the tribal families. Separate schools and residential schools have been established for the improvement of the educational standard of the Scheduled Tribes. Fair price shops, co-operative societies, large sized multipurpose co-operative societies (LAMPS), State Tribal Development Co-operative Society Ltd. (TDCOL) and a number of other such institutions have been established from time to time to purchase the surplus products and NTFPS from tribal to ensure payment of fair price for the products to them and to supply their necessities at a reasonable rate. A number of employment guarantee schemes have been introduced from time to time to ensure provision of employment to the Scheduled Tribes. In order to check the land alienation, Regulation (2) of 1956 has been promulgated. Twenty-point economic programme was launched by Mrs. Indira Gandhi to safeguard the interest of tribals. Various constitutional safeguards have been adopted for socio-economic and political development of the tribes. A number of medical institutions have been established to meet the health problems and various other development projects have been adopted for improving communication facilities to inaccessible pockets.

In spite of all these efforts made by the Government both at the Central and State level, the socio-economic conditions of the tribal have not improved up to our expectation. The educational development of the tribals is also not up to mark. Even today more than 80 per cent of the tribals in Koraput region are living below the poverty line. Hence, it has become necessary to evaluate the various schemes and programmes which have been implemented from time to time for the socio-economic development of tribals.

1.31 Objectives

1. To analyze the important schemes and programmes of tribal development by the Central and State governments from time to time.
2. To examine the effectiveness of implementation of Tribal Development Programmes and to find out the reasons of their success and failure.
3. To suggest some valuable strategy for better implementation of the tribal development schemes and programmes .

1.32 Hypothesis

The following are the hypothesis proposed to be tested in the study:

1. The schemes and programmes undertaken by the government from time to time have failed to achieve their objective.
2. People participation as a major input for the success of the programme has not been taken into account.
3. Findings of the evaluation on different schemes and programmes has not been taken into consideration.
4. The programme implementing agencies and financial institutions have not taken keen interest for successful implementation of the programmes.

1.33 Methodology

The study is based on both the primary data collected from the beneficiaries, village leaders and extension officials as well as the secondary data available in published literature, i.e., evaluation studies made by scholars and Government agencies taken up from time to time. Six blocks from Koraput region have been selected on the basis of multi-stage sampling method.

1.34 Tools and Technique

The following tools and technique will be adopted by the investigator to collect the detailed data relating to the research study:

1. Secondary information relating to the study has been collected from different implementing agencies.
2. A structured questionnaire was administered to the officers heading of different implementing agencies.
3. Another structured questionnaire was also administrated to the extension official who is directly connected with the implementation of the programme.
4. Interview schedule is administered on the sample beneficiaries.

1.35 Sample Study

Out of four districts in the Koraput Region, i.e., Koraput, Rayagada, Nabarangpur and Malkangiri two districts have been selected on the basis of purposive sampling. Koraput district has been selected because of the fact that Koraput was the district headquarters for the entire region before division of the district and it is also the headquarters after the division of the district. The programmes have been implemented under the direct supervision of the department officers and district administration.

On the other hand, Malkangiri district has been selected because the functioning of two Primitive Tribal Development Agency, i.e., Bonda Development Agency in Khairput Block and Didayi Development Agency in Kudumulugumma Block. The presence of other backward tribes like Koya and the absence of railway line and Large Scale Industries in the District would provide a true picture of the development activities taken up in the district.

In the second stage of sample, the two blocks, i.e., Kudumulugumma and Khairput blocks have been taken because of the functioning of the Micro Projects in Malkangiri district. The third block was selected on the basis of highest tribal concentration out of the remaining five blocks. Mathili Block with 75.06 per cent of tribal concentration was selected as the sample.

A simple random sample method was adapted to select three blocks, Boipariguda, Kundra and Narayanpatna Blocks in Koraput district.

Thus in the 2nd stage of sample six blocks of two districts, i.e., Khairput, Kudumulugumma and Mathili Blocks of Malkangiri district and Boipariguda, Kundra and Narayanpatna of Koraput district constituted the study areas.

In the third stage, two gram panchayats of each block were selected on the basis of simple random sample method and 12 gram panchayats were selected in total from the two districts.

From each of the gram panchayats so selected 24 villages were selected again on the basis of simple random sample method.

Form each of the 24 villages so selected 10 to 12 households were selected on the basis of systematic random sample method so as to make a sample of at least 300 households.

Twelve Schemes which are very important from the point of view of enhancing the level of living of the tribals of the area were taken for intensive study in the study areas. The functioning of educational institution, hostel management and pre-matric scholarship, the participation of PRI members in the Development programmes, Income generating schemes, Indira Awas Yajana, Gramin Banks, Women Self Help Groups, Public distribution system, Social Security Schemes and study on the Non-Bankable Income generating schemes and water harvesting structures have been studied in the study area to provide an idea about the effectiveness of these programmes in enhancing the living standard of the tribals within a period of one decade, i.e., 2001-10.

1.36 Statistical Tools Used

Only simple statistical tools like Percentage, Ratio and Diagrams have been used for the purpose of understanding the effectiveness of the schemes implemented in the study areas.

1.37 Limitations

The study has been conducted in only 24 villages of two districts.

In the entire Koraput Region only two districts have been selected for the purpose of the study. Out of the four new districts carved out from undivided Koraput, only two districts, i.e., Koraput and Malkangiri have been taken for study.

The study has concentrated only on 12 schemes and programmes implemented during the plan period, i.e., 2001-10. However, efforts have been made to make the study representative so that it can present all the aspects of tribal development in the region.

1.38 Reference Period

The reference period for which the sample variables are studied from 2001 to 2010.

1.39 Structure of Study

The structure of the study is briefly designed as fellows:

- The **first chapter** is introductory with the objectives and hypothesis of the study, the sampling technique adopted and a background of the study area.
- The **second** chapter deals with a brief review of literature.
- In chapter **three**, the different schemes and programmes implemented from time to time by the Government for the all-round development of the tribals particularly in Koraput region is analyzed.
- In chapter **four**, an attempt should be made to evaluate the performance and effectiveness of the schemes and programmes introduced and implemented by the government for tribal development.
- The outcome of the research is discussed in chapter **five** and the consequential suggestions for the effective implementation of the schemes and projects have been discussed.

2
Review of Literature

A number of studies have been made on specific problems concerning Tribal issues and their development. (However, systematic studies on the functioning of different schemes and programmes by individual scholars are very much limited). Studies have been made by Anthropologists, Economists, Sociologists and Experts from other disciplines on individuals' tribes and their problems of development.

Tribal Research Institutions and other institutions have also taken up periodical studies on socio-economic problems of tribes and their development. A brief review of some of the available literature dealing with tribal problems, tribal economy and tribal development schemes and programmes are attempted in this chapter.

2.1 Verrior Elwin (1943, 1950, 1964, 1965) provides reference to the socio-economic life of tribals in the country which are mostly anthropological in nature, particularly, during his tours in the tribal areas of Keonjhar, Pallahara, Ganjam and Koraput of Orissa. He studied the socio-economic life of the tribes like Juangs, Sauras, Kuttia Kondhs and Bondas. Among the socio- economic aspects, he described the exploitation of tribals in Ganjam and Koraput (undivided) districts by the Scheduled Caste Doms, Patro, landlords, Kumuti businessmen and Sundhi wine venders and also officials of the Forest Department. Further in the book *Bondo High lander* (1950) he described the socio-economic and cultural life of Bonda tribe of undivided Koraput district specifically.

2.2 L.K. Shrikant (1959-60), the then Commissioner of SC & ST described the administrative setup in the offices of the Commissioner, Central and State Governments. Further he recommended Advisory Boards/ Committee for Harijan and Tribal welfare and democratic decentralization, basing upon the recommendation of community project and National Extensive Service of the Committee on Plan Projects setup by the Planning Commission. The State Government and Union Administration have decided to set up Panchayat Samiti and Zilla Parisad for better implementation of new schemes and maintenance of the institution meant for Scheduled Castes and Scheduled Tribes and Backward Classes. In the field of economic development of the tribes legislative and executive measures have been taken up in various states and Union territories. In order to safeguard the interest of Scheduled Castes and Scheduled Tribes, in Madhya Pradesh, the Land Revenue Code, 1959, Land Alienation Act, 1916 (Allotment and Transfer of Land) Regulation, 1954 has been formulated and implemented. Land Settlement in Andhra Pradesh, Assam, Kerala, Madhya Pradesh, Orissa and Rajasthan has been operated. Improved seeds, plough bullocks and many other agricultural implements have been supplied in the year 1959-60. Further, it is reported that the co-operative institution have been launched in various tribal and backward areas of the country. The total expenditure incurred on this programme since inception of the Second Five Year Plan comes about Rs. 90.37 lakh which represent approximately 42 per cent of the plan allocation made for this purpose. In the Andaman & Nicobar Islands, a system of thrift deposit has also been introduced from July 1959 in all the 27 societies. The Commissioner has also dealt with the special multipurpose programme in the tribal blocks such as animal husbandry and agricultural extension, irrigation and land reclamation, health and rural sanitation, education, social education, communication, rural arts and crafts, co-operation, rural housing, child welfare and health centres, water supply and sanitation, teaching of tribals in nursing and herbal medicine, mobile dispensaries etc. There was progressive increase of expenditure on communication schemes from 143.06 lakh in 1958-59 to 158.11 lakh during 1959-60. In another report, the Commissioner has dealt with different schemes for the welfare of Scheduled Castes and Scheduled Tribes under Article 275(1) of the Constitution imposing special obligation on the Government to pay grant in aid to part A & B of the State Government for the purpose of promoting the welfare and development of scheduled and tribal area in the state and different schemes for the welfare of the Scheduled Castes and ex-criminal tribes.

2.3 Walter Fernandes and Mohammed Asif (1997) studies (funded by the Indian Council of Social Science Research) dealt with the state of displacement and rehabilitation of India, background of Orissa and the project area, extent of the type of land used by Development Projects, compensation and resettlement and its impact. It studied the state of rehabilitation and shocked to find that the country has displaced around 30 lakh people for whom no national rehabilitation policy has been formed till that date. The social as well as environmental cost of this negligence has been enormous. In this juncture it has been suggested both for better resettlement, new cost benefit analysis and technical alternatives, emphasis have been given towards more research on environmental consequences.

The needs of the village communities should be kept in view and the present approach of Government towards the tribal villages in forest area are revised. Steps should be taken up to eliminate the middlemen between the inhabitants of the forest and the Forest Department in relation to the exploitation of the forest. The system of ending monopoly was emphasized for which the State Government should organize Co-operative Finance and Development Corporation. Andhra Pradesh model for collection of forest produce were suggested. The programme covered all tribal areas by primary co-operatives which functioned as an agent of the central institute.

2.4 N.K. Bose (1967-68) dealt with various types of scholarships awarded for educational development of Scheduled Castes and Scheduled Tribes. Schemes on improving the working condition of the person engaged in unclean occupations including eradication of the practice of the carrying night-soil on head-load, the Government of India has introduced a scheme of wheel barrows, gum-boots etc. since 1957-58. For the development of nomadic and semi-nomadic tribes, Rs 7.00 crore were spent for their welfare in the first three plans under the central sectors. Special efforts have been made for educational development of the tribes like coaching facilities, health, housing and other schemes like drinking water facilities communication have been taken up. Regarding economic development, it has dealt with land and agricultural problems of Scheduled Castes and Scheduled Tribes, land alienation, shifting cultivation training and crafts promotion through cottage industries, small industries and grain gola.

2.5 Report of the Commissioner for Scheduled Castes and Scheduled Tribes (Twenty Second Report), 1973-74 dealt with the Fourth Plan (six pilot projects) for tribal development known as The Tribal Development Agencies which were taken up in the central sectors. These projects are implemented in the sensitive backward tribal area as such Srikakulam in Andhra Pradesh, Singhbhum in Bihar, Bastar/Dantewada, Bastar-II, Konta in Madhya Pradesh, Ganjam (Paralakhemundi), Koraput (Gunpur), Keonjhar (Bhuyanpur and Juangpirh) and Phulbani (Baliguda) in Orissa. All India Handloom Board and All India Handicrafts Board have given emphasis to promote the interests of Scheduled Castes and Scheduled Tribes. Further small scale and village industries in the plan have been emphasized for tribal areas.

2.6 Shankar Rao Mane (1974- 75), the Commissioner for Scheduled Castes and Scheduled Tribes in Twenty Third Report reflected that after launching the community development movement 43 Tribal Development Blocks have been established during the Second Five Year Plan as a pilot schemes and 43 special multipurpose Tribal Blocks were set up. In Third & Fourth Five Year Plan, 504 Blocks have been established in the country. Further, the report dealt with the establishment of Tribal

Development Agencies, Tribal Sub-Plan, Integrated Tribal Development Projects, Distribution of surplus land under the old ceiling land. The small farmer Development Agencies and Marginal Farmers and Agricultural Labourers Development Agencies were introduced during the Fourth Plan period. Further to wean the Scheduled Castes and Scheduled Tribes from the money-lenders quite a good deal of welfare and development work can be done among the weaker sections of the society through the formation and successful operation of the co-operative society. Such society render financial assistance to save them from exploitation at the hand of money-lenders and traders and also taken up various craft, trade oriented programmes for their economic development. The National Co-operative Development Corporation Act, 1962 was amended in 1974 to extend specifically the activities to assist co-operative for collection and marketing of minor forest produce. The tribal development corporations were formed in the respective states of Andhra Pradesh, Assam, Bihar, Gujarat, Karnataka, Kerala, Madhya Pradesh, Maharashtra, Orissa and Utter Pradesh.

2.7 National Commission for Scheduled Castes and Scheduled Tribes (1987-88) on dated 1.9.1987 the Government decided to demarcate the function of the special Officer for SC & ST and Commission for SC & ST. It was decided that only the Commissioner for SC & ST would be submitting the (Annual) Reports to the President and the Parliament and the Commission which was rechristened as the National Commission for SC & ST would conduct studies. The Ministry of Welfare Notification No. BC-13015/12/86-SCD. VI dated 1.9.1987 laid down the functions of the National Commission for SC & ST. The Constitution Amendment (Sixty Eighth Amendment) Bill, 1990 was passed unanimously by the Lok Sabha on 30.5.1990 and the Rajya Sabha on 31.5.1990. It received the President's assent on 7.6.1990 and was notified as the Constitutional (Sixty Fifth Amendment) Act, 1990 in the Official Gazette on 8.6.1990. The Commission was, however, reconstituted in accordance with these Rules only on dated 12.3.1992. The functions of the Commission have been laid down in clauses (5), (8) and (10) of the amended Article 338 of the Constitution. The Commission is required to monitor all matters relating to the safeguards provided for SC & ST under the Constitution or under any other law for the time being in force or under any order of the Government and to evaluate the working of such safeguards. The Commission has dealt with the Fifth Schedule and Sixth Schedule to the Constitution. In the Fifth Schedule provisions regarding the administration and control of the Scheduled areas and Scheduled Tribes have been discussed. The Sixth Schedule contains provisions relating to the administration of the Tribal Area in the State of Assam (North Cachar Hills District and Karbi Anglong

District), Meghalaya, Mizoram and Tripura (Autonomous Hill District). Besides these, the Commission has to monitor about the educational and cultural safeguards under Articles 15(4), 16(4), 29(1) and 350(A) of the Constitution. The Commission is also designated to monitor the political safeguard of the SC and ST people under Articles 164(1), 330, 332, 334, 371(A), 372(B), 371(C) and 371(F) containing special provision with respect of Nagaland, Assam, Manipur, and Sikkim respectively. Further, the Commission also dealt with the service safeguards under Articles 16(A), 335, and 320(4) of the Constitution of India.

2.8 The Dhebar Commission Report (U.N. Dhebar 1960-61) studied about the tribal development in Andhra Pradesh, Maharashtra, Assam, Mysore, Bihar, Orissa, M.P., West Bengal, Madras, Andaman & Nicobar Islands. Further, it evaluated the Land Reform measures taken up by different status of land transfers, displacement as a result of land alienation, rehabilitation of displaced tribes, tribal and forest policy, agriculture, shifting cultivation, soil conservation, village and cottage industry, community development, problems on indebtedness, and role of corporation in the tribal area educational development, health, housing and communication impact of industrialization, different training programmes and representation etc.

2.9 The Tribal Research Bureau of Orissa (ST-SC-RTI) carried out a few specific studies on various aspects of tribal economy and tribal development in Koraput district. The findings of the report were that a large proportion of the settlers had deserted the colonies, gone back to their own villages and reverted back to shifting cultivation due to lack of adoptability on the part of tribals in the new environment, unfamiliar to settled cultivation and in some cases due to lack of irrigation facilities. In another study on *Goti* System (Bonded Labour System) in Koraput district (1966-67), the focus was on analyzing the causes, extent and consequences of bonded labour system in the region and suggested the provisions and measures to save the tribals from such exploitations. Another study on *Goti* system in Koraput was made by Mohanty (1978) on the basis of the data collected by the research staff at the Bureau. His findings were more or less similar to that of the earlier one. The report suggested that legal provisions to abolish *Goti* (i.e. the Orissa Debt Bondage Abolition Regulation, 1968) should be implemented vigorously and *Gotis* should be resettled by the Government. The report further suggested formation of credit co-operative societies to supply credit to the tribal at easy terms. The Bureau had made a study on socio-economic life of Koyas, a primitive tribe living in Malkangiri area (1970). It focused on the agricultural practices adopted by the Koyas, their cattle wealth as well as indebtedness etc. and impact of Bengali settlers on the economic life of the Koyas. Other research institutes like Nabakrushna Choudhary Centre for Development Studies, Bhubaneswar and Council of Analytical Tribal Studies (COATS), Koraput, have taken micro-level studies on various socio-economic problems of the tribals of the region in recent years. The research publications of such institutions are of immense help to the scholars and administrators. The Tribal and Harijan Research-cum Training Institute, Orissa, has published a book entitled *The Tribes of Orissa* (1990) in which one can have an idea about the socio-economic condition of the tribals of Koraput region.

2.10 S.P. Rout (1963-64) study was based on review of 86 exploitation cases in Kondha village of Kumbhikota and Laxmipur area of Koraput district. The study focused on the extent of such type of exploitation, the mode of exploitation, its consequences etc.

2.11 J. Samal (1992) studied about economic life of the tribals of Koraput region in particular. It focused on the details of the agricultural and non-agricultural pursuits of tribals with the relative efficiency and productivity of it. It was a detailed micro level analysis of 365 days of engagement of the tribal household (1983-84) living under three different ecological situations like tribals' various activities, the level of income and poverty and also the seasonality of their operations.

2.12 Shishir Kumar, Commissioner, Scheduled Caste & Scheduled Tribe (1978-79) on the eve of the Fifth Plan, the tribal development scene was again reviewed through Shilu Ao Committee by the Planning Commission and examined in detail the working of the Tribal Development Blocks in all the states. The Committee came to the conclusion that the tribal development block programme had become too rigid and schematic as a result of which there was not much consonance between the problems of the area and the programme undertaken. The Committee also observed that the Tribal Development Block was too smaller a unit for planning and implementation of development programme in those areas. In view of the large number of units, it was difficult to get suitable personnel for key position for effective monitoring and supervision. The Committee, therefore, recommended a complete overhauling of the programme.

2.13 Bhikha Bhai (1985-86), Commissioner for the Scheduled Caste and Scheduled Tribe reported that during the Fifth Five Year Plan development efforts were made for the general sectors of the economy. The tribal sub-plan which was started during the Fifth Plan aimed at area development of the tribal concentrated pockets. Special attention was given to the primitive tribes, shifting cultivation, tribal displaced by projects, tribal women, improving the quality of tribal environment and upgradation of their resources. During the period under report State plan resources, special Central Assistance were provided by Ministry of Welfare, Central

Government and centrally sponsored schemes and institutional finance adopted by the Government for the development of tribal communities.

2.14 Mahanty (1998) in his research study on financing of non-farm sector for rural development has selected three tribal dominated districts of Sundargarh, Mayurbhanj, Koraput (undivided). At micro level, Mahanty surveyed twenty tribal blocks of Koraput region and it was found that beneficiaries financed under non-farm sector had partially used the money for the purpose and there has been an increase in the economic standard of such beneficiaries. On the other hand, the beneficiaries who have not properly utilized the fund have diverted the money so sanctioned. Finally, they have not shown any improvement in their economic standard.

2.15 Behera (2000) conducted a research study on the marketing habits of tribal and the role of marketing institution in the tribal areas of Koraput. It was found that almost all the marketing activities of the tribals were carried on the weekly *hats* only. Due to ignorance of the tribals, they are very often cheated by outsiders and non-tribal middlemen and traders. It was further revealed that marketing institutions like LAMP, TDCC and RMCS have been established for the better marketing of the tribals of Koraput region.

2.16 The Commission for Scheduled Caste and Scheduled Tribe in their Twenty Seventh Report (1979-81) has focused on the tribal development of the country. The Commission has recommended different schemes and programmes as well as dealt with the safeguard of the Scheduled Tribe and Scheduled Caste such as Abolition of unsociability under Article 17 of the Constitution, the Practice of Unsociability is forbidden in any form. In accordance with Article 35(a) II, the Unsociability (Offence) Act, 1955 was enacted which is called Protection of Civil Rights Act, 1955. The Commission has also recommended Employee Guarantee schemes, land, agricultural development, reservation of seats for Scheduled Castes and Scheduled Tribes in the Post-Graduate Medical courses, Pre-Metric and Post-Metric scholarship to the SC & ST students, Crafts based education in Ashram schools, Scholarship to SC & ST children/students staying in states other than their Home States. Further provisions were recommended for National Talent search scholarship, National overseas scholarship to Notified, Nomadic and Semi-Nomadic Tribes. Further, it is suggested that backward tribal communities known as Primitive Tribal Groups should be identified and financed on hundred per cent basis by the Ministry of Home Affairs.

2.17 Shisir Kumar (1975-77): The Twenty Fourth Report of the Commissioner for Scheduled Caste and Scheduled Tribe suggested the elimination of exploitation should be taken up on priority basis as an integral part of the plan of social and economic development of the tribal people. Programmes for prevention of land alienation, rehabilitation of bonded labours should also be taken up on priority basis. Further, it has aslo suggested that a network of educational institutions consisting of residential Ashram schools, lower primary, primary, middle and high schools, along with hostel facilities and other incentives with necessary likeness amongst them should form a package to be provided in each tribal area depending upon the social, educational and economic conditions. A study was undertaken in the Integrated Tribal Development Project, Sundargarh, Orissa. A similar study was undertaken on the working of Integrated Tribal Development Project KUKSHI DHAR in Madhya Pradesh which revealed that 17 units of sheep on exchange basis, were distributed to persons who were non-tribals. It is, therefore, suggested that benefit of the developmental programmes involving subsidy elements should be made available to Scheduled Tribes only. Further, it was suggested in the report that it is necessary to take steps to set up small and medium scale primary processing units in the tribal areas to provide gainful employment to the tribals through the collection of minor forest produce. The Twenty-fourth Report of the Commissioner for Scheduled Castes and Scheduled Tribes 1975 to 1977 gave more attention to the safeguard of Scheduled Castes and Scheduled Tribes. Safeguards have been extended in public sector undertakings, public sector and national banks, university and technical university, High Courts and judicial services, voluntary agencies receiving Grant-in-Aid from the Government and appointment in the private sector. In the promotional cases, Scheduled Castes and Scheduled Tribes working as sweeper and farashes in Government offices utilization of vacancies reserved for Scheduled Castes and Scheduled Tribes and *vice versa* in the event of suitable candidate of that particular communities are not available. Relaxation of standard in qualifying examination for promotion, encouragement of Scheduled Castes and Scheduled Tribes Training and employment, association of Scheduled Caste and Scheduled Tribe members in departmental promotion/selection board meeting and discussed on complaint regarding denial of justice in service matter. In the social development, it has been reported by the Commission about the observance and abolition of untouchables, Atrocity and Harassment, Monetary relief to the Scheduled Caste and Scheduled Tribe victim atrocities. Further, it has been discussed about the rendering the service by Non-Official Agencies like All India Harijan Sevak Sangh, Bharatiya Depressed Classes League, Hindu Sweepers Sevak Samaj, Ramakrushna Mission Ashram etc. Further the Commission has reviewed about the different tribal development programmes implemented by the Tribes, discussion has been made about the formulation of Sub-Plan, Integrated Tribal Development Projects and their basic problems, Primitive

Tribal Groups and their problems, tribals and forest, shifting cultivation, Industrialization impact on Tribal. Administration in the Tribals area and different Tanning Programmes and attention has been given on the impact of 20 point economic programme on Scheduled Castes and Scheduled Tribes.

2.18 Bhola Paswan Shastri (1979-1980): The Report of the Commissioner for Scheduled Castes and Scheduled Tribes (Second Report—April 1979 to March 1980) dealt with the special component plan for Scheduled Castes and Scheduled Tribe, emphasis has been given on reservation in services, eradication of untouchables, land reforms, economic development, constitutional safeguards as well as social and educational development of the Scheduled Castes and Scheduled Tribes.

2.19 The National Commission for Scheduled Castes and Scheduled Tribes (1997-98): In its Fourth Report presented to the President of India has tried to evaluate the implementation of special component plan and tribal sub-plan strategy adopted by the government for the socio-economic development of the Scheduled Castes and Scheduled Tribes. Safeguard and protection provided to them under the Constitution and various other laws and the extent of benefits accrued to them under the government policy of reservation in service and in educational and professional courses. In addition an attempt has been made to assess the availability of basic minimum needs to these communities and the impact of poverty alleviation programme on their economics status.

2.20 Dileep Sing Bhuria (1998-99), Chairman, National Commission for Scheduled Castes & Scheduled Tribes, presented report on social justice and empowerment instead of confining its area to only welfare oriented activities. Through the 73rd Amendment to the Constitution, provision has been made for reservation of seats for SC & ST in the Panchayati Raj Institutions and Urban Local Bodies. In 1997, the Ministry of Welfare was rechristened as the Ministry of Social Justice and Empowerment. A separate Ministry of Tribal Affairs was carved out in 1999 for giving more focused attention to the socio-economic development of tribal communities through PESA Act, 1996. The Scheduled area covered under Schedule-V, the Constitution have also been brought under the purview of the Panchayati Raj system. The provision for specific powers and responsibilities to the Gram Sabha to ensure closer participation of Tribal communities. In preservation of their cultural heritage and accelerated socio-economic development, an effort has been made in this report to analyze the impact of this measure in enabling the communities to overcome their social disabilities and their assimilation in their national mainstream.

In the year 2001, a report on Orissa about functioning of welfare schemes for the Scheduled Castes and Scheduled Tribes has been submitted by the Naba Krushna Choudhaty Centre for Development Studies, Bhubaneswar, Orissa. The main objective of the study was to evaluate whether the programme formulated for the welfare of the Scheduled Castes and Scheduled Tribes are being implemented properly in conformity with the avowed objective and to record such observations as might help in improving and strengthening the programme implementation with a view to ensuring better social returns from such investment. Secondly to examine whether the special components Plan special central assistance, Tribal sub-Plan funds earmarked for welfare programme of Scheduled Castes and Scheduled Tribes are being apparently, effectively and fully utilized to identify areas of slippage which came to notice and record suggestion that might help to mitigate any distortions in achieving the designated purpose of the schemes and thirdly to determine the constraints and bottleneck in the investigation and finalization of cases under the Scheduled Castes and Scheduled Tribes (Prevention of Atrocities) Act, 1989 and the Protection of Civil Rights Act, 1955 and suggest measures to correct such lacunae.

2.21 Bell (1945) and Senapati and Sahu (1966): There are two available District Gazetteers on Koraput, viz. one by Bell (1945) and other by Senapati and Sahu (1966). These Gazetteers in their usual ways deals with location, population, cultural practices, geology, forests, land, minerals, communication etc. and also focus on the Tribal communities, their economy and economic practices, earlier to these two Gazetteers, the Vizagapatnam District Gazetteer by Francis (1907) also covered Koraput reign and its people, as Koraput was a part of Vizagapatnam district until 1936 . One can have a clear picture of socio-religious practice of Koraput tribe including the "Mariah" (Human sacrifice) among Kondhas which was prevalent in the past in order to appease the supernatural spirits for good harvest in the Gazetteer by Francis.

2.22 Sahu (1942) in his book *Hill Tribes of Jeypore* study on Koraput District that is mostly anthropological in character and one can get some useful information about their economic life. He observed that the podu cultivation (Shifting Cultivation) by the tribes posed serious problems in the district. He estimated that the Tribal people hardly supported their livelihood for the five months from podu cultivation and for the rest of the year they had to live on other minor produce. Sahu like Elwin also referred to the economic exploitation of tribals in Koraput by Dombs Sundhis (wine-vender) and Kumuties (Trader and Money-lenders).

2.23 Tribals Research Bureau (1963-64) has taken up a study on the exploitation of tribals by Dombs in Kondha village in Koraput. The study prepared by S.P. Rout was based on the review of 86 exploitation cases in Kondha Villages of Kumbhikota and Laxmipur area of Koraput district. The study reveled that a few families of Dom numbering one to ten might be found in each Kandha village but they could manage to keep the innocent and ignorant tribal suppressed by their notorious activities of cheating, stealing, robbery and attacking. The Dombs were believed by the tribals to command much power and authority by virtue of which they could command the Kandhas to obey them. In the past, the Rajas entrusted the Dombs to collect taxes from the Kondha. Again in the days of British rule the converted Dombs were getting ample support from the missionaries to defend themselves in spite of various nuisances committed by them. Even today the Dombs act as spokesman of the villages when any Government official visits them, because the Kondha are shy of outsiders.

In the year 1970, the Tribal Research Bureau had taken another study on the socio-economic life of Koyas, a primitive tribe living in Malkangiri sub-Division of undivided Koraput district. The study revealed that the Koyas were shifting cultivators but after the ban on shifting cultivation and forest being progressively declared reserved, they were forced to take up wet and settled cultivation. The Koyas generally distinguish between the types of land for cultivation, viz. (i) Low land which can hold water for a considerable period, (ii) Land situated at a comparatively higher level which can be irrigated by making small earthen dams on all sides, and (iii) The slope lands full of trees and bushes where water can never be stored. The study revealed about the techniques used in their cultivation and economic life and cultural activities and day-to-day life.

Bangladeshi refugees have been resettled in Malkangiri area after implementation of Dandakaranya Development project though a lot of changes have taken place in the area with infrastructure development. The Koyas who are resettled in the colonies are found unchanged on the other hand the Bengali settlers are quite happy with a higher standard of living and the doors of exploitation have slowly opened.

In the year 1964, the report on survey of the submersible villages under Balimela project prepared by the Tribal Research Bureau give an insight on the colony of the tribals, the nature and causes of migration and attitude towards rehabilitation of the tribals. The report stated that the portion of the Machhkund valley which was going to be submerged was completely desolated for pretty long time being covered with forests, except a few hamlets. The Kondhas reported that their forefathers had migrated to the valley from Kalyanisingpur in Rayagada sub-Division and Narayanapatna in Koraput sub-division. The main attraction to choose this valley for them was the availability of land for cultivation. In course of time along with the Kondhas, a few families of other Castes like Gouda, Damba and other service classes had migrated to the valley.

2.24 Mishra and Mohapatra (1980-81): The evaluation report of the Malkangiri Integrated Tribal Development Project of Koraput district was prepared by Mishra and Mahapatra on the basis of field study. The study discussed the pattern of tribal agriculture, crop yields and level of income etc. The analysis was similar to tribal agriculture already discussed earlier in the chapter. The study further revealed that no change had taken place either in the cropping pattern or in the method of cultivation in the area after the functioning of the project. Similarly, other schemes like animal husbandry, cottage and small scale industries etc. had not been able to bring any improvement in the tribal economy in the area.

2.25 Mahapatra (1987) in his doctoral dissertation titled " Economic Development of Tribal India" has taken undivided Koraput District as his area of study. The main objectives of the study were to study the existing economic conditions of tribals in the district, to assess the impact of development strategy implemented and to suggest an appropriate strategy to develop the tribals in the district. Out of 42 blocks, 17 villages and 373 households were covered in the study. In the study, two strategies have been suggested for tribal development in the district. They are : (1) socio-economic development strategy, and (2) spatial development strategy. The scholar has given separate strategies for development of agriculture, both settled and shifting cultivation, livestock development, forest, indebtedness, non-agricultural economic activities, appropriate technology and spatial development strategies.

2.26 P.K. Acharya, Ramesh Mishra, Nilakantha Panigrahi and Ramesh Prasad Mahanty (2001) undertook a case study on functioning of welfare schemes for the Scheduled Castes of Kandhamal, Rayagada and Dhenkanal district, on random sampling basis. The study deals with the Tribal Sub-plan, special components plan and Atrocity and Civil Right Act.

2.27 Kulamani Padhi (2005) in his article "Tribal Development in India—Case study of Human Development" in *Orissa Review* states about the development plans for tribals during plan period. From the review of plans it is pertinent that special programmes for tribal development have been implemented in our country to benefit the tribal population under backward classes sector during the plan period.

In this article, various reports of the Commissioner of Scheduled Castes and Scheduled Tribes which is rechristened as National Commission of Scheduled Castes and Scheduled Tribes, the Annual Administration Report published by SC & ST Development Department, Orissa, where different tribal development schemes and programmes have been discussed and recommended for better formulation and implementation of the Tribal development schemes and programmes. Besides this, the Tribal Research Bureau and other scholars have also undertook studies on the adoption formulation and implementation of the different schemes and programmes meant for the tribal development.

A number of schemes and programmes have been adopted for the socio-economic and educational development of the tribes. But no systematic evaluation has been made so far. Hence, detailed evaluation and assessment of adoption, implementation and effectiveness of the different Tribal development schemes and programmes is necessary to be evaluated. Even the implementation of Panchayat Extension to the Scheduled Area (PESA) Act, 1996 and its impact on the tribal society has to be evaluated. In this regards out of four districts of the Koraput region at least two districts have been selected on the basis of purposive sampling, i.e., Koraput and Malkangiri district because of functioning of two primitive tribal development agencies, i.e., Banda and Didayi development agency. Koraput district have been selected as it is the headquarters before division of the districts. Three Blocks from each District and Two Gram Panchayats from each Block have been selected for the present study. Two revenue villages from each Gram panchayat so selected have been taken up and more than 300 respondents have been interviewed in the evaluation process. Besides this, the implementing agencies and financial institutions have also been associated on the random sample basis for better assessment of Tribal Development Schemes and programmes, percentage of successfulness and reasons for failure of the schemes have been presented.

From the review of various literatures on tribal development plans and policies above, the following summarization can be made:

1. Most of the research studies are based on the problems relating to tribal development as a top down approach.
2. Specific studies on the recommendations of various commissions for the implementation of different schemes and programmes are not being evaluated from the viewpoint of tribal need and aspirations.
3. Literatures relating to economic life of tribals impact of different schemes and programmes on tribals are being studied on a general perspective.
4. Evaluation of implemented programmes in respect to the beneficiaries on location and tribe specific has been limited.
5. Contemporary developmental role of programme implementing agencies and the financial institutions though studied are restricted to government level but not available to the general public.
6. Different schemes and programmes meant for the socio-economic and political development of the tribes (e.g. PESA Act, 1996, Forest Rights Act, 2006) need to be highlighted on a time variation scale.

Thus, it was felt that few important schemes desired to increase the level of living of the tribals in the Koraput region need in-depth study. Hence, the present study has been made.

3
Tribal Development Schemes and Programme
Retrospect and Prospect

3.0 Introduction

The tribal areas constitute a very significant part of backward areas of Orissa state. Except for the north, east Orissa occupies a unique position for the highest concentration of Scheduled Tribe next to Madhya Pradesh and Maharashtra. The rural predominance, low density due to unfavourable geographical location, inaccessibility, increasing trend of landlessness, restriction of use of forest rights have led them to lead a poor life. Various studies, reports of Government in Central and State governments present that in spite of the several constitutional safeguards provided for the protection and development of Scheduled Tribe, a lot of efforts are still to be made for their development.

Therefore, it becomes necessary to make analysis of the efforts made in different Five Year Plans for their development. It is also necessary to analyze to different programme and schemes implemented during the plan period for the development of the Scheduled Tribe in Koraput region.

3.1 Condition of the Tribes in the pre-Independence Period

The tribal people living in their remote hills and forests led a life of their own. On the entry of the missionaries into these areas that Administration started paying some attention to them. But the tribal people were neglected. Dr. J.H. Hutton, a distinguished member of the ICS, who made a deep study of the problems of tribal people wrote that, "Far from being of immediate benefit to the primitive tribes, the establishment of British Rule in India did most of them much more harm than good." It may be said that the early days of British Administration was detrimental to the economic position of tribes through ignorance and neglect of their rights and customs. Many changes have been caused incidentally by the penetration of the tribal country, the opening up of communications, the protection of forests and the establishment of schools, more so of the openings given in this way to

Christian Missions. Many of the results of these changes have caused acute discomfort to the tribes (Dhebar Commission Report, 1960-61)

The British policy of isolating the tribes resulted in exploitation. The technique was simple, Zamindars, landlords, money-lenders and contractors exploited the tribals to the maximum. Conservation and preservation of forests resulted in a progressive encroachment on the rights enjoyed by the tribals. Retired soldiers were granted land in the foot of the hills and forest. Implementation of forest policies compelled the tribals in different parts of the country to revolt against the exploitation. The Indian Mutiny of 1857 was preceded by the Santal Rebellion in 1855 which was excited by the oppression of the money-lenders and rapacious landlords. In 1869 and 1870, there was a unrest in Dhanbad between the Zamindars of Tundi and Santals on the question of enhancement of rent and Forest Right. This was followed by the Sardari Agitation of 1887 against compulsory labours, periodical contributions, and illegal enhancement of rent by landlords. In the Agency area of Andhra Pradesh, the revolt was led by Alluri Sitaram Raju against corruption and exploitation. This insurrection was proceeded by the uprisings in 1862 and 1879. The exploitation of tribals was the cause of many other disturbances such as the Rampa Rebellion in east Godavari, the Bastar Rising of 1911 and the civil disobedience by the Kond Maliahs of Orissa and by Tana Bhagat in 1920. In the Adilabad district of Hyderabad, Gonds and Kolams rebelled in 1941. In Orissa, Mundas revolted under the leadership of Birsamunda in the north Orissa and in the south Bhumias and other tribes revolted under the leadership of Laxman Nayak of Koraput district against the exploitation and land alienation in the tribal area (Report of the Scheduled Areas and Scheduled Tribes Commission, Volume I, 1960-61).

3.2 Condition of the Tribes in the Post-Independence Period

After independence, the Government of India has evolved different formula in the Constitution to deal with the tribal problems with adequate safeguards for their smooth integration. The Constitution arranged for the provision of resources and provided the required institutional apparatus. Further during the plan period, several development activities has been formulated and adopted for the all-round development of the tribes which we shall discuss as under.

3.2.1 Administrative institutional mechanisms

The execution of amelioration measures for the welfare of Scheduled Tribes and the development of Scheduled areas were initially carried out by the Tribal and Rural Welfare Development through Panchayati Raj Institutions. During 1965-66, the combined field organization of both Tribal and Rural Welfare and Gram Panchayats Departments was bifurcated. Thereafter, the Tribal and Rural Welfare Department and its own field organization at the district level worked under the direct supervision of Collector.

The Scheduled Tribe and Scheduled Caste Development Department is the nodal department of the State for the welfare and development of Scheduled Tribe and Scheduled Caste communities. The Department is headed by a senior Cabinet Minister. Likewise, a senior level IAS officer head the office of Secretary-*cum*-Commissioner in the Department and two senior officers of Additional Secretary rank head the two wings of the Department (ST & SC and OBC and Minority) as Directors. The Department has an elaborate arrangement at the field level with a District Welfare Officer in every district, Assistant District Welfare Officers in most of the sub-divisions and Welfare Extension Officers in every Block. There are 21 Integrated Tribal Development Agencies (ITDAs) in Odisha. Senior administrative officers are in position as Project Administrators of the Integrated Tribal Development Agencies with engineering wings. Besides 17 micro projects have been established in 12 tribal districts of the state and the Special Officers have been posted for all-round development of primitive Tribal groups. Especially for the educational development wings Circle Inspector of School and District Inspector of School have been posted (Annual Report, 2008-2009).

In order to ensure tribal development, the participation of Scheduled Tribes in planning and implementation of various schemes and programmes are essential. In this context, Pandit Jawaharlal Nehru, the first Prime Minister of India had enunciated five guiding principles for Tribal Development. These are:

1. Tribal people should develop along the line of their own genius and we should avoid imposing anything on them. We should try to encourage in every possible way their traditional art and culture.
2. Tribal rights in land and forest should be protected.
3. We should try to train and build up a team of their own people to do the work of administration and development. Some technical personnel from outside will no doubt be needed, especially in the beginning but we should avoid introducing too many outsiders into Tribal territory.
4. We should not over-administer these areas and work through their own social and cultural institutions.
5. We should judge the results, not by statistics or the amount of money spent, but by the quality of human character that is evolved.

(*Source*: *The Indian Tribes Through the Ages* by R.C. Verma, 1990.)

3.2.2 *Tribal Developments during Plan Period*

For the all-round development of the tribals, a number of efforts have been initiated during the plan period. During the beginning of the **First Five Year Plan**, when Community Development Approach was evolved, the areas inhabited by the tribals also received special attention. In the year 1954, Community Development approach in the tribal areas were initiated by setting up as several number of Special Multipurpose Tribal Development (SMPT) blocks covering a limited number of blocks of the State as pilot projects. Subsequently, in the year 1956, there was a reorientation in the approach to Tribal Development (TD) and the functioning of the SMPT blocks were reviewed at the end of the **Second Five Year Plan** and with the beginning of the **Third Five Year Plan,** the concept of Tribal Development Block was introduced and 75 T.D. Blocks were identified for extending special development programmes and this strategy continued until the end of the **Fourth Five Year Plan**. At the end of the **Third Five Year Plan**, it was revealed that the TD Block approach also did not yield any meaningful result as the problems of the tribals varied from place to place and were area specific in nature. During the Fourth Plan period, six Tribal Development Agencies were introduced on pilot basis in the country out of which two were started in Odisha including the Gunpur-Rayagada Tribal Development Agency. As a matter of fact till the end of the Fourth Five Year Plan period, the approach to the tribal development were basically generic in nature and were tried to be achieved through implementation of various sectoral programmes. With these backgrounds, it was decided to formulate a new strategy for the development of the tribal areas through area specific approach right from the beginning of the **Fifth Five Year Plan**. The tribal development problems during the Fifth Plan were visualized as two distinct categories, such as (a) areas inhabited by more than 50 per cent tribal population, and (b) tribals located in dispersed manner. During this Plan period, it was decided by the government to formulate an area development approach with focus on the tribals in case of the former categories of the tribals taking into consideration the local problems and felt needs of the tribals and for the dispersed tribals, family oriented programmes were decided to be extended. This is how the Tribal Sub-Plan approach came into force with the beginning of the **Fifth Five-Year Plan** in the State of Orissa. During this period for the implementation of the tribal development programmes, identification of development blocks in the state where tribal population was in majority and such places were covered under one Integrated Tribal Development Projects (TDPs) with a motive to adopt an integrated and area specific approach of development. For such projects, special fund provisions were made from State Government as well as from the Government of India under special central assistance. But during the **Sixth Five Year Plan**, the effort shifted to beneficiary oriented development schemes and during this phase, the scope of the Tribal Sub-Plan approach became more focused and Government adopted the Modified Area Development Approach (MADA) for smaller contiguous areas with a total population of 10,000 where tribal concentration is 50 per cent or more. The same development approach continued during the **Seventh Five Year Plan** and only the dispersed tribals were brought within the purview of the Tribal Sub-Plan during this Plan period. It is observed that during the above plan periods, until the end of the Seventh Plan period, the basic approach of development followed was socio-economic development of tribal through a number of income generating schemes and through Infrastructure development programmes. Despite all these efforts, it was revealed that the pace of development of the tribals was far from satisfactory and therefore, during the **Eighth Five Year Plan** period, the State started adopting the Maharashtra Model of Tribal Development through a single line demand through the Tribal Development Department. Under the changed system, instead of the past practice of planning from top to bottom, the exercise got reversed and the approach became from bottom to top. Thus, the decentralized system of planning was made for each tribal area with the ITDA as the base. Under such a changed arrangement, the tribal development department could be able to decide the priorities of the schemes to be implemented in the tribal areas on the basis of eliciting their felt needs. This approach adopted during the **Eighth Five Year Plan** proved to be relatively more beneficial as compared to the earlier plan periods. During the **Ninth Five Year Plan** spanning from 1997-2002, the major thrust of tribal development has been shifted to accelerate growth in employment, provision of basic minimum services to the people, eradication of poverty, and provision of food security. In order to guarantee that the above objectives are achieved and the quality of life of the tribals is increased, the Government of Orissa has given high priority to as many as seven basic services in the tribal inhabited areas. Along with these emphasis has been laid on the Agriculture and Rural Development Sectors for the tribals with a view to bringing them to the mainstream. During the **Tenth Five Year Plan 2002-2007** special attention was given for the all-round development of tribes in this regard Horticultural activities, effective irrigation facilities, animal husbandry and housing schemes are introduced for the interest of tribes. More funds have been provided to micro projects for all-round development of Primitive tribal Groups. The expenditure proposed on infrastructure development under SCA may be at least 70 per cent instead of 80 per cent as proposed in the guideline. This means up to 30 per cent may be used for income generating beneficiaries' schemes. During **Eleventh Five Year Plan 2008-**

2012 emphasis has been given towards the educational development of tribal students. The discussion on the schemes and programme formulated and adopted in different plan period has been elaborately discussed in this chapter.

Despite various poverty alleviation programmes and special strategies for economic development, poverty among Scheduled Castes and Scheduled Tribes is not reducing up to the mark. Among the special schemes undertaken by the government, the establishment of Special Multipurpose Tribal Development Blocks for giving special attention to neglected areas and population in the country, as laid down in Articles 46 and 275 of the Constitution which were based on the general pattern of Blocks and were to be as far as possible co-terminus with them and were to bring about rapid improvement in the economic and social standards of the tribals by selecting specially underdeveloped, but compact areas for multipurpose development. Initially on experimental basis four special multipurpose Blocks in Orissa were selected out of 43 Special Multipurpose Blocks established in the country for intensive Tribal welfare measures on the lines of the Community Development programme during the Second Plan period. Four backward Tribal areas were selected for establishment of these Blocks in 1956-57 as follows:

1. Bhuyanpirh in Keonjhar District.
2. Narayan patna in Koraput District.
3. Kashipur in Kalahandi District now transferred to Rayagada District.
4. Roruan in Mayurbhanj District.

The Scheme was executed in coordination with the Community Development Organization. The Government of India in the Ministry of Home Affairs gave Rs. 15 lakh and the Community Development Ministry Rs. 12 lakh for each of the Blocks. The funds of the Home Ministry passed through the Tribal and Rural Welfare Department and were placed at the disposal of the Community Development Department for execution of the scheme. However, the SMPT Blocks served as a pilot projects for taking up intensive welfare measures for the Tribals. In May 1959, the Ministry of Home Affairs, Government of India, appointed a committee under the chairmanship of Dr. Verrier Elwin to examine the work of the programme of these Blocks. This Committee examined the problems carefully and submitted a detailed report in 1960. The Committee felt that the experiment had succeeded and recommended it to be continued and extended during the Third Five Year Plan. In consideration of the committee's recommendations, the Government of India in the Ministry of Home Affairs in the letter No. 25/6/60-SCT-III (B), dated the 27th May,

1961, decided to open Tribal Development Blocks in Tribal concentrated areas with 66.23 per cent or more of Tribal population. Such Block would be covered out with an area of about 200 sq. miles and having roughly a population of 25,000 or 5,000 families on the basis of 1951 Census (*Sources*: Tribal and Rural Welfare Manual, Volume-2, Government of Orissa OGP 09.12.1966, Chapter – VI - II). It was decided that, there will be two stages of five years each for Tribal Development Blocks. In the 1st stage, the Tribal Development Block will get grants from Ministry of Home Affairs Rs. 10 lakh and in second stage Rs. 5 lakh. In addition these will get a sum of Rs. 12 lakh in stage-I and 5 lakh in stage-II as Community Development from the Ministry of C.D. (*Source*: Tribal and Rural Welfare Manual, Volume-II).

3.3 Co-operative Schemes and Projects

During the **First Five Year Plan,** the State Governments undertook schemes involving financial commitments in the field of co-operative societies. 310 multi-purpose societies, 350 grain banks and 653 forest labourers co-operative societies were formed in the tribal areas in order to tackle the problems of indebtedness of the tribals. The Government of Orissa decided to open different co-operative schemes during the **Second Five Year Plan** period in certain tribal areas to ensure supply of their daily necessity and to purchase their surplus produce at a fair price to wean the tribals away from the village *sahukars* and money-lenders from their economical exploitation (Tribal and Rural Welfare Manual, Vol. II, Government of Orissa).

3.4 Multipurpose Co-operative Societies

By the end of **Second Plan Period,** 34 multipurpose co-operative societies were established in different tribal inhabited areas of Orissa. The main object was to ensure supply of their daily necessaries and to purchase their surplus produce at a fair price. Besides, Craft-*cum*-Night School Teachers were appointed for spread of literacy among them to improve their economic conditions. Most of the societies were located near Ashram Schools for convenience of transactions as well as for enabling the tribal students to be acquainted with co-operative activities. The control of these societies was entrusted to the District Welfare Officers who were instructed to organize these societies in the first instance with the assistance of co-operative department and then get them registered under the Co-operative Societies Act. A manager was appointed to be in direct charge of the society. There was also a Salesman (The general instructions issued for control and management of these societies are given in GO No. 4405 (G) Tribal and Rural Welfare 1961). During the year 1961-62, the performance of these societies were reviewed. By that time 26 societies had been registered under the Co-operative Societies Act. On review it was found that, only 15 of the registered societies were functioning satisfactorily. The remaining 11 registered and 8 unregistered societies were found deficient and were closed down with effect from 30 April, 1961. The remaining 15 societies were allowed to run under the control and supervision of Registrar of Co-operative Societies. Government continued to give annual grant-in-aid to these societies according to bare need for some time to meet the minimum establishment cost (GO No. 5948-Co-Op-Misc 21/61(13), dated the 15th/17th April, 1961).

Even after reorganization some of the societies were found not to be serving the purpose for which they were meant. It was, therefore, suggested to the Registrar of Co-operative Societies for closing down these societies and to start fair price shops in their place. The Registrar of Co-operative Societies suggested amalgamating of such societies which are working satisfactorily with graingola co-operative societies to supply consumer goods to the tribals on barter system.

The multi-purpose co-operative societies initiated during the 1st Plan could not succeed. It was stated as an "Example of launching a ship without rudder and campus". (It was criticized in a study made by the NCAER). These organizations failed after they were transferred to the Community Development and Panchayati Raj (G.P.) Department of Government of Orissa. When they were administered on the same lines as Communities Development and Panchayati Raj Grain Golas. An evaluation study conducted by Tribal Research Bureau, Orissa pointed out the following main reasons for failure of these Grain Golas:

(a) It could attract only educationally and economically advanced groups of people to enroll as members of these societies.
(b) The members of Board of Governors were mainly from non-tribal groups.
(c) The percentage of loans offered by the Grain Golas were negligible as compared to the total volume of loans offered by the money-lenders.
(d) A high rate of interest, i.e., 25 per cent charged in short-term loans put a heavy burden on the borrowers as they take paddy loan generally for a period of six months.

Hence, these societies gradually became defunct (*Adivasi* – Vol. XIII, 1971-72).

3.5 Forest Co-operative Society

Tribal people generally were exploited by the forest contractors who took lease of the forest produce and make better profit using Tribal labour on low wages. In order to check this exploitation and to help the *Adivasis* to take substantial advantage of the forest wealth, government sponsored the Forest Co-operative Societies in Tribal area under the centrally sponsored programme during the **Second Plan** period. Under this scheme, co-operative societies were formed with tribal members. It was contemplated that these societies would take lease of the forests and minor forest produce. To protest the tribal labour 25 such societies were established in different tribal areas in Orissa for collection and marketing of forest products. But it was noticed that the societies are unable to pay back the loan amount without severally affecting the working of the society. So it was decided to provide the working capital to the societies in shape of subsidy and also to reward additional grants for the working capital to the extent required for smooth management and this was decided upon and adopted during the **Third Plan** period. The profit was distributed among the members of the societies in accordance with the approved bye-law (Tribal and Rural Welfare Manual, Vol. II, Government of Orissa).

3.6 Labour Contract Co-operative Societies

In tribal areas, the work was actually executed by Tribal labour but the profit was enjoyed by the contractor. In order to promote the economic improvement of the labour classes, Government was encouraging settlement of contracts through labour Co-operative Societies. To enable the tribal to take advantage of the facilities, in the year 1962, Government of Orissa sanctioned funds for organizing seven Lobour Contract Co-operative Societies of Tribals in different tribal areas (Tribal and Rural Welfare Manual, Vol. II, Government of Orissa, OGP, 9-12: 1966).

3.7 Forest Marketing Co-operative Societies

The Forest Marketing Co-operative Societies (FMCS) were organized in 1956-57 to check exploitation of the tribals by the Forest Contractors. But a review committee appointed by the Government has observed that these societies suffered from inadequacy of working capital, imperfect organization and severe competition from private traders. The apex forest producing marketing Society which was formed in 1968 to overcome the difficulties also suffered from similar limitations and had to run at a loss due to low turn over (Tribal and Rural Welfare Manual, Vol. II, Government of Orissa, OGP, 9-12: 1966).

3.8 Purchase, Sale and Fair Price Shop Scheme

The purchase, sale and fair price shop schemes were organized in 1963-64 with the main objectives to protect the tribal from exploitation of unscrupulous money-lenders to provide them with ready marketing facilities, ensure fair prices for their agricultural, forest produce and supply them credit both for production and consumption needs. But these societies could not extend their activities on account of inadequacy of funds, insufficient working capital, lack of flexibility in financial matters and absence of adequate system for collecting market reports and disposing of goods on larger wholesale markets (Tribal and Rural Welfare Department, Government of Orissa, 1976).

3.9 Orissa State Tribal Development Co-operative Society

The Orissa State Tribal Development Co-operative Society Ltd. was set up in April, 1972 with the main objectives of disbursement of production and consumption loans to the tribals, procurement of tribal produce, supply of basic consumers goods and other necessities to the tribals and to arrange marketing of produce of primary societies of the tribals. The Apex Forest Producing Marketing Co-operative Societies were merged under the newly formed society. The authorized share capital of the society was Rs. one crore and it has been observed that there was manifold increase in the share capital and working capital of the society in between 1971-72 to 1973-74. But the T.D.C.S. suffered from a number of limitations. It was pointed out that the society was losing sale of all controlled goods, because of heavy transport cost and inaccessibility of the areas, low turnover and heavy establishment cost. Hence, a further modification of Bye-laws was made in October 1975 and this society was registered as the Tribal Development Co-operative Corporation of Orissa Limited (T.D.C.C.O.L.) with the objective of further intensifying its activities. In spite of all these changes made, now the TDCCOL is in the process of disintegration (*Source*: Report of the Commission of Scheduled Castes and Scheduled Tribes, 1976).

3.10 Soil Conservation and Watershed Management Units

Under these schemes, the available resources near the habitation of the Tribals on the hill slopes were utilized with the objective of improving the economic condition of the Tribals and to wean them from shifting cultivation. Eroded lands near villages and road side were selected and anti-erosion measures were taken. Land having slope of above 10 per cent was set apart for preeminent (outstanding) vegetation, fruit farming or pasture development and land having slopes below 10 per cent were contour-bounded and used for crop production. Demarcation of cultivable land was done by planting rows of guava and cashew nut. Cultivation was discouraged on slopes above the demarcation lines. After the area for location of the Watershed Management Unit was demarcated, comprehensive soil conservation measures recommended for different lands were undertaken. The scheme was executed under the general control of the Joint Director of Soil Conservation who was under the administrative control of the Agriculture Department. The intention of the scheme was to provide Soil Conservation measures mainly contour bunds on lands belonging to tribals in the watershed areas affected by soil erosion in order to grow improved crops (Tribal and Rural Welfare Manual, Vol. II, Government of Orissa).

3.11 Grant for Development of Cottage industries

During the year 1956 -57, the scheme for development of cottage Industries especially for uplift of Scheduled Tribes was initiated. It was intended that the scheme would be able to help primarily Scheduled Tribes through training in crafts in the Ashram Schools, Industrial and other institutions. For imparting this kind of training, funds were provided in the State Sector Plan. The responsibility of selecting candidates for grant of subsidies and amount of grant to be given in them was entrusted to be the District Magistrates. During the year 1960-61, the principle was changed and it was decided to allot funds for purchases of tools, implements and registered under the Society Registration Act. For giving financial help to deserving person in the year 1961-62, the grant was placed at the disposal of Zilla Parisad. During the year 1963-64, the grant was placed at the disposal of the District Magistrate for sanctioning necessary grants-in-aid to the needy Scheduled Tribes Craftsmen to settle in trades. The grant was limited to Rs. 150 for an individual for purchase of tools and equipments as would be approved by sanctioning authority. It was continued as a special scheme in the Second Plan. In the Third Plan no special scheme could be included for this purpose. During the First Plan period, some Scheduled Tribe and Scheduled Caste candidates were deputed for training to different institutions both inside and outside the State and Government paid stipends for them. During the Second Plan Period, Government in the Tribal and Rural Welfare Department opened special training institutions of their own as well as sanctioned stipends to the Scheduled Tribe and Scheduled Caste and other Backward Class students for training in various industrial institutes. The schemes were started as centrally sponsored scheme for imparting training to the Scheduled Tribe students in various types of trades. The institution was started in the year 1957-58 with a sanctioned strength of 96 trainees and it has been expanded during the Third Five Year Plan period with the addition of 164 seats (Tribal and Rural Welfare Manual, Vol. II, Government of Orissa).

3.12 Poultry Rearing

The tribal are very fond of poultry rearing. They often need fowl for sacrifice in religious and social purposes. Further with the growth of civilization, the demand for fowl and eggs is increasing from time to time throughout the state. It was, therefore, felt necessary to encourage scientific poultry rearing among the tribals with a view to improve their economic condition and to make fowl and eggs easily available in backward areas. Government have, therefore, established poultry units in tribal areas in different districts which served both as demonstration centres as well as centres for supply of eggs and bird of improved breed. During the First Plan period for the encouragement of poultry rearing twelve poultry units were established in the tribal areas near Tribal and Harijan Welfare institutions like Ashram Schools, village welfare centres etc. During Second Plan period, the scope of the scheme was expanded by starting poultry units in all the Ashram Schools managed by the students on roster arrangement and a teacher was kept in charge of the supervision of the unit. In course of time most of the Ashram Units did not function properly. Hence, the Ashram school units were scrapped altogether and a new pattern of poultry development units was introduced in the following 5 Ashram schools such as Nuagan under Phulbani district, Sunabeda and Gobindapali under Koraput district, Chandragiri at Ganjam district and Suakati under Keonjhar district with appointment of veterinary staff (Tribal and Rural Welfare Manual, Vol. II, Government of Orissa).

3.13 Pisciculture

In order to provide improved method of fish rearing in the tribal areas government sponsored a scheme to open small pisciculture centres in different tribal areas. During the Second Plan period, six such centres were started, one in Phulbani, two in Mayurbhanj, two in Koraput and one in Keonjhar district by the end of 1960-61. Out of this, one centre located at Kotpad in the Koraput district was transferred to Dandakaranya Development Authority in 1960-61 and in its place another centre was started in the district of Keonjhar. Besides one Composite fish seed centre on a big scale was started at Bomelei in the Sambalpur district in the year 1961-62 for research, demonstration and supply of fish seed and fries to the people as well as to other small centres. All these schemes were executed through the Director of Fisheries. For the execution of work, the Director of Fisheries has been empowered to sanction plan and estimates up to Rs. 50,000 for non-residential buildings and up to Rs. 20,000 for residential building in Finance Department Resolution No. 5394-Codes-16/63F dated the 18th February, 1963). He has also empowered to sanction the projects of reclamation of tanks up to Rs. 50,000. There are a good many number of fishermen among the other backward classes but due to their poverty they did not get adequate opportunity to improve their trades. During the 1958-59, a scheme for improvement of pisciculture among them was sponsored by the Government under Central Sector of the plan with the objective to (1) renovate selected swamps and to allot them to local fisherman's co-operatives. (2) To take up a special pogramme for giving equipments to coastal fishermen and to give equipments to fishermen's co-operative to enable them to fish in tanks and rivers to improve their trade. However the scheme was dropped during the Third Plan Period (*Source*: Tribal and Rural Welfare Manual, Vol II).

3.14 Bee Keeping

Honey is a valuable wealth in agency areas. In order to train the Adivasis in scientific method Apiculture, two bee-keeping instructors were appointed one in Phulbani and the other in Koraput for the purpose. There were two bee-keeping centres in each of these district, viz. Nuagan and Phiringia in Phulbani district and Govindapalli and Gompakonda in Koraput district opened in 1951 and the bee-keeping instructor appointed for the district remained in charge of these centres in the respective districts. These centres served as demonstration centres for the areas. Bee boxes were supplied not only to these centres but also to various other welfare institutions like Ashram Schools, Sevashram, and Village Welfare Centres etc. The Instructors were collecting honey by taming bees at the Centres under their control and also were going round different institutions which have been supplied with bee-boxes, to impart necessary instructions in bee-keeping and production of honey. The honey collected was sold and the sale proceeds were deposited in treasury. Out of the 4 centres opened previous, two centres in Koraput district have been closed down. Only one Bee-keeping instructor was attached to Nuagan Centre. He functions under the control and supervision of the District Welfare Officer (*Source*: Tribal and Rural Manual, Vol. II).

3.15 Graingola

During the year 1951-52, the scheme of construction of graingolas was introduced. Funds for this purpose were given by Gram Panchayat Department and Tribal and Rural Welfare Department. In order to have a uniform pattern of Graingola the scheme has been co-coordinated with that of the Community Development and Gram Panchayat Departments (*vide* Community Development Department Letter No. 2 (C.D.F.) dated the 2nd January, 1959 (Tribal and Rural Welfare Manual, Vol. II). The idea behind setting up of Graingolas was to ameliorate the economic conditions of the

Scheduled Tribes by providing cheap credit in the form of grain loans and by eliminating usurious money-lenders. Graingolas or grain banks were functioning in the States of Bihar, Orissa, and West Bengal. The paddy stocked in the gaingolas was advanced on loan to needy villagers at an interest of 25 per cent. In Co-operative Graingolas, generally paddy loans were advanced in 3 instalments. First instalment was distributed in the month of May or June for the purpose of exchanging it with seeds. The second instalment was given in July or August for purchase of agricultural inputs and the third was made available for consumption during the lean Months. Where Graingolas were not organized into Co-operative Societies and was under departmental management, a local committee of the leading persons of the villages was formed for each Graingola and where Gram Panchayats have been constituted, the members of the Gram Panchayats were the members of the committee. The Committee meet at the time of issuing loan and recommends genuine applications for grant of loans.

The Paddy loan advanced by the Graingolas should as a rule was to be repaid in paddy with usual rate of interest but in every special circumstances where the Board of Directors of the society were satisfied that for exceptional reasons, such as natural calamities, the borrowers were not able to repay the loan in form of paddy, repayment may be allowed in cash. While allowing such repayment in cash, the principal and the interest due from the borrower should be calculated in paddy terms and its value recovered in shape of cash at the current market price. This procedure was not, however, to be restored to as a matter of course. The loanee must repay the entire quantity of grain loan given to him together with the interest at 25 per cent of the principal just after the harvest of the agricultural year in which the loan is taken. If the loan is not reapid in time, it becomes recoverable under the "Public Demand Recovery Act" in case of Co-operative Graingola an award is issued by the R.C.S. for recovery of the loan.

Although the primary objective of the Graingolas was to supply paddy loans to cultivators, it may also take up loan in the shape of distributing the fertilizers, seeds and manure (Report of the Scheduled Area and Scheduled Tribes Commission, Volume I, 1960-61 under the Chairmanship of U.N. Dhebar).

3.16 Rehabilitation Schemes of Tribes

For the establishment of different projects in the tribal areas, a number of tribal families were displaced. In the construction of Balimela Projects 72 villages were projected to be submerged. About 2000 families mostly Scheduled Tribes were affected. Like-wise ten villages in Sunabeda areas were acquired in connection with the establishment of Aero Engine

Factory. A number of tribal families were affected in the establishment of Kolab Irrigation Project in the undivided Koraput district.

Government in the Centre and State Government have taken a number of rehabilitation measures for socio-economic development of the tribals during the plan period. Dandakaranya Project was set up by the Ministry of Rehabilitation, Government of India for resettlement of displaced persons. Under the provision, the following principles were approved:

(1) Each family should be given 7 acres of land.
(2) The State Government was responsible to provide house buildings, supply of seeds, agricultural implements, bullocks etc., which was limited to a maximum of Rs. 1300 per family as a grant not as a loan.
(3) A maintenance grant up to Rs. 200 per family to enable the family to subsist till the crops were harvested should be paid through the state Government.
(4) A number of houses to be constructed in each new tribal village should be as suggested by the respective State Government.
(5) In respect of school, community building etc. the general principles followed in establishing such colonies for displaced persons were to be followed (*Source*: Tribal and Rural Welfare Manual, Vol. II).
(6) Besides affording rehabilitation facilities to the Scheduled Tribes under the colonization schemes, Government have given other help to poor Scheduled Tribes and Scheduled Castes for agricultural operation such as distribution of bullocks, seeds and implements. This was a non-recurring grant given to selected Scheduled Tribes and Scheduled Castes people who were unable to afford purchase of bullocks, seeds and implements for their cultivation. The grant was placed at the disposal of Zilla Parishad/Panchayat Samitis or the Collectors as the case may be for distribution among the deserving persons (*Source:* Tribal and Rural Welfare Manual, Vol. II).

3.17 Baipariguda Pilot Project

During the year 1959, Shri Anna saheb Sahasrabuddhe, a prominent member of Akhil Bharat Sarva Seva Sangha discussed with the Deputy Minister of Community Development and Co-operation about the possibility of launching a special pilot scheme in Baipariguda areas to be executed through non-official agency. The matter was then taken up at a Government level and the Community Development Ministry agreed to the proposal. Then a detailed report in this regard has been submitted by the Akhil Bharat Sarva Seva Sangha amounting Rs. 32.29 lakh, which was to be operated over a period of 6 years. The aim of the scheme was to improve the economic standard of the Tribal people of Baipariguda area comprising the limits of the Baipariguda panchayat samiti. The following gram panchayats were included in the project area:

1 Baipariguda Gram Panchayat
2. Ramgiri Gram Panchayat
3. Kenduguda Gam Panchayat
4. Dasamantpur Gram Panchayat
5. Majhipada Gram Panchayat

The scheme was approved by the Government of India to be executed through the Akhil Bharat Sarva Seva Sangha. The pilot project was started in October 1959 as the Project authorities were authorized to utilize a sum of Rs 1.22 lakh out of the unspent balance of the Grant given to the Sangha previously for development of Sarva Sadan villages. During the year 1960-61, a sum of Rs. 6,59,480 was given to the project in two instalments. Thus total amount Rs. 7,81,480 was given to the Sangha by the Tribal and Rural Welfare Department up to the end of 1960-61 against the scheme out of the saving under other centrally sponsored schemes provided during the Second Five Year Plan. An agreement was executed by the Sangha to execute the scheme as stipulated by Government. While releasing grant-in-aid for this scheme, the Home Ministry, Government of India, stipulated that the grant given by them for the scheme should not be utilized for giving loans. As the proposal of the Sangha included item of loan amounting to Rs. 8,52,500, the Sangha was intimated to restrict the expenditure out of the Government grant to non-loan items only and to meet the cost of loan item from their own resources (*Source*: Tribal and Rural Welfare Manual, Vol. II).

It also laid down that there would be an Advisory Committee called the Project Development Committee to advise an implementation of the programme. This was to be reviewed when Panchayat Samiti would be set up.

Due to introduction of Panchayati Raj, the committee of direction had no function as envisaged in the original resolution. So the committee of direction was abolished and in its place a advisory committee was set up in resolution No. 6658 TRW, dated the 5th May, 1961 consisting of two representatives of A.B.S.S.S. (Akhil Bharat Sarba Seva Shangha), Revenue Divisional Commissioner, Southern Division, Collector Koraput, Chairman Zilla Parishad, Koraput and Chairman Panchayat Samiti, Baipariguda. Subsequently, a few members were taken and the committee was constituted. The main function of the committee was to advise Government on the policy to be followed in the pilot project and to formulate if any detailed scheme for consideration by Government Zilla Parishad or Panchayat Samiti. The proposed project development committee was dropped since there was no scope for the body.

After the commencement of the Block, the Project Officer was appointed as Block Development Officer as laid down in the resolution of the Tribal and Rural Welfare Department and the other staffs were absorbed in the Block pattern as far as practicable. In pursuance of the Government of India another committee was constituted by Community Development and Panchayati Raj (C.D.) Department in the resolution No. 293/C.D. dated the 16th January, 1962, with a view to co-ordinate the activities of Akhil Bharat Sarva Seva Sangha and the Community Development Organization. This was more or less meant to review the progress of the joint programme of the Sarba Seva Sangha of Baipariguda Block.

In the first meeting of the State level Committee held on the 14th February, 1963, the question of transfer of the Block for the management by Panchayati Raj Institution under the control and guidance of Government was discussed and agreed. Accordingly, the transfer was given effect from the 1st April, 1963, a regular B.D.O. was appointed to the Block by Government. The Sangha according to the decision would continue their work in the view of Co-operative Societies. The question of giving financial help from Government would be considered on the merit of work taken up (Tribal Rural Welfare Manual, Vol. II).

3.18 Large Sized Multi-purpose Co-operative Societies (LAMPS)

On the recommendation of Bawa Committee, LAMPS were established in Tribal areas to provide integrated credit and other services. It was based on the objective that a tribal requires a package of services, the main components of which are production as well as consumption credit and marketing of his agricultural and forest produce. These area need to be protected through a co-operative structure. Secondly, a tribal should not be required to approach too many institutions for assistance and all necessary assistance be made available under a single umbrella. In order to meet all these needs, LAMPS were established in tribal areas of the State.

Keeping in view the above recommendation of the Bawa Committee, the State Government decided to organize LAMPS only where no primary societies exist at that time or where the primary societies were defunct. LAMPS were to be serviced for credit purposes by the Central Co-operative Banks and commercial banks where Central Co-operative Banks did not exist. LAMPS provide service for supply of inputs and marketing of agricultural produce by Regional Co-operative Marketing Societies (RCMS). The TDCCOL were to serve them for marketing of non-agricultural produce and minor forest produce.

Initially, till 1980 these societies played an important role in supplying credit to villages. However, due to lack of adequate staff in the LAMPS and its branches, these institutions failed to provide necessary services. (*Source*: Sub-Plan for Tribal Regions of Orissa 1974-79. Tribal and Rural Welfare Department, Government of Orissa, Bhubaneswar, January, 1975).

3.19 Scheduled Caste/Scheduled Tribe Research and Training Institute (SCSTRTI)

The Institute is functioning since 1952 at Bhubaneswar with the broad objectives of research activities, identification of Primitive Tribes, preparation of Action Plan for the Socio-economic Development of STs and SCs, Organization of various training programmes, preparation and publication of various Evaluation Reports and the Journal '*Adivasi*' during 2002-03, the institute has completed Base Line Survey of all 13 PTGs residing in 17 Micro Project areas. Besides, evaluation study of 85 Grain Banks operating in TSP areas has been completed during 2002-03. It has also conducted 7 training programmes for field functionaries of ITDAs, Micro Projects and functionaries of PRIs. A workshop on "Customary Law in Primitive Societies" and one seminar on "Tribal Medicine and Medicine Men" have also been organized by the Institute (SCSTRTI, Bhubaneswar). Further this institution is organizing the different training programmes on skill development, life skill development training programme etc. among the field functionaries of the department.

3.20 Communication

Particularly the Tribal area badly lack in communication facilities which stands as a great hurdle in the implementation of welfare programmes. Generally, the tribal villages lie in interior areas away from the main roads, public institutions like Sevashrams. Village welfare centres have been established in the interior villages. People of surrounding localities are not able to take full advantages of these institutions owing to lack of good communication system. In order to provide good communication facilities in the inaccessible area the tribal and rural welfare department have been sanctioned funds every year to improve the communication by constructing village roads and link roads to connect main roads such as market places, hospitals, institutions and many other essential places, under SGRY, NFFWP & NREGS and a number of Cement Concrete roads have been constructed in interior villages during the last decade (*Source*: Tribal and Rural Welfare Mannual, Vol. II, Government of Orissa, OGP 9.12.1966).

3.21 Tribal Sub-plan Approach

From the beginning of the Fifth Five Year Plan, a new strategy has been introduced for the development of the Tribals. The problem of Tribal development was broadly classified into two categories— (1) Area having more than 50 per cent tribal concentration, and (2) Dispersed Tribals. In respect of the former it was decided to accept an area development approach with focus on Tribals. For dispersed Tribals, family oriented programmes were decided for being taken up. Thus, the strategy for Tribal sub-plan area came into operation on the eve of the Fifth Five Year Plan. The strategy composed of (i) Identification of development Block in the state where Tribal population was in majority and their Constitution into ITDPs with a view to adopting therein an integrated and project based approach for development, (ii) Earmarking of funds for the Tribal Sub-plan and ensuring flow of funds from the State and Central plan sectoral outlay. Special central assistance from financial institutions, and (iii) Creation of appropriate administrative structure in Tribal areas and adoption of appropriate personal policy.

3.22 Constitutional Provision

In order to uplift to the tribals various holistic efforts have been made since independence for their socio-economic development. Article 46 of the Constitution specially guarantees the Education and Economic interest of the weaker section people. Particularly of the Scheduled Tribe and shall project them from social injustice and all forms of exploitation. For achieving these objectives various safeguards relating to protection and development of tribals have been made under the Constitution, like (a) Social safeguards in Articles 17, 23, 24 and 25(2), and (b); Educational safeguards in Articles 14(4), 29 and 46; Political safeguards in Articles 164, 320(4), 332, 334, 243(d), 243(T), 371(A) (B) (C) (F) (G) and 371(H); Service safeguard: Article 16(4), 335 and 338. Provision relating to development, economic safeguard are contained under Article 275(I) and 339(2).

The Fifth Schedule to the Constitution contains provision relating to the administration and control of scheduled areas and Scheduled Tribes. The eight States, i.e., Andhra Pradesh, Bihar, Gujarat, Himachal Pradesh, Madhya Pradesh, Maharastra, Orissa and Rajasthan having Scheduled Tribe population are to constitute Tribal Advisory Council for all development policies of Scheduled Tribes. The Governor of States have been vested with special powers and responsibilities towards the all-round development of Scheduled Tribes. Further reservation in seats and special representation in State Legislature and Parliament have been ensured under Article 334 and reservation of services under 335 of the Constitution.

In order to ensure Socio-economic development of the Tribes different efforts have been taken up. During the plan period, the schemes for development of cottage industries, poultry rearing, pisciculture, graingola, bee keeping and other so many schemes and programmes have been taken up for the upliftment of tribal people. To tackle the problems of indebtedness of the tribals, 34 multipurpose Co-operative Societies have been opened during the Second Plan Period. Further to safeguard the tribes from the forest contractors, Co-operative Societies have been set up. Co-operative Societies were also initiated to help the economic improvement of the labour class. The tribal village welfare centre have been formulated with a view to educate the rural mass in various development measures taken for them to improve their socio-economic condition (*Source*: *The Indian Tribes Through the Ages,* R.C. Verman, 1990, p. 120).

3.23 Integrated Tribal Development Agency (ITDA)

Under the umbrella of Tribal Sub-Plan, ITDAs were set up in mid-seventies as nodal agencies for plan formulation programme, implementation and operationalisation of the TSP concept. At present 21 ITDAs are functioning in the 12 districts of the state of Orissa covering 118 Blocks having 50 per cent or more tribal population. Prime concern of ITDAs is to minimize the gap that exists between them and the rest of the society, to improve socio-economic conditions of tribals and to strengthen infrastructure in Tribal areas through various schemes that aim at income generation, asset creation, education, administrative and legal protection from exploitation (Annual Report 2008-09, ST & SC Development Department and Minorities and Backward Classes Welfare Department, Government of Orissa).

3.24 Modified Area Development Approach (MADA)

Modified Area Development Approach (MADA) was adopted during Sixth Plan. It was intended for development of the tribal population residing in contiguous area outside the TSP area having a population of 10,000 or more with at least 50 per cent Tribal concentration. 46 such MADA pockets in 47 Blocks in 17 districts in Orissa having 5.68 lakh population (2001Census) are functioning in the State in these pockets. Individual family oriented income generating schemes and also critical infrastructural development programmes are being implemented. There is MADA project level committee for each MADA pocket under the chairmanship of the Sub-Collector and official and non-officials including the local MLA and MPs as members. The Committee draws up programmes and oversees their implementation (Tribal and Rural Welfare Manual, Vol. II, Government of Orissa, OGP. 9.12.1966, Chapter VI. II).

3.25 Clusters Approach

The cluster approach was introduced during the middle of the Seventh Plan period to bring smaller areas of tribal concentration beyond the MADA pockets into the mainstream of development contiguous areas having population of 5000 or more with at least 50 per cent tribal concentration are identified as clusters.14 such clusters of the state covering 13 Blocks in 10 districts of the State covering 62,021 ST population (2001 Census) have been functioning under cluster approach. The administrative arrangement for these 14 clusters is similar to that of MADA pocket. For development of Tribals in these clusters in addition to the normal programme SCA is being provided for implementation of income generating schemes in group mode and community benefit-oriented programme (Annual Report 2008-09, ST & SC Development Department and Minorities and Backward Classes Welfare Department, Government of Orissa).

3.26 Dispersed Tribal Development Programme

Dispersed Tribal Development Programme (DTDP) is being implemented in the State of Orissa. Scheduled Caste and Scheduled Tribe Development Finance Co-operative Corporation Limited for the benefit of tribal families living outside the special project areas like ITDAs, MADA pockets Clusters and micro Projects. Currently 23 districts and 197 Blocks are covered under this programme. The following activities are undertaken under DTDP for which assistance is provided to the Tribal population living below Poverty line: (a) Provision of economic assistance under various bankable income generating schemes under margin Money Loan programme, (b) Community Minor Irrigation Project such as LIPs, WHS etc., (c) Training Programme for self-employment and wage-employment, (d) Enrolment of STs as members of co operatives (Annual Report 2008-09, ST & SC Development Department and Minorities and Backward Classes Welfare Department, Government of Orissa).

3.27 Micro Projects

The primitive tribal communities are considered as a special category in view of their distinctly different social, cultural and occupational practices and traits. Primitive Tribes are distinguished from other tribal communities with regard to their pre-agricultural economy, extremely low level of literacy, isolated habitation etc. During the Fifth Five Year Plan, it was decided by the Government of India to plan and implement specific programmes focused on the all-round development of the primitive tribes. In this regard, the Government of India has recognized 13 Primitive tribes in Orissa. The total population of the primitive tribes in Orissa as per the

was released as Tribal Co-operative Marketing Federation did not make sufficient procurement to make higher claims.

It will be observed that the performance of TRIFED has been showing downward trend in all respects. It should review the functioning of various units and initiate corrective measures as to play the important role of ensuring remunerative prices to the tribals for their produce. The present level of turnover is far too low and it needs to be significantly enhanced for playing a meaningful rule. The paid up share capital for the corporation has caught up with the authorized share capital. The TRIFED may take urgent action to enhance the authorized share capital so that it can continue to get share capital contribution from the Government to increase its activities. (*Source*: National Commission for Scheduled Caste and Scheduled Tribe Fifth Report 1998-99, Vol. I, pp. 209-211).

3.33 Tribal Development in Ninth Plan Period

The Ninth Five Year Plan has commenced from 1.4.1997 and the year 2000-2001 was the fourth year of this plan period. As per the guidelines of the Planning Commission, Government of India, Ministry of Tribal Affairs now lays emphasis on accelerated growth in employment, provision of basic minimum services to the people, or eradication of poverty through provision of food security. In order to ensure that the quality of life of the people is enhanced, seven basic minimum services, like drinking water, primary health services, primary education, housing to the shelterless, mid-day meal in primary education, rural road connecting the villages and public distribution system has been given high priority as focused in the Chief Ministers Conference organized by the Planning Commission. Special attention has been given in the Ninth Plan to agriculture and rural development sectors. For achieving the goal, an outlay of Rs. 5240 lakh have been proposed in the Annual Plan Estimate of the ST & SC Development Department during 2000-2001. The Tribal Sub-plan approach envisages the integrated development of the Tribal Area in which all programmes irrespective of their sources of funding operate in unison to achieve a common goal of bringing the area at par with the rest of the state and to improve the quality of life of the Tribals. Since mid-seventies the Tribal Sub-plan approach is in operation and on the basis of experience gained, the strategy and the methodology are refined from plan to plan so as to confront new challenges and to take care of new situations (*Source*: *Primitive Tribes of Orissa and Their Development Strategy,* 2005 by Nityananda Pattnaik and Annual Report, 2008-09).

3.34 Special Plan for KBK District (RLTAP)

Since implementation of the Revised Long Term Action Plan (RLTAP) for KBK districts in 1998-99, major thrust area of activity has been promotion of literacy among the ST & SC in general and promotion of female literacy in particular by way of providing scholarship to SC/ST students to pursue their studies, providing hostel accommodation from primary level arranging amenities in these hostels and taking up special repair/renovation of existing schools and hostels infrastructure. Keeping in view the special development of KBK districts, as many as 364 numbers of 100 seated ST girl hostel have been established in the year 2008-09 out of 1004 established in the state. The trend has been maintained by proposing further 372 new 100 seated ST Girl's hostel during the year 2010-11 out of 1040 in the state as a whole. Construction of 120 boys' hostels in the KBK districts is also in progress out of 288 proposed for the state. Of the 250 seated 19 numbers of ST Girl's educational complexes 8 nos. are located in the KBK districts and are functional. Located in the KBK (Annual Report 2013-14, ST & SC Development Department).

3.35 Janashree Bima Yojana (JBY)

Janashree Bima Yojana (JBY) of L.I.C. of India Ltd. was introduced in the year 2004-05 under Central Sector Scheme for development of PTG with 100 per cent grant-in-aid by Ministry of Tribal Affairs, Government of India, for insurance coverage of PTG families of the state. Total 18,722 PTG families have been insured under JBY by the end of 2007-08 (*Source*: ST & SC Development Department, Orissa).

3.36 Economic Rural Rehabilitation Programme (ERRP)

In order to eradicate poverty among the tribals Economic Rural Rehabilitation Programme has been introduced and steps have been taken for their socio-economic development. Various income generating schemes have been implemented for socio-economic development of rural people living under below poverty line. In partial modification of CD & RR Department letter No. 14102 Dt. 7.10.85 and No. 9417 dt. 6.11.85 in view of large scale failure of goatery and sheep rearing units taken up under ERRP programme in the past Government have been pleased to decide that goat rearing and sheep rearing shall no more be admissible under ERRP programme.

Similarly, dispersed poultry units scheme have not been successful. Government have, therefore, decided that individual poultry units shall no more be admissible under ERRP programme. Instead of mini poultry complexes should be developed around township and growth centres and the beneficiaries have been organized into co-operative society. The Tribal families who were the traditional poultry keepers ordinarily are given this scheme for better management.

Further, it has been decided that for pisciculture, excavation and renovation of private tanks of Scheduled Caste and Scheduled Tribe will be taken up. In the TSP and MADA areas, the Tribal beneficiaries have been provided 50 per cent subsidy for development of psciculture activities and economic development of the Tribal people. (CFSC) (*Source*: CD & RR Department, Letter No. 14102 dated 7.10.1985 & Letter No. 9417 dated 6.11.1985).

3.37 Grain Bank

A centrally sponsored scheme of the Grain Banks in tribal villages was launched during 1996-97 by the Ministry of Tribal Affairs in 13 states and was implemented through Tribal Co-operative Marketing Federation of India Ltd., an autonomous body under the Ministry of Tribal Affairs. During the Tenth Plan period, the standing committee of Union Ministers and State Chief Minister on Food Management and Agricultural experts in its meeting on 31st October, 2001 decided to expand existing Grain Bank schemes and extend it to all the endemic drought and migration prone areas with non-tribal area. Accordingly, it was proposed to include all eligible families living below poverty line in the grain bank schemes for which the Planning Commission had agreed to provide Rs. 250 crore.

The main objective of the scheme was to provide safeguards against starvation during the period of natural calamity or lean season when the marginalized food insecure households do not have sufficient resources to purchase the rations. Such people in need of foodgrain will be able to buy foodgrain from village grain bank. Gain banks have been established in the different interior villages for food security to the people in the tribal area. Further, a revised village Grain Bank scheme has been established in the different villages in the ITDA/MADA/DPAP/PTG and Micro project area and other remote and inaccessible pockets. The grain bank was functioning with its committee. Generally, the village grain bank committee consist of 7 executive members. The committee members were selected in a palli sabha in presence of PAITDA/BDO or WEO as per the Government guideline. 6 members should be of Scheduled Tribe and one member from Scheduled Caste community, out of which 5 are the female and 2 members are male (*Source*: Tribal and Rural Welfare Mannual, Vol. II, Government of Orissa, OGP, 9-12:1966).

3.38 Schemes for Tribal Education

Education is the backbone of a sound society. Generally, the Scheduled Tribe people are very backward in education. As they are the forest or hill dwellers and are inhabited in inaccessible pockets they are far from school education. In order to ensure educational development of the tribals, Government has initiated a number of schemes and programmes after independence and during the plan period. Just after independence,

Government has established a number of Ashram schools, Kanyashrams, Sevashrams and Residential Sevashrams with boarding and lodging facilities to the Tribal students.

3.38.1 *Educational Facility in Pre-Independence Era*

The Census figure of 1931 disclosed that among the tribals the literacy percentage was as low as 0.7 per cent . As regards the literacy is concerned, the condition of the tribal people was worse than that of the Scheduled Castes. The late Shri A.V. Thakker observed in 1941 that educational grant to aboriginal area have been meager and inadequate hitherto, middle school, higher school and college education among the Adivasi is of course negligible if not altogether zero. (Report of the Scheduled Area and Scheduled Tribe Commission, Vol. I, 1960-61).

3.38.2 *Educational Facilities in Post-Independence Period*

For educational development of tribals educational institutions have been established in the tribal concentrated area. From the period of 1948-49 to 1963-64, 85 nos. of Ashram and Knyashram schools have been established in the 13 undivided districts of Orissa. Out of these, 17 nos. of schools have been opened in the undivided Koraput district. Subsequently, many more educational institutions have been established for educational development of tribal children. At present 1585 educational institutions are running under the administrative control of ST & SC Development Department. Table 3.1 the detailed position of educational institutions of Orissa.

Table 3.1: List of the Educational Institutions Under SSD

Sl. No.	*Category of School*	*Number of Institution*
1	Eklavya Model Residential School	11
2	Higher Secondary Schools (Commerce & Science)	8
3	High School	155
4	Girls High School	143
5	Ashram School	109
6	Secondary Teacher Teaching School	2
7	Residential Sevashram	142
8	Sevashram	1026
	Total	**1585**

Source: Annual Report 2008-09, ST & SC Development Department and Minorities Backward Classes Welfare Department, Government of Orissa.

3.38.3 *Upgradation of Primary School under Sarbasikhya Abhiyan*

As per the decision of Government all the 109 Ashram schools, 142 residential Sevashram and Sevashram where ST girls hostel and primary school hostels have been opened. Out of remaining sevashrams of a district located in thickly populated area and in places where upper primary, middle English schools are not available within 3 km have been upgraded to upper primary school up to class VIII from the academic year 2008-09 under Sarba Sikhya Abhiyan letter No. 22641, dated 29.5.2008, Director ST & SC-*cum*-Additional Secy. to Government, Government of Orissa, ST and SC Development Department.

3.38.4 *Construction of New Residential Girls High School*

In the year 2001-02 keeping in view of the educational development of the Scheduled Tribe girls children, forty seated (KBK) girls hostel have been opened attaching to Sevashram school. Where 40 ST girls boarders students up to class V are allowed to reside in the hostel. Further 100 seated girls hostel have been opened during the financial year 2007-08 for better education of tribal girl students up to class X. Besides the Model School have been established for the higher education of the tribal students. During Eleventh Five Year Plan, the ST, SC Development Department has established 52 nos. of new Residential Girls High School from class VI to X in tribal blocks in the year 2008-09. Each school has a strength of 250 girl students (Annual Report, 2008-09).

3.38.5 *Educational Complexes in Micro Project Area*

In order to ensure educational development of children of primitive tribal groups and to arrest the dropout rate 19 educational complexes have been opened in 2008-09 in micro project area. Educational Complex of Arishkani at Bisamcuttack for Dongariakandha, Parsali at Kalyansingpur, Kereba at Gunpur for Lanjiasoura under Rayagada district, Badbel at Khairput for Bonda, Nandinipada Educational Complex at Kudumuluguma for Didayi and Badapada Educational Complex at Khirput for low-literacy pockets of Malkangiri district under study area has been opened and functioning with its own buildings (Annual Report, 2008-09).

3.38.6 Opening of Higher Secondary School

For the Higher educational facility to ST & SC students, 8 nos. of Higher Secondary Schools have been established in the year 2006-07 in different tribal populous block of the State having the Commerce and Science Faculty (ST & SC Development Department, Orissa, Bhubaneswar).

3.38.7 *Teaching in Tribal Language*

Government in ST & SC Development Department have taken steps to impart teaching in tribal language in Santali, Saora, Munda, Bonda, Kul, Kuvi, Juang, Koya, Kisan and Oram in primary section of some schools of this department which are located in the most remote tribal areas. The Tribal language teachers have been engaged in the school selected for imparting teaching in the local tribal language during the year 2007-08 (Annual Report, 2008-09).

3.38.8 *Opening of Teachers Training Institutions*

Teachers training school at Kodigan under Phulbani district has been functioning and one B.Ed. Training College has been established in the Kandhamal district in the year 2009-10 for imparting training to the un-trained teachers posted by the ST & SC Development department. In spite of various measures taken for improving the educational facilities and literacy level among the tribal communities, the rate of literacy among the tribals is far from satisfactory. As a result they have not been able to take full advantage of various development programmes and benefit of reservations in the educational course and in services. To supplement the efforts of normal programme of Education Departments in the Central and State Governments, certain specific programmes have been launched exclusively for the benefit of Scheduled Tribe communities. In view of the peculiar socio-cultural environment of the tribal communities, a centrally sponsored scheme of Ashram Schools was launched in 1990-91. The objective was to extend educational facilities in an environment which is conducive to learning by the tribal children. Under this scheme, 50 per cent of the cost of construction of school buildings, hostels, staff quarters etc., is provided by the Central Government. The balance 50 per cent of the capital cost as well as the recurring expenditure is to be met by the concerned States from their own resources. Similarly, the Central Government provides 50 per cent grant for construction of hostels for tribal boys and girls. In addition, the Central Government provides post-metric scholarship to the tribal children for higher education, including for professional courses. There are also facilities for coaching, book banks etc. so as to see that the tribal children are enabled to get the benefit of higher education (Annual Report, 2008-09).

3.38.9 *Scheme for Scholarship to SC/ST Students*

Pre-metric Scholarship is given to the Scheduled Caste and Scheduled Tribe students studying in the residential schools of ST & SC Development Department, UP/M.E. schools and High schools of School and Mass Education Department and the educational institution run by NGOs. The detail rate of Pre-Matric Scholarship awarded to the ST and SC students studying in class I to X is shown in Table 3.2.

Table 3.2: Chart of Pre-Matric Schlarship

Sl. No..	*Type of scholarship*	*Fund provided by*	*Hostellers*		*Day Scholars*		
			Boys	*Girls*	*Class*	*Boys*	*Girls*
1	Pre-matric Scholarship	State Government	620 p.m.	650 p.m.	VI-VII	150 p.a.	200 p.a.
					VIII	200 p.a.	250 p.a.
2	Pre-Matric Scholarship to ST & SC students of Class IX & X	Govt. of India	350 p.m.	350 p.m.		150 p.m.	150/p.m
3	*Adhoc* grant to ST & SC students of Class IX & X	Govt. of India	1000 p.a.	1000 p.a.		750 p.a.	750 p.a.
4	Top-up amount to ST& SC girl students of class IX & X within the family income cap of Rs. 200000 p.a.	DFID under OGIP		95 p.m.			95 p.m.
5	Top-up amount to ST & SC girl students of class IX & X beyond the family income cap of Rs. 200000 p.a.	DFID under OGIP		95 p.m.			95 p.m.

Source: Govt. Order No. 22804 SSD Bhubaneswar, Government of Orissa, ST & SC Development Department.

3.38.10 *Orissa Model Tribal Education Society*

Establishment of Model Residential School was launched during 1997-98. To provide quality education to the tribal students. It was decided by the Ministry of Tribal Affairs to utilize a part of the funds under Article 275(1) of the Constitution, for setting up of 100 model residential schools from class VI to XII in different tribal concentrated states of the country. As per the latest decision, the CBSE course has been introduced from class VI from the year 2011-12. The school have been affiliated to CBSE Board w.e.f. 2012-13. The Model Residential School have been named as Eklavya Model Residential Schools (EMRS). In Orissa, a society called the Odisha Model Tribal Education Society has been established and registered with the Secretary to the Department as its chairman and the director (ST & SC Development Department) as member Secretary. Eklavya Model Tribal Residential School has started functioning since 2000-01. In its 14th year of functioning 13 EMRS have been established across the state covering 9 districts. The Eklavya Model Tribal Residential School at Pungar under Similiguda Block of the district of Koraput has been established in the year 2000-01 in my study area.

3.38.11 *Scheme of Post-Matric Scholarship for ST & SC Students*

In order to provide Financial Assistance to ST & SC students studying at Post-Matriculation/Post-Secondary stage to enable them to complete their education. Centrally Sponsored Scheme of Post-Matric Scholarship has been implemented by the Government in ST & SC Development Department. The scheme is not limited with the ST & SC students, subsequently scholarship has been extended to the students of OBC/SEBC and Minority community. With a view to avoid delay in payment of Post-Matric Scholarship electronic mode of payment has been implemented from the academic year 2011-12. Students of Post-Matric stages are being divided into four groups – Graduate/Post-Graduate level courses in Engineering, Medical, Agriculture and Veterinary, PL course, P.G. Diploma course in Management and Medicine, Courses relating to Accountancy, M.Phil. Ph.D. and Post-Doctoral programme (D.Litt. D.Sc. etc.) LLM coming under group I.

Graduate, Post-Graduate courses leading to Degree, Diploma, Certificate areas, like Pharmacy, Nursing, Paramedical, LLB, Mass Communication, Hotel Management, Interior Decoration etc. PG Courses MA/MSc/M.Com./M.Ed., M. Pharma etc. belong to group II. +3 courses are group III and +2 . ITI, 3 years Diploma and 2 years vocational courses are group IV. The rate of maintenance fees per month is shown in Table 3.3.

Table 3.3: Scheme of Post-Matric Scholarship for SC ST Students

Type	*Group-I*	*Group- II*	*Group -III*	*Group- IV*
Day Scholar	550	530	300	230
Boarders	1200	820	570	380

Source: Information Brochure 2011, Scheme of Post-Matric Scholarship for ST/SC/OBC/SEBC and Minority Students, ST& SC Development and Minorities and Backward Classes Welfare Department, Government of Orissa.

3.39 Tribal Land Alienation and Constitutional Safeguards

Land is the most important productive resource base for the tribals and it is the mainstay of their social and religious practices. As per 2011 Census, 80 per cent of tribals depend on land either as cultivators or as agricultural labourers for maintaining their livelihood. Large scale land alienation from tribals to non-tribals has taken place during and after the British rule. Indebtedness, *benami* transactions and tempering of records by influential landlords are some of the important reasons for such land alienation.

The Orissa state have promulgated legislations from time to time to check land alienation. They are :

1. The Orissa (Scheduled Areas) Transfer of Immovable Property (by Scheduled Tribes) Regulation, 1956 (Regulation 2 of 1956).
2. The Orissa Scheduled Areas Transfer of Immovable Property (By Scheduled Tribes) Amendment Regulation, 2000.

Under the provisions of the Regulation 2 of 1956, any transfer of immovable property by a member of Scheduled Tribe shall be null and void and will have no force or effect what so ever unless made in favour of another member of Scheduled Tribe or with previous permission in writing of the competent authority. This regulation came into force from 4th October,1956. Regulation 2 of 1956 has been further amended on 4th September, 2000 to empower the Gram Panchayat and Gram Sasan in the prevention of land alienation in the Scheduled Areas as envisaged under Section 4 (m) (iii) of the provisions of Panchayat (Extension of Scheduled Areas) Act, 1996. The Amendment Regulation, 2000 has made provision for total prohibition to transfer of tribal land in the Scheduled Areas from members of Scheduled Tribes to others, if the land remaining after transfer will be reduced to two acres in case of irrigated land and five acres in case of unirrigated land. The Amendment Regulation, 2000 has also provided for restoration of land transferred from a member of a Scheduled Tribe to others without permission of the competent authority after 4th October, 1956. 2449 land alienation cases were pending at the beginning of the year 2001-2002 and 848 cases were instituted during 2001-2002. Out of these 1096 cases were disposed of by the end of March, 2002 and 201.253 acres of land were restored to the tribals. In spite of the legal provisions, the progress of restoration of tribal land has been very slow. The restoration of land transferred after 4th October, 1956 has posed a big challenge to the administration.

3.40 Forest Rights Act, 2006

Forest Rights Act, 2006 and Amendment Rules, 2012 are the significant landmarks and an important measure to provide Records of Rights to

Scheduled Tribes and other traditional forest dwellers. This is an epoch making legislation announced and promulgated by the Government of India, Ministry of Tribal Affairs. The Act envisages a number of provisions which enable the landless tribes to become legal landholder of such forest land which they have been customarily enjoying for considerable length of time. The Act in fact need to be understood by all Government functionaries of line Department such as ST & SC Development Department, Panchayati Raj Department, Revenue and Disaster Management Department and Environment and Forest Department who are actively involved in the implementation of the Act. In the process of this Act, many committees have been constituted in different levels. In the village level Forest Right Committees (FRCs) have been formed in each and every revenue village. This committee plays a vital role to recommend the landless people those who have been occupying the forest land before 13.12.2005 are to submit their application to the forest right committee of their respective villages and after approval of the same in the palli sabha. Approved applications can be submitted to the Sub-Divisional level Forest Right Committee (SDLC). After proper scrutinization by the Sub-Divisional level forest right committee all eligible applications with other necessary documents can be submitted to the District Level Committee for its final approval then right of records are being prepared and distributed among the beneficiaries concerned. Besides this state level monitoring committees are also functioning to expedite and implement the Forest Rights Act. Under the Act individual as well as community claims are to be taken into consideration. 13 Primitive Tribal Groups residing in the 12 districts of the state of Orissa are also availing the facility of the Forest Rights Act, 2006. Out of total households, 18,581 of the Primitive Tribal Group 16,822 families have been distributed the certificate of title. In this connection, 26,008 acres of land has been allotted in favour of them.

Thereafter, as on 31.3.2014, a total number of 3,31,939 titles have been settled and distributed which consist of 3,28,808 individual titles and 3,131 community rights title holders. The total area covered towards distribution of titles is 6,70,689.58 acres which includes 5,19,525.49 acres for individual titles and 1,51,164.09 acres for community right holders. Distribution of titles includes 17,798 individual certificates of titles to Particularly Vulnerable Tribal Group (PVTG) (*Source*: Annual Report, 2013-14).

3.41 National Scheduled Caste and Scheduled Tribe Finance and Development Corporation (NSFDC)

The National Scheduled Castes and Scheduled Tribes Finance and Development Corporation was established on 8th February, 1989, as a non-

First Plan were the establishment of 4000 schools including 1000 Ashram and Sevashram schools especially in Bihar, Madhya Pradesh and Orissa and the erstwhile State of Bombay and about 650 Shankar Kendras, Balwadis and Community centres in Bihar, Madhya Bharat, Rajasthan and Pre-organised Bombay State. Assistance was given to about 4,50,000 tribal students by way of scholarships, grants for books, hostel fees, etc". (Dhebar, U.N., 1961).

As far as Orissa is concerned 91 Ashram Schools were established in the State out of which 18 Ashram Schools, were established in Koraput region during the first two plan periods (Tribal and Rural Welfare Manual, Vol. I-II, 1966).

During the year 2004-05, there were 33,777 primary schools in the State out of which 18,320 primary schools were located in Scheduled Areas of the State. Similarly out of 13,225 Upper Primary Schools in the State of which 6,389 Upper Primary Schools were located in the Scheduled Areas of the State (Annual Report on the Administration of Scheduled Areas in Orissa, 2004-05).

The number of Ashram Schools functioning in the State increased from 91 in 2004-05 to 766 in 2011-12 and Sevashram Schools increased to 506 in 2011-12. The number of schools functioning under the administrative control of ST and SC Development Department in the year was 1619 including 156 High Schools, 143 Girls High Schools, 13 Eklavya Model Residential Schools and 19 Educational Complex for Primitive Tribal Groups (Annual Report, 2011-12).

4.1.2 *Collection of Data*

Primary data were collected from 24 educational institutions of the study area covering Koraput and Malkangiri districts to make an evaluation of the functioning of residential schools. The sample educational institutions consist of 8 residential schools functioning under School and Mass Education Department and 16 residential schools running under SC and ST Development Department.

The study has been made separately on the school and on the hostel. Investigation was made on the functioning of the school. Both internal factors and external factors were taken into account while evaluating the functioning of the school. From among the internal factors, the language of instruction, content and pedagogy, timing of the school, right type of teacher, stagnation and wastage, students' enrolment, play ground and provision of sports material, water supply and electricity facility, supply of books and writing materials etc. were taken into account. Among the external factors, geographical communication factors, gender bias, parental migration, community participation and ownership were taken into account.

4.1.3 *Students' Enrolment*

Student strength collected from different schools have been indicated at Col.11 of Table 4.1. The table reveals that the student strength varied between 86-595. There has been a substantial improvement in the enrolment of students over the past years. This situation indicates that the tribals have developed interest towards education. Due to determined efforts of the government at the Central and State levels, the Gross Enrolment Ratio (GER) of ST children has increased considerably at elementary levels of education, even more as compared to their non-tribal counterparts, e.g. the (GER) of ST children at primary stage is 137 as against 116 of their non-tribal counterparts. The corresponding figures for Upper Primary stage are 88.9 as against 85.5, and for elementary stage is 119.7 as against 104.3 (Chandramauli, 2013). Thus, the participation of ST children is now more or less in proportion to their share in population at elementary school level.

4.1.4 *Dropout of ST Children*

However, dropouts, though declining over years, are significantly large at the elementary level, the dropout rates of ST children at primary school level is 35.6 per cent as against 27 per cent of their non-tribal counterparts. The corresponding figure for elementary school stage is 55 per cent as against 40.06 per cent (Chandramauli, 2013). The factors responsible for the high rate of dropout among ST children of Koraput district of Orissa, as revealed from a DPEP sponsored study conducted by Pradhan in (2001) are : teachers absenteeism, lack of adequate teaching-learning materials in schools, irregularity in the supply of mid-day meal, lack of participation of VEC in school programme, poverty and illiteracy of parents etc.

It was reported by the Head Masters and other teachers present during the course of investigation that due to functioning of the mid-day meals programme, the dropout position of the students are being arrested (Col. 21). but it has been observed in the villages that there are few dropouts in the primary class and number of dropouts are more among ST girls. In addition to the socio-economic reasons, the temporary migration of parents in search of their livelihood is also another reason for dropout of ST children.

4.1.5 *Language of Instruction*

One of the major problems in tribal education is that of language. The text-books used in tribal areas are written in regional languages, with which the tribals are not familiar. The language used by the tribals vary from tribe to tribe and from place to place and therefore, the state government is facing a lot of difficulties. However, during the last decade steps have been taken to prepare primers for the Class-I and II students in tribal spoken language written in the regional language. Primers have been prepared in Koya, Bonda and Kandha during the last decade and it is expected that the children in these schools will perform better.

The use of tribal language in the initial years can develop a sense of comfort for the tribal child. The first language must be taught as a means of acquiring knowledge of tribal culture, ethnicity, literature and the Arts. "More importantly, class room transaction must be such that they show respect for child's language, identity and social background. The child can be exposed to State language steadily which is imperative for integration into mainstream schools and society". (N.N. Pradhan, 2014). Local language only cannot be used as a medium of instruction because of practical constraints. The study conducted by Pradhan and Pattanaik (2011) revealed that tribal students did not show interest to pursue formal education in their home language(s). They are of the opinion that education in the medium of their home languages (tribal languages) would not help them to expand the horizon of knowledge.

The scholar also found similar views expressed by the parents and children in Malkangiri and Koraput district. However, there was an unanimous opinion that at the beginning stage the use of tribal language written in local language can help a lot to the tribal children to create interest for education in their mind.

4.1.6 *Content of Pedagogy*

Research in child development and pedagogy has indicated that a young child learns concepts better if they are presented in the local contexts. Educational content should be moulded in the relevant culture of the community. Language resources of the tribal community can be tapped for this purpose. The Government of Orissa has provided tribal primers of tribal children, supported by picture dictionary, teachers' handbook, conversational chart and language training modules for non-tribal teachers (Educational Resource Unit, 2006).

4.1.7 *Timing of the School*

The attendance of the students in schools in tribal areas depends to a greater extent in the timings of the school hours and seasons. Absenteeism is found to be more during the seasons of agricultural operations and on the occasion of socio-religious festivals and rituals. The school timing, holidays and vacations are planned according to the general pattern followed in the non-tribal region all-over the state instead of planning them according to local needs. Hence, the attendance of students in schools are poor in tribal areas. The Dhebar Commission and Elwin Committee have recommended that the handicap of low attendance can easily be removed by observing vacations and holidays to fit in with the agricultural and forest operations and social festivals. The harvesting periods and festival period in Koraput region vary from tribe to tribe and sometimes from village to village within the same tribe. Hence, the village teacher should be given a free hand to plan his holiday list in consultation with the parents.

4.1.8 *Right Type of Teachers*

A number of teachers working in tribal areas are non-tribals and they do not have identification with the people and the area. Such teachers neither know the language of the people, nor their cultures and traditions. Adequate orientation is not provided to these teachers to equip with necessary knowledge of the language and culture of the people. They are also occasionally transferred to new schools where the culture and tradition of the people as well as the language may be different.

The recent effort made by the Government of Orissa to prepare primers in the regional language with the use of their own oral language, teachers' handbook and conversational chart, self-learning materials for teachers have partly solved the problem. However, it is desirable that tribal teachers are posted in their own area to provide better teaching to their own people.

Table 4.1 in column (13) reveals that there are a number of vacancy of teachers in Tribal areas of Koraput. The students of High schools are facing a lot of difficulties due to the lack of subject teachers in a number of subjects. The findings of the survey in the study area indicated that except in Government High School, Mudulipada at Bonda Hills, subject teacher posts are vacant in most of the schools in the study area.

4.1.9 *Playground and Sports Materials*

It has been found in the study area that the absence of games and sports facilities in the school fail to attract a tribal boy to the school. It was suggested by the Village Education Committee (VEC) members and teachers that in addition to football, volleyball, cricket, the traditional games and sports of their own area should be introduced in the school. It was held that this would be an additional attraction to tribal boys to attend the school and the dropout will be reduced.

During the survey it was found that there are no playground facilities available in the schools. Table 4.1, column 10 reveals this picture. Hence, it is suggested that playground facilities are to be provided in every school

Table 4.1: Evaluation of Educational Programme

Sl. No.	*Name of the Educational Institution*	*Year of Establishment*	*Village*	*GP*	*Block*	*Communicational facility*	*Distance from Block/ Dist. H.Q.*	*Area of Institution*	*Play-gound availa-ble/no*	*Student srength*	*Teaching Staff*	*Subject Teacher for H/S*	*No. of Class Rooms*
1	2	3	4	5	6	7	8	9	10	11	12	13	14
1	Report no collected		Kadam-guda	Pangam	Mathili	-	-	-	-	-	-	-	-
2	Pungam primary school S and ME	1953	Pangam	Pangam	Mathili	All weather	8 km	0.70 Ac.	No	326	5	No	4
3	Upgraded High school, Ambaguda	2008	Ambaguda	Ambaguda	Mathili	All weather	6 km	1.50 Ac.	No	150	2	No	4
4	Primary Sevashram, Matkamiguda	1954	Matkami-guda	Ambaguda	Mathili	All weather	5 km	1.23 Ac.	No	224	4		7
5	Govt. Girls High School	1994	Purunu-guma	Kadamguda	Kudumulu-guma	All weaher	12 km	4.00 Ac..	No	250	6	No	5
6	Primary School S and ME (Deptt)	1954	Siripeta	Parkanmala	Kudumulu-guma	All weather	15 km	0.97 Ac.	No	175	2	No	3
7	Sindhiguda Residenial School	1965	Sindhi-guda	Parkanmala	Kudumulu-guma	All weather	4 km	2.00 Ac.	No	411	4	No	5
8	U.P. School (Edun.)	1964	Kandel	Somnathpur	Kudumulu-guma	All weather	20 km	0.30 Ac.	No	96	2	No	2

(contd.)

(contd.)

Sl. No.	Name of the Educational Institution	Electricity Facility	Sports article	Drinking Water	Book Supplied	Note Book suppl-ied	Writing Materials	Drop-out position	Stipend per month				Annual HC Result 2009-10		
									VI-VII		VIII-X		Students appe-ared	Student passed	Percen-tage
									Boys	Girls	Boys	Girls			
1	2	15	16	17	18	19	20	21	22	23	24	25	26	27	28
1	Report no collected	-	-	-	-	-	-	-	-	-	-	-	-	-	-
2	Pungam Primary school S and ME	No	Nc	1 tube-well	Partly	No	No	5					NA	NA	NA
3	Upgraded High School Ambaguda	No	No	1 tube-well	No	No	No	3	15	20	20	25	Nil	Nil	Nil
4	Primary Sevashram, Matkamiguda	Yes	No	2 tube-wells	Partly	No	No	2							
5	Govt. Girls High School	Yes	Yes	3 tube-wells	Yes	No	No	2	15	20	20	25	NA	NA	NA
6	Primary School S and ME (Dept.)	No	No	1 tube-well	Partly	No	No	2					51	35	
7	Sindhiguda Residential School	Yes	No	1 tube-well	Partly	No	No	Nil					NA	NA	NA
8	U.P. School (Edun.)	No	No	No	Partly	No	No	Nil					NA	NA	NA

(contd.)

(contd.)

Sl. No.	Name of the Educational Institution	Year of Establishment	Village	GP	Block	Communicational facility	Distance from Block/ Dist. H.Q.	Area of Institution	Play-gound available/no	Student srength	Teaching Staff	Subject Teacher for H/S	No. of Class Rooms
1	2	3	4	5	6	7	8	9	10	11	12	13	14
9	Educatinal Complex, Kadamguda		Kadam-guda	Kadamguda	Khairput	All weather	5 km	4.00 Ac.	No	250	5	Partly	5
10	Kadamguda Sevashram	1972	Kadam-guda	Kadamguda	Khairput	All weather	10 km	2.00 Ac.	No	230	3	No	5
11	Govt. Girls High school	1996	Muduli-pada	Mudulipada	Khairput	All weather	14 km	2 .00 Ac.	No	301	7	Yes	10
12	Govt. High School for Boys	1984	Muduli-pada	Mudulipada	Khairput	All weather	14 km	3.00 Ac.	No	595	8	Partly	10
13	U.P. School S and ME, Jantaput	1972	Jantaput	Masigan	Kundra	All weather	17 km	0.50 Ac.	No	133	2	No	5
14	Primary Sevashram, Massigan	1947	Massigan	Massigan	Kundra	All weather	15 km	1.70 Ac.	No	315	4	No	5
15	U.P. School (Upgraded to H/S)	1960	Kalapada	Ghumar	Kundra	All weather	33 km	0.12Ac.	No	146	2	No	6
16	Ghumar Sevashram	1947	Ghumar	Ghumar	Kundra	All weather	30 km	2.00 Ac.	No	350	5	No	6

(contd.)

(contd.)

Sl. No.	Name of the Educational Institution	Electricity Facility	Sports article	Drinking Water	Book Supplied	Note Book suppl-ied	Writing Materials	Drop-out position	Stipend per month				Annual HC Result 2009-10		
									VI-VII		VIII-X		Students appe-ared	Student passed	Per-centage
									Boys	Girls	Boys	Girls			
1	2	15	16	17	18	19	20	21	22	23	24	25	26	27	28
9	Educatinal complex, Kadamguda	Yes	No	Running water	Partly	No	No	2					NA	NA	NA
10	Kadamguda Sevashram	Yes	No	1 tube-well	Partly	No	No	Nil					NA	NA	NA
11	Govt. Girls High school	Yes	Yes	2 tube-wells	Partly	No	No	Nil					NA		
12	Govt. High School for Boys	Yes	No	2 tube-wells	Partly	No	No	Nil					NA		
13	U.P School S and ME, Jantaput	Yes	No	1 tube-well	Partly	No	No	Nil					NA	NA	NA
14	Primary Sevashram, Massigan	No	Yes	2 tube-wells	Partly	No	No	5					NA	NA	NA
15	U.P. School (Upgraded to H/S)	No	No	1 tube-well	Partly	No	No	Nil					NA		
16	Ghumar Sevashram	Yes	No	2 tube-wells	Partly	No	No	2					NA	NA	NA

(contd.)

(contd.)

Sl. No.	Name of the Educational Institution	Year of Establishment	Village	GP	Block	Communicational facility	Distance from Block/ Dist. H.Q.	Area of Institution	Play-gound available/no	Student srength	Teaching Staff	Subject Teacher for H/S	No. of Class Rooms
1	2	3	4	5	6	7	8	9	10	11	12	13	14
17	Kanyashram, Baligan	1955	Baligan	Baligan	Baipari-guda	All weather	20 km	7.00 Ac.	No	415	8	Partly	10
18	U.P. School (S & ME)	1947	Sindhigan	Baligan	Baipari-guda	All weather	21 km	1.00 Ac.	No	135	2	No	3
19	Minarbali Sevashram	1952	Majhi-guda	Doraguda	Baipari-guda	All weather	8 km	2.50 Ac.	No	86	2	No	4
20	Doraguda R.S.	1956	Doraguda	Doraguda	Baipari-guida	All weather	15 km	3.00 Ac.	No	363	5	Partly	7
21	Kumbhari Sevashram	1947	Kumbhari	Kumbhari	Narayan-patna	All weather	10 km	2.00 Ac.	No	345	4	Partly	4
22	UG high School S & ME Deptt	1993	Siribeda	Kumbhari	Narayan-patna	All weather	8 km	1.50 Ac.	No	150	3	No	3
23	Palaput Sevashram	1952	Palaput	N.Patna	Narayan-patna	All weather	20 km	2.00 Ac.	No	237	3	No	3
24	Information not Available	Not available	Odepentha	N.Patna	Narayan-patna	All weather	4 km	NA	No	NA	NA	NA	NA
25	Balipeta SS	1947	Balipeta	N.Patna	Narayan-patna	All weather	3 km	NA	No	267	5	NA	5

(contd.)

(contd.)

Sl. No.	Name of the Educational Institution	Electricity Facility	Sports article	Drinking Water	Book Supplied	Note - Book suppl- ied	Writing Materials	Drop- out position	Stipend per month				Annual HC Result 2009-10		
									VI-VII		VIII-X		Students appe- ared	Student passed	Per- centage
									Boys	Girls	Boys	Girls			
1	2	15	16	17	18	19	20	21	22	23	24	25	26	27	28
17	Kanyashram, Baligan	Yes	No	2 tube-wells	Partly	No	No	Nil					NA	NA	NA
18	U.P. School (S & ME)	No	Yes	1 tube-well	Partly	No	No	Nil					NA	NA	NA
19	Minarbali Sevashram	Yes	No	1 tube-well	Partly	No	No	2					NA	NA	NA
20	Doraguda R.S.	Yes	No	1 tube-well	Partly	No	No	Nil					NA	NA	NA
21	Kumbhari Sevashram	Yes	No	1 tube-well	Partly	No	No	3					NA	NA	NA
22	UG high School S & ME Deptt	No	No	1 tube-well	Partly	No	No	Nil					11	11	
23	Palaput Sevashram	No	No	1 tube-well	Partly	No	No	2					NA	NA	NA
24	Information not Available	NA	NA		NA	NA	NA	Nil					NA	NA	NA
25	Balipeta SS	Yes	Avail.	2 tube-wells	Partly	No	No	5					NA	NA	NA

and games and sports facilities are to be introduced. The data collected also revealed that sports materials are available only in Government Girls High School, Purunagumma under Mathili Block, Government High Schools, Mudulipada under Khairaput Block, and Baligaon Kanyashram under Boipariguda Block and Masigaon Sevashram of Kundra Block of Koraput district. Except these schools no other schools are having sports article.

4.1.10 *Supply of Reading and Writing Materials*

In order to ensure joyful teaching method, adequate teaching, reading and writing materials need to be provided to every school. Essential Maps, Charts and Teaching aids along with an Almirah to store them carefully need to be provided to all the schools in the study area.

However, it was found in the study area that only Government High School, Purunagumma have been supplied with all necessary books and all other schools in the area have received books which are less than the requirement during September and October. Column-18 of Table 4.1 has presented this picture.

It was also noted that none of the educational institutions in the study area have been supplied with writing materials and notebooks. It has been found that different incentives like free uniforms, reading and writing materials and boarding and lodging facilities have resulted in higher enrolment of SC and ST students including girls. Hence, special attention needs to be paid for the provision of these incentives in time.

4.1.11 *Drinking Water Facility*

Safe drinking water facilities in the schools are a prime requisite for the health of the students. The Government of Orissa has given special attention for this aspect. The District Water and Sanitation Mission has been given this responsibility in the districts.

The present study revealed that except U.P. School of Kundel in Somnathpur Gram Panchayat of Kudumulugumma block, all educational institutions of the study area are running with its own tube well. No running water facility is available except in the educational complex at Kadamguda under Khairaput Block. This has been indicated in column-17 of Table 4.1.

4.1.12 *Electricity Facility*

In order to impart education as per the present syllabus electricity facility is a must in every school. The students and teachers use computer and the data base of the school are to be maintained in the computer. It has been found in the study that almost all educational institutions running under ST and SC Development Department are electrified. However, most of the schools run by School and Mass Education Department are not electrified till date. Hence, special attention has to be paid by the department to provide electricity facilities in these schools.

4.2 External Factors

External factors lie outside the education system. These, *inter alia*, include gender bias, difficulties of communication and distressed migration.

4.2.1 *Gender Bias*

Gender imbalance is an important issue at all levels of education, placing tribal girls at a disadvantage. Tribal girls have a higher tendency to drop-out and a lower tendency to enroll in schools. In many tribal communities, parents give minimal importance to girls' education due to economic and social limitations. Most frequently, girls apart from taking part in agricultural activities, forest produce collection devote their time for helping their mothers in household activities and sibling care. They are often compelled by their parents not to attend schools to extend cooperation in household work.

Efforts have been made by the Government as well as Non-Governmental Organizations to address the problem. Government schemes such as NPEGEL (National Programme of Education for Girls at Elementary Level) and KGBV (Kasturba Gandhi Balika Vidyalaya) are aimed at improving quality of education in tribal concentrated areas. These programmes have largely contributed for reducing drop-outs in respect of tribal girls in the study area.

4.2.2 *Difficulties of Communication*

In any isolated backward region, the geographical and communication factors are the important constraints in the spread of formal education. There are many villages in the district which have no primary school within a radius of 1.5 km due to geographical conditions, sparse population, and inaccessibility of tribal villages or migratory character of the tribals.

However, in the study area it is found that all weather communication facility is available in all the schools. Students do not face any trouble to go to the school regularly. But it is also noted that in the Nandapur and Semiliguda blocks, there are schools where the students have to cross the streams during the rainy season. Boat facility is to be provided in such stream to enable the students to attend the school regularly. It is learnt from the school teachers of these areas that the students/their parents have demanded boat facility from the district administration to enable the students to cross the river during rainy season to attend the school.

The above analysis and findings reveal that proper educational facilities are not provided in the tribal areas till today. In spite of the difficulties, a gradual increase in the awareness among the tribal parents about the value of education has been able to attract the tribals to the schools. Free boarding and lodging facilities provided in residential schools and provision of mid-day meal system have been attracting the tribals to the schools and there has been a substantial decline in the drop-out rate among the tribal students. The priority given by the government both at the Central and State levels for girls education and provision of 100 seated ST girls hostel has been responsible to attract ST girls to the schools.

However, all efforts are needed to be taken by the government to provide required number of subject teachers, playground and games and sports facilities, reading and writing materials, drinking water and toilet facilities, electricity and other facilities to enable these backward populations to compete with their counterparts in other developed areas.

4.3 Evaluation Study of PRI Members

Panchayat system is as old as India's civilization, politics, philosophy and culture (N. Das, 1967). Village Panchayat and Caste Panchayat were the symbol of socio-characteristics of the rural politics. Settlement of disputes through peaceful means were mainly done by village panchayats. The principle of Panchayat was 'Panch Parameshwar', i.e. God speaks through the five which in other words means that a unanimous decision of the Panchayat was respected as the verdict of God (H.D. Malaviya, 1956). 'Panch' was taken as the symbol of God and each member of the 'Panch' which originally consisted of five persons were considered impartial, judicious and their decisions were guided by the principles of natural justice. The decisions of 'Panch' were respected and honoured. Defiance of such decisions resulted in excommunication of the offender. The prerogatives of the 'Panch' were extended over all domains of social life (N. Das, 1967).

Scholar interacting with Sarpanch at Ambaguda GP of Mathili Block

The Kautilya's *Arthashastra* contains brilliant reference to the system of village Administration during the Maurya period. During the Vedic period, reference has been made to the existence of popular assemblies like the 'Sabha' and the 'Samitis'. These assemblies provided the democratic element in the administration of rural areas. (Harihar Das, 1993). Panchayat system also prevailed in Muslim period, Marathas period, and British period. Even to-day, the traditional Panchayats look after the administration of justice in the village and inter-village disputes.

4.3.1 *Statutory Panchayats in Orissa*

After independence, the concept of democratic decentralization was materialized in the State. The Orissa Gram Panchayat Act was passed in year 1948 which provided for the establishment of Gram Panchayat as units of local self-government. This Act had only set up Gram Panchayats in the villages. However, on the basis of Balwant Rai Mehta Committee Report, the three tier Panchayati Raj system was adopted in Orissa. The Orissa Legislative Assembly passed the Orissa Panchayat Samit and Zilla Parishad Act in 1959 and it received the assent of the Governor in January 1960. But in 1968 this Act was amended and Zilla Parishad was abolished (P.K. Behera, 2011).

A Photograph of Gram Sabha

Consequent upon the implementation of 73rd Amendment in the Constitution, the Panchayati Raj Institutions have received constitutional status. The Orissa Panchayat Act, 1985 has been amended in all respects in conformity with the Seventy Third Amendment in order to suit the needs of the people. The extension of the 73rd Amendment Act, 1993 and the election process were challenged in the High Courts of some of the States. As a consequence of this, as per the recommendation of the Bhuria Committee, the Parliament have passed the provisions of the Panchayats (Extension to Scheduled Areas) Act, 1996 (P.C. Mohapatro, 2013).

Scholar interacting with PRI Members

The Panchayats Extension to Scheduled Areas (PESA) Act, 1996 has made it mandatory for the state having Scheduled Areas to make specific provisions for giving wide ranging powers to the tribals on matters relating to decision making and development of their community. The Act has bestowed consultative powers to the Gram Sabha with regard to acquisition of land. It has also bestowed recommendary powers to the Grama Sabha and Panchayats for grant of prospective licence or mining lease for minor minerals in tribal areas and for grant of concession for the exploitation of minor minerals by auction. It has also bestowed wide powers to enforce prohibition or to regulate or restrict the sale and consumption of intoxicants, ownership of Minor Forest Produce, prevent alienation of land, control over money-lending, and central institutions functioning in tribal areas.

The provisions of the Central Act were adopted in Orissa State by amending the Orissa Gram Panchayat Act, 1964, Orissa Panchayat Samiti Act, 1959 and Orissa Zilla Parishad Act, 1961. The provisions of the Act were followed from February, 2002 PRI elections. Despite all the Constitutional Amendments on the political empowerment of the tribes, the empowerment of tribes in Koraput Region is not up to mark. Hence, an evaluation study has been conducted in the six blocks of Malkangiri and Koraput district which is the study area of the scholar.

4.3.2 *Data Collection*

During the course of field study detailed interaction has been made with the PRI members in the study area. 16 Ward members, 8 Sarpanches, one Panchayat Samiti Chairman and two Zilla Parishad members have been interviewed about their function, powers enjoyed and responsibilities for the development of their area. As the scholar could not meet with the Chairman, Panchayat Samiti of the study area, interview was made with the Chairperson Smt. Demai Nayak of Panchayat Samiti, Jeypore of Koraput district to assess the functions, powers enjoyed and responsibilities of the PRI members of the scheduled area.

4.3.3 *Educational Qualification*

A qualified PRI representative can represent the problems of his area in a better way and can understand his powers, responsibilities and functions properly However, the data collected about the qualification of the PRI representatives revealed that only three of them have passed HSC examination, six of them have failed in 10th class, eleven of them were in the range of class-2 to class-8 and others were just literate. Column-10 of Table 4.2 represents the educational qualification of each PRI member.

Thus, it is found that none of the PRI members in the study area is a graduate.

In the study area there are a number of HSC qualified candidates, a few graduates and one or two post-graduates. Hence, it is necessary to fix up a minimum qualification for the PRI members in the future elections to improve the functioning of the PRI members for the development of their area as well as to appreciate their powers and responsibilities.

4.3.4 *Category of PRI Members*

Column-8, 9 and 11 of Table 4.2 reveals that out of the 28 PRI members 9 were females and 19 were males. Out of 9 lady members, it was found that two were Chairman, one was a Sarpanch and the balance of 6 were Ward members. During the PRI training programmes organized by the State Institute of Rural Development (SIRD) through District Administration or NGOs, the lady PRI members were accompanied by their husbands. It was also found that in case of lady PRI members, their husbands enjoy the powers of their wife's office and take decision in many issues. This aspect need to be seriously considered by the Government and appropriate measures are to be taken for empowerment of women in political field.

4.3.5 *Primary Occupation of PRI Members*

It was found that almost all the PRI members belong to cultivator's family. Their main occupation is agriculture. Only two of them were landless and they were mainly engaged as agricultural labourers. One of the two have encroached Government land for cultivation purpose.

4.3.6 *Knowledge of PESA Act*

The State Institute of Rural Development have made arrangements for imparting training on three tier system of PRIs through Non-Governmental Organisations. Training have also been given by the DRDA on the PESA Act, 1996 to the Zilla Parishad members and Sarpanches. However, during the interaction among the PRI members, the scholar found that none of the members have complete knowledge on the PESA Act. One of the respondents was completely ignorant about the Act. Others have limited knowledge on the Act varying from 15 per cent to 50 per cent. This information has been presented in Column-15 of Table 4.2. It was learnt from the organizations who imparted training on PESA to PRI members that only 50 to 60 per cent of the PRI members attend the training. Few of these members attend only one day in the training programme.

The SIRD and the concerned district administration have to take adequate steps for the attendance of PRI members in the training programme.

4.3.7 *Attendance in the Meetings*

During the course of discussion it was learnt from the PRI members that the Ward members and the Sarpanches attend the Gram Panchayat meetings regularly. It was also found that they are attending the Palli Sabha and Grama Sabha meetings regularly. Even the Panchayat Samiti members and Zilla Parishad members try to attend the Palli Sabha meeting without fail. But it becomes difficult on the part of Zilla Parishad and Panchayat Samiti members to attend the Palli Sabha meeting as they are organized on a single day (Col. 16 of Table 4.2).

4.3.8 *Participation in the Meetings*

In the course of interaction with the PRI members it was learnt that even though the PRI members attend the meeting, some of them are not able to highlight the problems of their respective area. In many cases, the husbands of the lady PRI members are acting as proxy PRI members and the female members are set aside. Even the Panchayat Samiti Chairman of Jeypore block who is a tribal woman said that she is unable to play an active role in the decision making process in her Panchayat Samiti. Therefore, the Government has to find out the ways to empower the women representatives in the process of independent decision making.

4.3.9 *Functioning of the Traditional Village Panchayat*

Broadly speaking, functions and responsibilities of the tribal village Panchayats are the following:

(i) Upholding the social customs, traditions, mores, codes governing matrimonial alliances, divorce and family disputes etc.

(ii) Safeguarding and promoting the economic interest of the villages or member of the tribe in allocating community lands, and Government waste lands for cultivation as well as land for shifting cultivation, allotment of non-timber forest produce, community assets and protection of common property resources.

(iii) *Religious notes festivals:* Celebration of annual religious notes, ceremonies, festivals in order to appear the Gods and Goddesses and Spirits both benevolent and malevolent.

(iv) *Political safeguard:* It includes the development and encouragement of right type of leaders among the tribals, maintenance of organic linkages with statutory and traditional leaders at different levels and administration of justice as per traditional law, hereditary rights etc.

(v) *Protection of cultural heritage:* The traditional Panchayat also look after the maintenance and continuity of folk dance, songs, music, folklore, traditional skills and knowledge etc. (Gopinath Pradhan, 2009).

The traditional village panchayats in the study area are still performing some of their traditional functions. Fixing the days for observation of different festivals, settling the disputes inside the village between two persons or two groups of persons, disputes regarding marriage and divorce, appeasing Gods and Goddesses and Spirits both benevolent and malevolent are still performed by the traditional Panchayat. The statutory Panchayats perform the functions of development of the village, construction of roads and official buildings, identification of poorest of the poor people in the village etc.

In tribal areas of the study area, there is a good relationship between the traditional panchayats and statutory panchayats. The traditional Naik invites the Sarpanch to settle the disputes. On the other hand, the new leaders sometimes invite the traditional Naik for selecting a Sarpanch or Ward Members. The Sarpanch does not generally intervene in the performance of functions of the traditional council.

4.3.10 *Broad Implications*

With the introduction of statutory Panchayats, the traditional Panchayats have lost the functions of development of the village. But it has still retained its functions of deciding the cases brought before it relating to the theft, quarrel, divorce, sex offences and the like. The land dispute cases and murder cases are not taken by the traditional panchayats. The traditional Panchayats still play an important role for observation of tribal festivals, fixing the period of observation of a festival. In recent times, the period of observation of Pusa Purnima and Chitra festival has been reduced to few days due to the economic necessities.

The implementation of Panchayat Extension to Scheduled Areas (PESA) Act, 1996 has given wide powers to Palli Sabha and Gram Sabha. The State Government has delegated powers to Gram Panchayat, Panchayat Samiti and Zilla Parishad. However, due to illiteracy of the Ward members and lack of awareness among the Sarpanches, they are unable to exercise their powers in controlling the activities of different departments to the benefit of their respective area. In respect of Zilla Parishad President and members also, it is found that they are unable to exercise their powers. The district level officers and members of the Zilla Parishad should work together for formulating schemes and programmes for the development of the district. But it is found in the study area that a cordial relationship between the officials and elected members is lacking.

Table 4.2: Evaluation of PRI Members

Sl. No.	Name	Father Name	Village	GP	Block	Post holding	Sex		Educational Qualification	Tribal Group
							Male	Female		
1	2	3	4	5	6	7	8	9	10	11
1	Damuru Bhumia	Ram chandra	Kadamguda	Pangam	Mathili	Ward member	Male		Literate	Bhumia
2	Indra Nayak	Ishwar	Pangam	Pangam	Mathili	Sarpanch	Male		H.S.C.	Bhumia
3	Banamali Baraja	Mangala	Ambaguda	Ambaguda	Mathili	Sarpanch	Male		H.S.C.	Bhumia
4	Umakanta Nayak	Bhadra	Matkamiguda	Ambaguda	Mathili	Ward member	Male		10th Fail	Bhumia
5	Somanath Dora	Biswanath	Kandel	Somnathpur	Kudumuluguma	Ward member	Male		5th	Bhumia
6	Samara Pujari	Jhitru	Siripeta	Parkanmala	Kudumuluguma	Sarpanch	Male		10th Fail	Bhumia
7	Phula Kusa	w/o Sanu	Sindhiguda	Parkanmala	Kudumuluguma	Ward member		Female	Literate	Bhumia
8	Urdhaba Dora	S/o Sana	Pilakusum	Somnathpur	Kudumuluguma	Ward member	Male		10th Fail	Poraja
9	Manglu Sisa	Madhusudan	Kadamguda	Kadamguda	Khairput	Sarpanch	Male		10th Fail	Bonda
10	Sukru Kirsani	Shankar	Pusuguda	Kadamguda	Khairput	PS member	Male		Literate	Bonda
11	Shanti Kirsani	Laba	Mudulipada	Mudulipada	Khairput	Ward member		Female	Literate	Bonda
12	Sukru Sisa	Manglu	Andrahal	Andrahal	Khairput	Ward member	Male		Literate	Bonda
13	Arjun Pujari	Dayanidhi	Jantaput	Massigan	Kundra	Ward member	Male		3rd	Bhumia
14	K.Marichapulia	W/o Meena	Massigan	Massigan	Kundra	Sarpanch			4th	Bhumia

(contd.)

(contd.)

Sl. No.	Name	No. of Contestent	Occupation	Percentage of knowledge on PESA	Mode of Attending Meeting	Discuss with Govt. Official Freely or not	Functioning the Traditional Village Panchayat	How many meeting held in a year	Participated in Palli Sabha / Gram-sabha	Aware about Palli Sabha and Gram-sabha	No. of Voters casted their vote	Percentage of Votes
1	**2**	**12**	**13**	**14**	**15**	**16**	**17**	**18**	**19**	**20**	**21**	**22**
1	Damuru Bhumia	4	Cultivation	Nil	Regular	Freely	Functioning	4 to 5	Yes	20%	217/261	
2	Indra Nayak	5	Cultivaion	30%	Regular	Freely	Functioning	3 to 4	Yes	50%	4500/5000	
3	Banamali Baraja	5	Culivstion	35%	Regular	Freely	Functioning	3 to 4	Yes	50%	1800/2500	
4	Umakanta Nayak	2	Cultivation		Regular	Freely	Functioning	3 to 4	Yes	45%	140/260	
5	Somanath Dora	2	Cultivation	25%	Regular	Freely	Functioning	3 to 4	Yes	50%	240/280	
6	Samara Pujari	6	Cultivation	45%	Regular	Freely	Functioning	4 to 5	Yes	56%	3571/3855	
7	Phula Kusa	3	Cultivation	20%	Regular	Not freely	Functioning	3 to 4	Yes	30%	215/251	
8	Urdhaba Dora	2	Cultivation	50%	Regular	Freely	Functioning	3 to 4	Yes	49%	192/248	
9	Manglu Sisa	4	Cultivation	40%	Regular	Freely	Functioning	3 to 4	Yes	45%	3895/4270	
10	Sukru Kirsani	3	Cultivation	20%	Regular	Freely	Functioning	2 to 3	Yes	24%	1823/1756	
11	Shanti Kirsani	2	Agr. labour	31%	Regular	Not freely	Functioning	3-Apr	Yes	20%	90/120	
12	Sukru Sisa	1	Agr. labour	20%	Regular	Not freely	Functioning	3-Apr	Yes	23%	110/149	
13	Arjun Pujari	1	Cultivation	20%	Regular	Freely	Functioning	3 to 4	Yes	25%	1900/2300	
14	K. Marichapulia	2	Cultivation	21%	Regular	Freely	Functioning	2 to 3	Yes	27%	2579/2998	

(contd.)

(contd.)

Sl. No.	Name	Father Name	Village	GP	Block	Post holding	Sex		Educational Qualification	Tribal Group
							Male	Female		
1	2	3	4	5	6	7	8	9	10	11
15	Bholanath Majhi	Krupa	Kalapada	Ghumar	Kundra	Sarpanch	Male		7th	Bhumia
16	Susila Nayak	W/o Sobha	Paknaguda	Ghumar	Kundra	Ward member		Female	5th	Bhumia
17	Nanda Kendu	Budra	Baligan	Baligan	Baipariguda	Sarpanch	Male		2nd	Bhumia
18	Bhagabati Pujari	W/o Jai	Sindhigan	Baligan	Baipariguda	Samiti member		Female	HSC	Bhumia
19	Janki Poraja	W/o Sunadhar	Majhiguda	Doraguda	Baipariguda	Sarpanch		Female	Literate	Poraja
20	Lambodora Khara	Ram Chandra	Doraguda	Doraguda	Baipariguida	Ward member	Male		8th	Gadba
21	Budra Kunja	W/o Badadora	Kumbhari	Kumbhari	Narayanpatna	Ward member.		Female	Literate	Kanda dora
22	Girija Tu a	Kasinath	Siribeda	Kumbhari	Narayanpatna	Ward member	Male		4th	OBC
23	Narayan Saura	Kamollochan	Phampuni	Phampuni	Jeypore	Z P M	Male		5th	ST
24	Sadan Muduli	Ghenu	Kundra	Kundra	Kundra	Z P M	Male		10th fail	ST
25	Kanaklata Penthia	Arjun	Kundra	Kundra	Kundra	Chairman		Female	10th fail	ST
26	Gandabarni Gourt	Nariacha	Palaput	N. Patna	Narayanpatna	Ward member		Female	5th	ST
27	Chhalu Madingi	Sham	Odiapentha	N. Patna	Narayanpatna	Ward member	Male		8th	ST
28	Damai Nayak		Chhatarla	Pujariput	Kundra	Chairman		Female	5th	ST

(contd.)

(contd.)

Sl. No.	Name	No. of Contestent	Occupation	Percentage of knowledge on PESA	Mode of Attending Meeting	Discuss with Govt. Official Freely or not	Functioning the Traditional Village Panchayat	How many meeting held in a year	Participated in Palli Sabha / Gram-sabha	Aware about Palli Sabha and Gram-sabha	No. of Voters casted their vote	Percentage of Votes
1	2	12	13	14	15	16	17	18	19	20	21	22
15	Bholanath Majhi	6	Cultivation	30%	Regular	Freely	Functioning	3 to 4	Yes	45%	3523/3879	
16	Susila Nayak	2	Cultivation	29%	Regular	Freely	Functioning	3 to 4	Yes	40%	288/351	
17	Nanda Kendu	3	Cultivation	25%	Regular	Freely	Functioning	2 to 4	Yes	48%	2913/3125	
18	Bhagabati Pujari	2	Cultivation	60%	Regular	Freely	Functioning	3 to 4	Yes	80%	2723/3240	
19	Janki Poraja	3	Cultivation	19%	Regular	Freely	Functioning	4	Yes	40%	2861/3421	
20	Lambodora Khara	2	Cultivation	34%	Regular	Freely	Functioning	3 to 4	Yes	45%	221/245	
21	Budra Kunja	4	Cultivation	20%	Regular	Freely	Functioning	4 to 5	Yes	38%	198/245	
22	Girija Tula	3	Cultivation	35%	Regular	Freely	Functioning	3 to 4	Yes	40%	147/185	
23	Narayan Soura	3	Cultivation	50%	Regular	Freely	Functioning	3 to 4	Yes	50%	17800/20315	
24	Sadan Muduli	2	Cultivation	50 %	Regular	Freely	Functioning	3 to 4	Yes	50%	15678/18567	
25	Kanaklata Penthia	-	Cultivation	50%	Regular	Freely	Functioning	3 to 4	Yes	50%	3454/4231	
26	Gandabaini Gourt	3	Cultivation	20%	Regular	Freely	Functioning	3 to 4	Yes	35%	135/179	
27	Chhalu Madingi	4	Cultivation	40%	Regular	Freely	Functioning	3 to 4	Yes	40%	145/192	
28	Damai Nayak	2	Cultivation	40%	Regular	Freely	Functioning	3 to 4	Yes	40%	2113/3542	

4.4 Findings on Hostel Management

In order to reduce the dropout rate and for providing residential facility to the students belonging to ST families, the State Government have taken a special drive to establish hostels in approachable places. The first Ashram school in the State was started near Chandikhol temple in the year 1944 under the pioneership of Bhairabonanda Bramachari. This school was taken over by the Tribal and Rural Welfare Department in the year 1953. The Basipitha Ashram school was started as Sevashram school in the year 1950 and was upgraded as Ashram school in the year 1955 (Evaluation of Ashram Schools, 1971-72, *Adivasi*).

Girls Hostel, Bonda Development, Mudulipada

By March, 2003, 218 Residential High Schools were functioning in the State out of which 70 High Schools were in Koraput Region. During this period, out of 149 Residential Ashram Schools in the State 34 were functioning in Koraput region and out of 143 Residential Sevashram in the State 44 were functioning in Koraput region.

By the end of the year 2011-12, 3448 hostels were functioning in the State and 1383 were under construction. It consisted of different category of hostels, i.e., Primary School Hostels in ITDA blocks (1548), Primary School Hostels for ST Boys and Girls in KBK districts (400), ST Girls Hostels (1003 existing and 1040 under construction), ST Boys Hostels in 5 L.W.E. districts (388 under construction), Hostel for SC Boys and Girls

(438 existing and 55 under construction), Residential Ashram Schools in TSP area (52) and Special Adivasi Hostels (7) (Annual Report, 2011-12).

Forty seated hostels were constructed in each existing place of hostels for Scheduled Tribe girls during the Ninth Plan period. During the Eleventh Five Year Plan 100 seated ST girls Hostels have been established in the MADA and ITDA area.

Between 2009-10 and 2013-14, 817 Girls and Boys hostels were sanctioned most of which have been completed. The year-wise and district-wise allotment of hostels are detailed in Table 4.3.

Table 4.3: No. of Hostels for which funds were sanctioned during the period 2009-10 to 2013-14

Name of the District	*2009-10*	*2010-11*	*2011-12*	*2013-14*	*Total*
Koraput	61	20	80	24	185
Malkangiri	99	8	42	9	158
Nabarangpur	83	—	70	35	188
Rayagada	127	7	68	84	286
Koraput Region	370	35	260	152	817

Source: ST & SC Development Department, Annual Report, 2013-14.

It has been reported that all facilities like safe piped drinking water, sufficient number of toilets and bathrooms, kitchen, library rooms, play ground and high and properly fenced boundary walls. In addition boarders are provided with cots, blankets, mosquito nets, utensils, medicines, lady warden, lady cook-*cum*-attendants etc.

A series of instructions and guidelines has also been issued for efficient management of school and hostels by ST and SC Development Department as most of the schools of this Department are residential. Special emphasis has been given for management of the hostels. Sufficient funds are provided in the form of pre-matric scholarship for the boarders towards their food, accommodation, dress etc. Instructions are also issued from time to time for ensuring supply of qualitative food as well as quality education to the boarders along with their proper health care.

4.4.1 *Data Collection*

Primary investigation on management of hostels has been conducted in the study area of 11 different hostels and residential schools of Koraput and Malkangiri districts. During the course of field study both boy and girl boarders were examined. In the investigation process group discussions have been conducted among 260 boarders of 11 hostels, 24 teachers and

12 cook-*cum*-attendants (CCA) have been interacted about the functioning and management of hostels. As the Malkangiri district is coming under the study area, the educational complexes of primitive tribes of Bonda and Didayi are also included in the primary investigation of hostel management. The primary data so collected has been tabulated in Table 4.4.

During the course of investigation eleven numbers of residential schools running under ST and SC Development Department of Malkangiri and Koraput districts as well as the primary school hostels having 40 boarders, were covered. The two hostels functioning in Mudulipada for Bonda boys and girls under Khairaput block and the educational complex at Kadamguda were also included for collection of data. Thus, data has been collected from three blocks each from Koraput and Malkangiri districts. Kudumulugumma, Khairaput and Mathili blocks of Malkangiri district and Kundra, Boipariguda and Narayanpatna blocks of Koraput district have been covered to know the functioning of hostels.

4.4.2 *Water Supply Facility*

An investigation made on the supply of water to the inmates of eleven residential schools revealed that there is no tap water facilities in ten residential schools. Only the educational complex for Didayi students in Kudumulugumma block has this facility. The boarders are using water drawn from the tubewell. Absence of running water facilities in these schools create difficulties for the boarders to be ready in time for their classes. This also creates difficulties for supply of safe drinking water. The water facility provided in these institutions have been indicated in column 30 of Tables 4.4. Hence, it is suggested that pipe water facilities are to be provided in all the residential schools for the convenience of the inmates of the hostel.

4.4.3 *Electricity Facility*

It was found during the field study that the hostels run by the ST and SC Development Department are mostly electrified. This has been indicated in Column 15 of Table 4.4. But it has been reported by the boarders and concerned teachers that the electricity system is not functioning properly due to lack of proper maintenance. There is no provision of repair and maintenance in the school budget. Hence, it is suggested that adequate funds may be provided for the maintenance of electricity system in the schools.

4.4.4 *Toilet Facility*

Sufficient toilet facility has not been provided in the hostels as per the strength of the students. Columns 16 and 17 of Table 4.4 indicates the

Table 4.4: Evaluation of Hostels Functioning

Sl. No.	Name of the Hostel	Village	G.P.	Block	District	Year of estblish-ment	Condition of hostel building	Boarders Strength		Superintendent		Medical facilities	Distance from Hostel	Electri-fied or not
								Boys	Girls	Male	Female			
1	2	3	4	5	6	7	8	9	10	11	12	13	14	15
1	Hostel not available	Kadam-guda	Pangam	Mathili	Malkangiri	N.A.	N.A.	Nil	Nil	N.A.	N.A.	N.A.	N.A.	N.A.
2	Hostel not available	Pangam	Pangam	Mathili	Malkangiri	N.A.	N.A.	Nil	Nil	N.A.	N.A.	N.A.	N.A.	N.A.
3	Hostel not available	Ambaguda	Ambaguda	Mathili	Malkangiri	N.A.	N.A.	Nil	Nil	N.A.	N.A.	N.A.	N.A.	N.A.
4	Matkamiguda 110 seated	Matkam-iguda	Ambaguda	Mathili	Malkangiri	1,947	Need Rep.	40	150	1	1	Mathili	5	Yes
5	Hostel not available	Kandel	Somnathpur	Kudumu-luguma	Malkangiri	N.A.	N.A.	Nil	Nil	N.A.	N.A.	N.A.	N.A.	N.A.
6	Hostel not available	Siripeta	Parkanmala	Kudumu-luguma	Malkangiri	N.A.	N.A.	Nil	Nil	N.A.	N.A.	N.A.	N.A.	N.A.
7	Sindhiguda R.S. Hostel	Sindhi-guda	Parkanmala	Kudumu-luguma	Malkangiri	1994	Good	232	169	1	1	PHC K.guma	4 km	Yes
8	Hostel not available	Pilakusum	Somnathpur	Kudumu-luguma	Malkangiri	N.A.	—	—	Nil	Nil	Nil	Nil	Nil	
9	PSH/K.B.K/ 110 seated	Kadam-guda	Kadamguda	Khairput	Malkangiri	1,947	Good	40	150	1	—	Khairput PHC	10 km	elctr-ified
10	Hostel not available	Pusuguda	Kadamguda	Khairput	Malkangiri	N.A.	N.A.	Nil	Nil	N.A.	N.A.	N.A.	N.A.	N.A.

(contd.)

(contd.)

Sl. No.	Name of the Hostel	Toiletry facilities		Amenities						Schol-arship per month	System of pocket money	Reading and writing materials			Book supp-lied timely or not	Water supply
		Avail-able	*Requ-ired*	*Cots*	*M.Net*	*Blan-kets*	*Satar-anji*	*Plate*	*Water jug*			*Books*	*Note books*	*Pen/ pencil*		
1	**2**	**16**	**17**	**18**	**19**	**20**	**21**	**22**	**23**	**24**	**25**	**26**	**27**	**28**	**29**	**30**
1	Hostel not available	N.A.	N.A.	N.A.	N.A.	N.A.	N.A.	N.A.	N.A.	N.A.	N.A.	N.A.	N.A.	N.A.	N.A.	N.A.
2	Hostel not available	N.A.	N.A.	N.A.	N.A.	N.A.	N.A.	N.A.	N.A.	N.A.	N.A.	N.A.	N.A.	N.A.	N.A.	N.A.
3	Hostel not available	N.A.	N.A.	N.A.	N.A.	N.A.	N.A.	N.A.	N.A.	N.A.	N.A.	N.A.	N.A.	N.A.	N.A.	N.A.
4	Matkamiguda 110 seated	10	20	50	72	50	50	120	50	600	only girls	insuff-icient	not suppl.	not suppl.	not	2 tube wells
5	Hostel not available	N.A.	N.A.	N.A.	N.A.	N.A.	N.A.	N.A.	N.A.	N.A.	N.A.	N.A.	N.A.	N.A.	N.A.	N.A.
6	Hostel not available	N.A.	N.A.	N.A.	N.A.	N.A.	N.A.	N.A.	N.A.	N.A.	N.A.	N.A.	N.A.	N.A.	N.A.	N.A.
7	Sindhiguda R.S. Hostel	10	30	80	80	200	100	130	35	600	only girls	insuff-icient	not suppl.	not suppl.	No	2 tube wells
8	Hostel not available	Nil	Nil	Nil	Nil	Nil	Nil	Nil	Nil	Nil	Nil	Nil	Nil	Nil	Nil	Nil
9	PSH/K.B.K/ 110 seated	6	20	40	45	80	80	75	nil	600	only girls	insuff-icient	not suppl.	not suppl.	No	1 tube well
10	Hostel not available	N.A.	N.A.	N.A.	N.A.	N.A.	N.A.	N.A.	N.A.	N.A.	N.A.	N.A.	N.A.	N.A.	N.A.	N.A.

(contd.)

(*contd.*)

Sl. No.	*Name of the Hostel*	*Village*	*G.P.*	*Block*	*District*	*Year of estblish-ment*	*Condition of hostel building*	*Boarders Strength*		*Superintendent*		*Medical facilities*	*Distance from Hostel*	*Electri-fied or not*
								Boys	*Girls*	*Male*	*Female*			
1	**2**	**3**	**4**	**5**	**6**	**7**	**8**	**9**	**10**	**11**	**12**	**13**	**14**	**15**
11	Girls H/S Hostel	Muduli-pada	Mudulipada	Khairput	Malkangiri	1984	Good		301		1	Khairput PHC	14 km	elctr-ified
12	Boys H S Hostel	Muduli-pada	Mudulipada	Khairput	Malkangiri	1984	Good	595		1		Khairput PHC	14 km	elctr-ified
13	Hostel Not available	Jantaput	Massigaoan	Kundra	Koraput	Nil	N.A.	Nil	Nil	N.A.	N.A.	N.A.	N.A.	N.A.
14	PSH/ K.B.K/110 seated	Massigaon	Massigaoan	Kundra	Koraput	1,947	Good	40	150	1	1	Digapur PHC	3 km	elctr-ified
15	Hostel not available	Kalapada	Ghumar	Kundra	Koraput	Nil	N.A.	Nil	Nil	N.A.	N.A.	N.A.	N.A.	N.A.
16	Hostel not available	Pakna-guda	Ghumar	Kundra	Koraput	Nil	Good	40	150	1	1	Digapur PHC	3 km	elctr-ified
17	Baligan kanyashram	Baligan	Baligan	Baipari-guda	Koraput	1954	Good	nil	350		2	Baipari-guda	15 km	elctr-ified
18	Hostel not available	Sindhigan	Baligan	Baipari-guda	Koraput	N.A.	N.A.	N.A.	N.A.	N.A.	N.A.	N.A.	N.A.	N.A.
19	KB.K Hostel	Majhi-guda	Doraguda	Baipari-guda	Koraput	2002	Good	Nil	40	1	Nil	PHC Baipari-guda	10 km	elctr-ified
20	Doraguda R.S	Doraguda	Doraguda	Baipari-guda	Koraput	1954	Good	213	150	1	1	Baipari-guda	15 km	elctr-ified

(*contd.*)

(*contd.*)

Sl. No.	Name of the Hostel	Toiletry facilities		Amenities						Schol-arship per month	System of pocket money	Reading and writing materials			Book supp-lied timely or not	Water supply
		Avail-able	Requ-ired	Cots	M.Net	Blan-kets	Satar-anji	Plate	Water jug			Books	Note books	Pen/ pencil		
1	**2**	**16**	**17**	**18**	**19**	**20**	**21**	**22**	**23**	**24**	**25**	**26**	**27**	**28**	**29**	**30**
11	Girls H/S Hostel	15	15	130	60	120	145	301	nil	530	Rs. 30	Partly	Nil	Nil	No	2 tube-well
12	Boys H/S Hostel	15	25	192	73	185	163	595	nil	500		Partly	Nil	Nil	No	2 tube-wells
13	Hostel not available	N.A.	N.A.	N.A.	N.A.	N.A.	N.A.	N.A.	N.A.	N.A.	N.A.	N.A.	N.A.	N.A.	N.A.	N.A.
14	PSH/K.B.K./ 110 seated	9	20	55	60	100	100	120	Nil	600	only girls	insuff-icient	not supl.	not supl.	No	1 tube-well
15	Hostel not available	N.A.	N.A.	N.A.	N.A.	N.A.	N.A.	N.A.	N.A.	N.A.	N.A.	N.A.	N.A.	N.A.	N.A.	N.A.
16	Hostel not available	9	20	55	60	100	100	120	Nil	600	only girls	insuff-icient	not supl.	not supl.	No	1 tube-well
17	Baligan Kanyashram	20	15	130	144	165	79	171	Nil		Rs. 30	partly	No	No	No	3 tube-wells
18	Hostel not available	N.A.	N.A.	N.A.	N.A.	N.A.	N.A.	N.A.	N.A.	N.A.	N.A.	N.A.	N.A.	N.A.	N.A.	
19	K.B.K. Hostel	4	need rep	15	20	Nil	Nil	30	Nil	600	only girls	insuff-icient	not supl.	not supl.	No	1 tube-well
20	Doraguda R.S.	10	20	120	200	Nil	Nil	215	Nil	600	only girls	partly	No	No	No	2 tube-wells

(*contd.*)

(contd.)

Sl. No.	Name of the Hostel	Village	G.P.	Block	District	Year of estblish-ment	Condition of hostel building	Boarders Strength		Superintendent		Medical facilities	Distance from Hostel	Electri-fied or not
								Boys	Girls	Male	Female			
1	2	3	4	5	6	7	8	9	10	11	12	13	14	15
21	K.B.K./PSH/ 110 Seated SS	Kumbhari	Kumbhari	Narayan-Patna	Koraput	1,947	Good	195	150	1	1	N. Patna	10 km	electr-ified
22	Hostel Not available	Siribeda	Kumbhari	Narayan-Patna	Koraput	N.A.	N.A.	N.A.	NA	N.A.	N.A.	N.A.	N.A.	N.A.
23	Balipeta Sevashram	Balipeta	N. Patna	Narayan-Patna	Koraput	1,947		117	150	1	1	N. Patna	3 km	electr-ified
24	Information not available	Odia Pentha	N. Patna	Narayan-Patna	Koraput	NA	N.A.	N.A.	N.A.	N.A.	N.A.	N.A.	N.A.	N.A.
25	Educational Complex	Kadam-guda	Andrahall	Khairput	Malkangiri	2007-08	Functi-oning		250	1	1	PHC Khairput	5 km	electr-ified
26	Palaput SS	Palaput	N. Patna	Narayan-Patna	Koraput	1991	Good	40	150	1	1	N. Patna	1 km	electr-ified

(contd.)

(contd.)

Sl. No.	Name of the Hostel	Toiletry facilities		Amenities						Schol-arship per month	System of pocket money	Reading and writing materials			Book supp-lied timely or not	Water supply
		Avail-able	Requ-irea	Cots	M.Net	Blan-kets	Satar-anji	Plate	Water jug			Books	Note books	Pen/ pencil		
1	2	**16**	**17**	**18**	**19**	**20**	**21**	**22**	**23**	**24**	25	**26**	**27**	28	**29**	**30**
21	K.B.K./PSH/110 Seated SS	9	20	135	110	Nil	Nil	185	Nil		Rs. 30	Partly	No	No	No	2 tube-wells
22	Hostel Not available	N.A.	N.A.	N.A.	N.A.	N.A.	N.A.	N.A.	N.A.	N.A.	N.A.	N.A.	N.A.	N.A.	N.A.	
23	Balipeta Sevashram	10	15	130	100	Nil	Nil	150	Nil	600	Rs. 30	Partly	No	No	No	2 tube-wells
24	Information not available	N.A.	N.A.	N.A.	N.A.	N.A.	N.A.	N.A.	N.A.	N.A.	N.A.	N.A.	N.A.	N.A.	N.A.	
25	Educational Complex	15	10	nil	100	100	250	Nil	No	530/	Rs. 30 per girl	Nil	Nil	No	No	running water
26	Palaput SS	3	12	30	40	Nil	Nil	150	Nil	530	Rs. 30	Partly	Nil	Nil	No	2 tube-wells

existing number of toilets and the requirement. It has been found that the boarders are used to go outside for taking bath and to meet with their natural calls.

4.4.5 *Residing of Lady Teacher in the Girls Hostel*

During the field study, it was found that the lady teachers entrusted with the responsibility of Assistant Superintendent are not residing in the hostels. At some places these teachers in turn ask the lady cook-*cum*-attendant to look after the girls. This situation is found mostly in hostels situated in hilly and inaccessible areas. Such situation creates the problem of safety and security for the girls. Hence, it has to be ensured that the Assistant Superintendent should always be present with the students.

4.4.6 *Health Care of the Boarders*

It has been found in the study area that the sick boarders do not get any medical treatment. These hostels are located in inaccessible areas which are away from the PHC/CHC. Even health workers post are vacant in such areas. In such cases, the boarders are asked to go to their houses after preliminary treatment by the teachers. Ultimately, such boarders are taken to the traditional medicinemen by the parents of the students. Hence, it is necessary that at least a female health worker is posted in such areas and proper medical treatment is ensured to the boarders.

4.4.7 *Supply of Cot, Blanket and Bed*

The boarders should be provided with a cot, bed and a blanket. However, columns 18 to 20 of Table 4.4 provide the information in this respect. The boarders have not been provided with these minimum requirements for a comfortable stay in the hostels. Sufficient cots have not been provided to the inmates of the hostels. Even *Satrang* are not provided as per the requirement of the students. A number of boarders are sleeping on the ground. There is always an apprehension of poisonous snakes or reptiles in the hilly areas. The boarders feel difficulties to sleep in the iron cots if they have not brought any sleeping materials from their house. Mosquito nets have been provided in some of the hostels. Even in these hostels these nets are not sufficient to meet with the requirement of the students.

It is felt that the boarders are not given the minimum amenities for a sound sleep in the hostels. Hence, it is necessary on the part of the administration to ensure supply of these minimum requirements of a boarder.

4.4.8 *Reading and Writing Materials*

An interaction by the scholar with the boarders and teachers revealed that the reading materials are neither given in time nor in sufficient number as per the requirement of the boarders. The writing materials have not been supplied to any hostel in the study area. It has to be recognized by the administrators that these ST students are from poor families and the Government owns the responsibility for providing them quality education. The Central Government is providing enough grants for the educational development of these marginalized groups. Hence, every care has to be taken by the administration to provide the minimum requirement of these students.

4.4.9 *Pre-matric Scholarship*

Pre-matric scholarship is provided to the ST & SC students studying in the residential schools under SC and ST Development Department, ME schools and High Schools under School and Mass Education Department and the Boarders of Special Adivasi Hostels under the ST & SC Development Department. The Girl boarders are receiving Rs. 650 per month including Rs. 30 as their pocket money and the boy boarders are getting Rs. 620 per month. As regards the Days' scholars, students from class VI to VII are getting Rs. 15 and Rs. 20 per month in respect of Boys and Girls respectively in the schools run by ST and SC Development Department and School and Mass Education Department. Students from Class VIII to X are getting Rs. 20 and Rs. 25 per month for boys and girls respectively.

In the recent circular, the Department for International Development (DFID) has introduced a new scheme known as "Odisha Girls Incentive Programme" (OGIP) in the year 2012-13. In this programme, day's scholars of Class IX and X are getting the *ad hoc* book grant of Rs. 750 per annum and in respect of boarders they are getting Rs. 1000 per annum.

It is learnt from the pre-matric scholarship of different institutions that rate of scholarship are different for different institutions. The rate of pre-matric scholarship for Eklavya Model Residential School (EMRS) is Rs. 1000 per month for a boarder whereas it is Rs. 650 per girl and Rs. 620 per boy per month for a normal school run by the same ST and SC Development Department. In respect of Women and Child Development Department it is Rs. 750 per month per boarder (District Welfare Office, Koraput and District Social Welfare Office, Koraput). It is further learnt that all boarders of EMRS are getting pocket money which is not found in respect of boys in normal school.

4.4.10 *Sports Materials*

It was also found in the study area that sports materials are not available in all the residential schools. Provision of sports materials will provide an opportunity to the boarders to practice different games and sports like football, volley ball, Badminton, cricket etc. and enable them to represent their schools in different State level competitions. This is also a useful diversion of tribal students from their studies. Provision of sports facilities besides providing a useful diversion and sound health to the students will make them interested to study.

Scholar interacting with the Girls Boarder

4.4.11 *Health and Sanitation*

There is a saying that if wealth is lost, nothing is lost, but if health is lost everything is lost. The management of the hostels is an important aspect of providing quality education. It has already been found that running water/ pipe water facilities are not available in ten out of eleven hostels. In the absence of adequate toilet facilities the boys and girls are often found going to the nearby streams for meeting with their needs of natural calls. Even the girl students are compelled to take bath in the streams as they have to attend the classes in time. The sick students often go to the nearby PHC/ CHC as no medical staff is there to take care of them. During rainy season, the sick students face a lot of difficulties in the hostels situated in hilly and inaccessible areas. Adequate mosquito nets, cots, blankets, Satranj are not provided to the boarders, causing a lot of difficulties for a sound sleep.

Excepting in the hostel of Didayi area, the lady Superintendent/Assistant Superintendents are not staying with the boarders in the campus. All these combined poses difficulties for the students to maintain good health and sanitation facilities.

The introduction of residential schools in tribal areas during the early plan periods have attracted tribal boys and girls from different communities to read in these institutions. In course of time after the Third Five Year Plan period residential schools like Sevashrams, Kanyashram, Primary School Hostels, 40 seated ST girls hostels in KBK area and 100 seated hostels have been established in Tribal areas. The parents enjoy confidence if they get a seat in the residential schools. During the Eleventh Plan period Eklavya Model Residential complex have been established to meet with the quality education needs of the ST students.

However, there is an urgent need for quality management of the hostels. The students have to be provided with all their necessities in the hostels. Sound management of the hostels will be able to promote a larger number of ST students to compete with their counterparts in non-tribal areas. Hence, the State and the District Administration has to take all care for improvement of the hostel management in tribal areas.

4.5 Evaluation on Pre -Matric Scholarship

4.5.1 *Objective*

Keeping in view of the educational development of the Scheduled Caste and Scheduled Tribe student a holistic scheme of scholarship has been implemented during the First and Second Five Year Plan. The scholarship is being paid as day scholar and boarder rate wherever it is applicable. The Scheduled Caste and Scheduled Tribe students studying in ST & SC Development Department Schools and M.E. and High School of the School and Mass Education Department schools. This scheme was introduced to attract the students into the school and hostels, the poor parents will be willing to send their children into the school. As it is a successful programme, the Scheduled Tribe and Scheduled Caste students are taking the advantage of this scheme. The main object of the scheme is to provide financial assistance to children of Scheduled Caste and Scheduled Tribe community for their educational development. Subsequently, more emphasis have been given to the tribal women education and in order to encourage tribal women education 100 seated ST girls hostels are being established in the Eleventh Five Year Plan. It has been found during the primary investigation that maximum 100 seated girls hostels have been opened during the Eleventh plan period in the educational institution running under ST & SC Development Department schools. But gradually 100 seated girl's hostels have also been provided to the schools running under School and Mass Education Department School to provide better educational facility to the tribal women with boarding and lodging facilities.

Scholar interacting with students and teachers in the class-room

4.5.2 *Data Collection*

Primary and secondary data have been collected from the different educational institutions of Koraput and Malkangiri district, interaction have been made with the 24 teachers and around 50 Scheduled Caste and Scheduled Tribe students, 15 Cluster Resource Co-coordinators, 3 Block Resource Co-coordinators, 7 Welfare Extension Officers, Special Officer

Table 4.5: Pre-matric Scholarship for Day Scholar Students

Educational Level	*Rate per Pre-matric scholarship per annum as per the Govt. Resolution No. 70/94-29321 dated 29.9.94*		*Rate per Pre-matric scholarship per annum as per the Govt. Resolution No. 9082 dated 11.5.2010*	
	Boy	**Girls**	**Boys**	**Girls**
M.E. School Level Class VI & VII	100	150	150	200
High School Level Class VIII to X	150	200	200	250

Source: Government of Odisha ST & SC Development Department.

of Didayee Development Agency, District Welfare Officer, Koraput, Project Adminitrator ITDA, Jeypore and Koraput. The secondary data have been collected from the Government Guideline issued from time to time by the Government in ST & SC Development Department which has been tabulated in Tables 4.5, 4.6 and 4.7.

Table 4.6: Pre-Matric Scholarship for Boarder Students

Sl. No.	*Categories of educational Institutions*	*Existing rate of pre-matric scholarship*		*Revised rate of pre-matric scholarship*	
		Boys	*Girls*	*Boys*	*Girls*
1	**2**	**3**	**4**	**5**	**6**
	Categories of educational institutions of ST & SC Development Department e.g. H/S, A/S, R/S, PSH, 40 seated ST girls Hostels, up to100 seated ST Girls Hostel and 100 seated ST boys Hostel from Class 1 to X (boarders)	Rs. 600 pm for ten months	Rs. 630 pm for ten months	Rs. 620 pm for ten months	Rs. 650 pm for ten months

Source: Government of Orissa ST & SC Development Department Circular No. 22566 dated 17.7.2012).

Table 4.7: Pre-Matric Scholarship for Boarder students with detailed dietary expenses and other expenses

Sl. No.	*Details of materials*	*Qty. per time*	*No. of time*	*Price per kg*	*Amount per day*	*Amount per month*
1	Rice	250 gram	2	Rs. 2	Rs. 1	Rs. 30.00
2	Dal	40 gram	2	Vegetable according to prevailing market price		Rs. 355.00
3	Vegetables	135 gram	2			
4	Oil	20 gram	29.70			
5	Salt Fuel					
6	LPG and Fuel					Rs. 58.00

(contd.)

Sl. No.	Details of materials	Qty. per time	No. of time	Price per kg	Amount per day	Amount per month
7	Fish/Mutton/ Eggs/Chicken		Minimum Twice/ week			Rs. 65.00
8	Breakfast/Tiffin				Rs. 3.00	Rs. 90.00
9	TV/DTH connection					Rs. 2.00
10	Misc. Expenditure Oil/Soap/ Diesel/Corpus fund, etc.					Rs. 20.00
Total Expenditure						Rs. 620.00
	Pocket money including other expenses for girls					Rs. 30.00
	Total Expenditure for girls					Rs. 650.00

N.B: There is no provision of dresses during the year 2011.
Source: Government of Orissa, ST & SC Development Department, Circular No. 22566 dated 17.7.2012.

Tables 4.4 and 4.5 indicates the rate of pre-matric scholarships per month for food and other expenses per annum. In respect of food and other expenses, the scholarship has increased both for boys and girls. In spite of the increase, the students are not able to manage with the existing scholarship comfortably.

Table 4.6 indicates the pre-matric scholarship for boarders with detailed diatary expenses. It is found that only Rs. 3 has been sanctioned for breakfast student and Rs. 65 has been sanctioned for about eight times non-vegetable curry per month per student. Thus, per one non-vegetable curry, the average amount comes to Rs. 8. Rupees 8 for a plate of non-vegetable curry, Rs. 3 for breakfast is quite insufficient taking into account the current prices of goods and services.

Table 4.8 reveals that there has been discrimination among the day scholars and boarders in respect of book grant per annum. The book grant for day scholars should be equal to that of a boarder.

Table 4.8: Enhancement rate of pre-matric scholarship adhoc grant/book grant

Educational standard	*Category of students*	*Pre-Matric scholarship per month*	*Book/ad-hoc grant per annum for day scholar students*	*Book/adhoc grant per annum for boarders students*
I	ST & SC	NA	NA	NA
II	ST & SC	NA	NA	NA
III	ST & SC	NA	NA	NA
IV	ST & SC	NA	NA	NA
V	ST & SC	NA	NA	NA
VI	ST & SC	Rs. 15 per Boy, Rs. 20 per Girl	NA	NA
VII	ST & SC	Rs. 15 per Boy, Rs. 20 per Girl	NA	NA
VIII	ST & SC	Rs. 20 per Boy, Rs. 25 per Girl	NA	NA
IX	ST & SC	Rs. 150	Rs. 750	Rs. 1000
X	ST & SC	Rs. 150	Rs. 750	Rs. 1000

Source: Government of Orissa, ST & SC Development Departemnt, Bhubaneswar, Orissa

4.5.3 *Data Evaluation*

The primary data have been collected from different educational institutions of the Koraput and Malkangiri districts. The secondary data have also been collected from the District Welfare Office, Koraput and Malkangiri, which has been reflected in Table 4.5. The data presented in Table 4.5 reveals that the day scholar students belonging to Scheduled Caste and Scheduled Tribes are getting at very low rate of Pre-matric Scholarship. In Class VI and VII, the boys are getting Rs. 150 and the Girl students are getting Rs. 200 per annum, from class VIII to Class X the boys are receiving Rs. 200 and the Girl students are getting Rs. 250 per annum. But subsequently, the Government decided to introduce a new Centrally sponsored scheme of Pre-Matric Scholarship for students belonging to Scheduled Caste and Scheduled Tribe studying in Class IX and X with effect from 1.7.2012. The objective of the scheme is to support parents of ST & SC children for education of their wards studying in Class IX & X so that the incident of drop-out especially in the transition from the elementary to the secondary stage is minimized. Table 4.8 reveals that the day scholar students both boys and girls will get Rs 150 per month and book and *adhoc* Grant of Rs 750 per annum and in case of Boarders they will receive Rs. 1000 per annum with hostel facilities (*Source*: Government of Orissa, ST & SC Development Department). Further there is a provision of pocket money to the boys and girls boarders at the rate of Rs. 90 and Rs. 120 respectively.(*Source*: Letter No. 783/OMTES dated 24.11.1011 of Deputy Secretary, Government in ST & SC Development Department).

Further it is shown in Table 4.8 that the Boarders students are getting maximum Rs. 620 for boys and Rs. 650 for girl's boarders. This is meant for lodging and boarding facility of the boarders. A sum of Rs. 30 only is meant for the pocket money of the girl boarders out of Rs. 650. There is no provision of pocket money for boy boarders to study the provision of the diet chart provided by the Government. It is assessed that there is no provision of dresses to the boarders. Only pocket money is meant for girls but boy boarders are not receiving any pocket money. No dresses and electricity charges has been specified in the prescribed chart.

4.5.4 *Broad Implications*

The scholarship awarding system is being implemented since First Five Year Plan. In order to attract the Scheduled Caste and Scheduled Tribe students to schools, Government has implemented this scheme. The scholarship is given as day scholar and boarder rate. It is divided in two parts, as Pre-matric scholarship and Post-matric scholarship. From class I to X award of scholarship is called pre-matric scholarship and from Class XI onwards it is called post-matric scholarship. The scholarship for the Scheduled Caste and Scheduled Tribe students is enhanced from time to time. During the year 2010 after careful consideration of the existing rate of pre-matric scholarship provided to the Scheduled Caste and Scheduled Tribe boys and girls scholarship for day scholar students have been prescribed in the Department Resolution No. Sch(RS) 70/94-29321 and with due regard to the recommendation of departmental standing committee-VIII-2009-2010 (Fourteenth Assembly), the Government have been pleased to enhance the rate of pre-matric scholarship of the day scholar ST and SC students (Boys and Girls which has been applicable from the Financial Year 2110-2011). Another main impression on the pre-matric scholarship for the Scheduled Caste and Scheduled Tribe students is that, the boarding facility are being provided to them. Government in ST and SC Development Department has opened Residential school with lodging and boarding facilities K.B.K. 40 seated ST girls hostel, 100 seated girls hostel, Kanyashram, High school, Eklavya Modern Residential School, Primary school hostel even at college level up to standard XII with residential facility has been functioning for the educational development of the Scheduled Caste and Scheduled Tribe students in the tribal area. Because of these facilities, the Scheduled Caste and Scheduled Tribe students are getting free education with boarding and lodging facility. The poor parents are sending their children into the nearby school/hostel. The Scheduled Caste and Scheduled Tribe students are attracted towards the school because of hostel facility. The enrolment position of the school are rising. Students are availing the free lodging and boarding facility in the schools.

Scholar interacting with students in the classroom with Boarders

4.6 Conclusion

In tribal areas, the boys and girls are economic assets to their parents. A tribal boy helps his parents in a number of economic activities and a tribal girl helps her mother in household activities. A girl child also takes care of her younger brothers and sisters when her parents go out for work during the day time.

However, there has been a change in the attitude of the parents towards educating their children. They have now realized the value of education. The scholarship scheme which provides free boarding facilities and the hostels which provide free lodging facilities to their wards have attracted them to educate their children.

Dress for both boarders and day scholar pupils are being provided to create interest among them. Orissa Girls Incentive programme has been implemented, book and *adhoc* grant are being provided for the students of class IX and X. But the pre-matric scholarship for the student of class VI to VII is very low which need to be enhanced. Scholarship for girls incentive and *adhoc* grant should be extended to the students of class VI. Further it is found that when a boarder is getting in the EMRS Rs. 1000 per month the boarders residing in the hostel run under ST and SC Development Department school are getting a maximum of Rs. 650.

4.6.1 *Gaps in the Scholarship System*

Primary data and the secondary data have been collected from different Government offices of the ST and SC Development Department of Koraput and Malkangiri district, it is assessed that the holistic schemes meant for the Scheduled Tribe and Scheduled Caste students are not free from the defects. The lacuna found has been indicated as follows:

1. The rate of pre-matric scholarship is very low for the day scholar Boys and Girls students. For class VI and VII, the Boys are getting Rs. 15 per month and the girl day scholar student are getting Rs. 20 per month. The day scholar boy students of class VIII to X are getting Rs. 20 per month and girl students are getting Rs. 25 per month.
2. Whereas the SEBC and OBC students are getting Rs. 45 per month the Scheduled Caste and Scheduled Tribe students are getting minimum Rs. 15 and maximum Rs. 25 per month.
3. Whereas the children's home run by N.G.Os under Social Welfare Department are getting Rs. 750 per month, the Scheduled Caste and Scheduled Tribe students are getting only Rs. 620 for boys and Rs. 650 for girl boarders per month.
4. In the same department, the EMRS students are getting Rs. 1000 per month but there is no change in scholarship system of the SC/ST students they are getting only Rs. 620 for boy and Rs. 650 for girls per month.
5. The pocket money system is implemented only for the girl boarders but the boy boarders are not receiving any pocket money. But pocket money system is available both for boy and girl boarders in EMR schools.
6. The cost of dress of the boarders is not included within the scholarship, therefore, boarders are not getting dresses in time.

7. There is no provision of the medicine and electricity in the diet chart provided by the government.
8. New schemes of pre-matric scholarship is limited with the students of class IX and X.

4.6.2 *Prospects*

Implementation of the scholarship system is a holistic scheme of the Government for which more and more Scheduled Caste and Scheduled Tribe students are attracted towards the school and education. Even the parents are also very much interested to send their children into the school. The scheme is helping the poor Scheduled Caste and Scheduled Tribe students. They are getting free education with lodging and boarding facility. Students from class VI onwards are included in the scheme, and the boarders residing in the hostel are availing the pre-matric scholarship. With the continuation of this schemes, the tribal students are getting more benefit and their educational level as well as the educational standard are being improved. The main motto of the scheme is to support parents of ST & SC children for their education and to arrest the drop-out position. The scheme is not limited with class X students only. It is also available to higher education as post-matric scholarship. Only there is a provision that those parent's income range is below one lakh per annum will be entitled to avail the post-matric scholarship. But subsequently the income range of parents is enhanced to Rs. 2 lakh per annum.

4.6.3 *Concussion*

Under the right to education (RTE) Act passed in 2009 by the Government of India, a free and compulsory education is guaranteed for all children in the age group of 6 to 14 and most recent figures for primary school enrolment figures are impressive. Introduction of pre-matric scholarship for the Scheduled Caste and Scheduled Tribe students by the Government is encouraging students to take admission in schools. The parents are sending their children to the hostel anxiously for educational development of their wards. The primary and secondary data in respect of the pre-Matric Scholarship revealed that the rate of pre-Matric Scholarship for the students is very low in comparison to the present situation. Further it is not rationalized; different types of hostels are getting different rates of scholarship. There is no pocket money system for boy boarders; only girl boarders are getting pocket money. There should not be any discrimination in the rate of scholars in the pre-Matric scholarship among the boarders of different residential schools and hostels. Keeping in view of the present market rate, the Pre-Matric Scholarship for day scholars and boarders students should be enhanced. Pocket money system has to be implemented for the boy and girl boarders for all types of hostels to maintain parity. With the main objective of empowerment through education, Government of India is implementing scholarship schemes of pre-matric scholarship, post-matric and merit-*cum*-poverty scholarship to encourage parents and enable the students to pursue education. These schemes with the same guidelines are extended and implemented by Government of India to OBC and Minority students. Introduction of 100 seated ST girls hostel during Elevennth Plan period has better impact on the tribal women education. Scheduled Tribe girl students are getting free education with lodging and boarding facilities from class I to X. Likewise 40 seated girls hostels implemented in the tribal area stand for the development of tribal women education. Despite these hostel facilities, primary school hostels are functioning in the study area with a capacity of 40 boarders, Ashram schools and boys high schools as well as government girls high schools are functioning with lodging and boarding facilities out of pre-matric scholarship. Besides boarders, tribal students, day scholar students of Scheduled Caste and Scheduled Tribe communities have been covered under pre-matric scholarship schemes. This scheme is not only limited with Scheduled Caste and Scheduled Tribe students but also is extended to OBC and minority students. But from the primary and secondary investigation on the implementation of pre-matric scholarship it is observed that the rate of pre-matric scholarship meant for the Scheduled Caste and Scheduled Tribe day scholar students reading in different educational institutions from class VI to class X are getting very low rate of scholarship. The boys day scholar student of class VI and VII are getting Rs. 15 per month whereas the girl students are entitled to get Rs. 20 per month. In case of class VIII to Class X, the boys day scholar students are getting Rs. 20 per month and the girl students are awarded Rs. 25 per month. The rate of pre-matric scholarship awarded to the day scholar students is very low in comparison to the present market rate. If the rate of day scholar students will be enhanced at least up to Rs. 200 per month per boy student and Rs. 250 per month for girl students it can enable the students to purchase their study materials and encourage them to continue their higher education.

4.7 Evaluations Study on Income Generating Schemes (Bankable)

4.7.1 *Objective*

Eradication of poverty and increase in the standard of living of poorer sections of the society has been the primary objective of the States and Central Government in all the plans. The First Five Year Plan during 1951-52 believed in trickledown theory. It envisaged that programmes under various sectors of development would benefit all sections of population including the weaker section of society. During Second Plan over the year 1956-1961 was formulated with the promise to ensure that economic and social benefits of national developments will reach the backward classes. The Third Plan period during 1961-1966 annual plans during 1966-1969 advocated greater equality of opportunities and reduction in the economic disparities and differences in income and wealth in the society. The Fourth Plan 1969-1974 envisaged the basic goal of repaid increase in the standard of living of the people through measures which also promoted equality and social justice. The Fifth Plan (1974-1979) was a watershed for STs. In the year 1975-1976 Tribal sub-plan was launched by keeping aside plan funds for the development of Scheduled Tribe areas. Sixth Plan 1980-1985 continued with the SCP for SCs which become a significant feature of the Five Year Plan along with TSP for STs. The Seventh Plan 1985-1990 saw the strengthening of SCA to TSP within the flow of funds from the state plan, central plan and Special Central Assistance (SCA) and institutional finance, facilitating enlargement of infrastructures and expansion of their coverage to benefit more SCs & STs. In 1989, National SCs and STs Finance Development Corporation (NSFDC) was established to provide loan to SCs and STs for taking up gainful and profitable self-employment productive activities and business enterprise. The Eight Plan 1992-1997 aimed at bridging the gap between the development of the weaker sections and others by the beginning of the Twenty First century.

Individual Income Generating Schemes' beneficiary with Unit

The Ninth Plan 1997-2002 aimed to empower the socially disadvantaged groups to become self-sufficient. It was expected to create an enabling environment conducive for SCs & STs, minorities and OBCs to exercise their rights freely to enjoy all privileges and lead a life with confidence and dignity at par with the rest of the society.

So far as the Orissa state is concerned, resources have not been exploited adequately for income generating activities. As a result, Orissa ranks very low among the other Indian states in terms of per capita investment. Besides all these programmes implemented for the income generating Sampurna Gramina Rozgar Yojana (SGRY), Employment Assurance Schemes (EAS), Jawahar Grama Samriddhi Yojana (JGSY), Swarna Jayanti Grama Swarozgar Yojana (SGSY), are some of the important programmes. In addition income generating schemes have been adopted under Odisha Scheduled Caste Finance Development Corporation (OSFDC), Integrated Tribal Development Agency (ITDA) and Modified Area Development Agency Programme for raising the income level of Scheduled Caste and Scheduled Tribe people.

Tribal Women beneficiaries in Vegetable Cultivation Field

4.7.2 *Data Collection*

Basing upon the projects taken up in the study area primary information has been collected from 24 villages of 12 Gram Panchayats of Malkangiri and Koraput districts. In this connection, 24 Tribal beneficiaries from the villages indicated in column 3 of Table 4.9 have been interacted on the schematic loan taken under bankable projects. The process of getting loan

Table 4.9: Evaluation of Income Generating Scheme

Sl. No.	*Name of the Beneficiaries*	*Village*	*GP*	*Block*	*Distance from Block H.G.*	*Caste*	*Occupation*	*Name of the Scheme*	*Unit Cost*	*Loan*	*Subsidy*	*Year*	*Name of the scheme*	*S.B. A/c No.*	*Bank*
1	**2**	**3**	**4**	**5**	**6**	**7**	**8**	**9**	**10**	**11**	**12**	**13**	**14**	**15**	**16**
1	Kailash Majh.	Pakna-guda	Ghumar	Kundra	30 km	Bhumia	Cultivation	tea stall	40000	30000	10000	2004-05	SGSY	Tl - 7	UGBD-Igapur
2	Not found	Kalapada	Ghumar	Kundra	32 km										
3	Bhisma Minarbalia	Massigan	Massigan	Kundra	15 km	Bhumia	Cultivation	tea stall	30000	20000	10000	2006-07	SGSY	not shown	UGBD Igapur
4	Mukta Soura	Jantaput	Massigan	Kundra	12 km	Soura	Agr. labour	business	20000	10000	10000	2003-04	ITDA	TL. 19	UGBD Igapur
5	Rama Minarbalia	Minarbali	Minarbali	Baipar - guda	8 km	Bhumia	Agr. labour	business	20000	10000	10000	2006-07	SGSY	not Shown	UGBD Igapur
6	Hari Majhi	Majhi-guda	Minarbali	Baipar - guda	9 km	Bhumia	Agr. labour	business	20000	10000	10000	2007-08	SGSY	2438	Lamps Baipar-iguda
7	Padu Poraja	Baligan	Baligan	Baipar - guda	20 km	Poraja	Cultivation	veg. cult	20000	10000	10000	2005-06	SGSY	missed	Lamps Baipar-iguda
8	Hari Majhi	Majhi-guda	Doraguda	Baipar - guda	25 km	Bhumia	Cultivation	veg. cult	20000	10000	10000	2006-07	SGSY	2438	Lamps Baipar-iguda
9	Not found	Sindhi-guda	Baipar-iguda	Baipar - guda	20 km										

(contd.)

(contd.)

Sl. No.	Name of the Beneficiaries	Loan Disbursed	Subsidy disbursed	Scheme grounded or not	Unit grounded by		Monthly Income	Bank Loan repaid	Follow-up action by Bank	Follow up action by implementing Agency	Amount Saving	Annual Income from other sources	Annual Expenditure per Annum	Balance amount, if any	Financial Condition	
					On Will	By Force									Before financial asistance	After financial asistance
1	2	17	18	19	20	21	22	23	24	25	26	27	28	29	30	31
1	Kailash Majhi	30000	10000	No	Own will		1000		No	No		17000	19000	Nil	Weak	Not changed
2	Not found								Nil	Nil						
3	Bhisma Minarbalia	20000	10000	Grouned	Own will		1000		Nil	Nil		12000	14000	Nil	Weak	Weak
4	Mukta Soura	10000	10000	Yes	Own will		1000		Nil	Nil		8000	14500	Nil	Weak	Waek
5	Rama Minarbalia	10000	10000	No	Own will		500		Nil	Nil		12000	15000	NIl	Waek	Weak
6	Hari Majhi	10000	10000	No	Own will		700	7000	Nil	Nil		10000	14000	Nil	Weak	Weak
7	Padu Poraja	10000	10000	No	Own will		600		Nil	Nil		14000	14000	NIl	Weak	Weak
8	Hari Majhi	10000	10000	Grouned	Own will		800	10000	Nil	Nil	600	18000	17500	NIl	Weak	Weak
9	Not found								Nil	Nil						

(contd.)

(contd.)

Sl. No.	*Name of the Beneficiaries*	*Village*	*GP*	*Block*	*Distance from Block H.G.*	*Caste*	*Occupation*	*Name of the Scheme*	*Unit Cost*	*Loan*	*Subsidy*	*Year*	*Name of the scheme*	*S.B. A/c No.*	*Bank*
1	**2**	**3**	**4**	**5**	**6**	**7**	**8**	**9**	**10**	**11**	**12**	**13**	**14**	**15**	**16**
10	Sanu Khila	Pilaku-sum	Somna-thpur	Kudumu-uguma	10 km	Bhumia	Cultiv-ation	Business	20000	10000	10000	2007-08	SGSY	not shown	Mini bank
11	Sidheswar Kuradi	Pilaku-sum	Somna-thpur	Kudumu-uguma	not found	Bhumia	Cultiv-ation	Business	20000	10000	10000	2007-08	SGSY	not shown	Mini bank
12	Budra Poraja	Amba-guda	Amba-guda	Mathili	15 km	Bhumia	Agr. labour	Minihaller	50000	40000	10000	2007-08	ITDA	not shown	UGB GUMA
13	Damu Bbhumia	Phusur-guda	Amba-guda	Mathili	25 km	Bhumia	Cultiv-ation	Minihaller	45000	35000	10000	2009-10	SGSY	with bank	Mini bank
14	Rama Patataka	Kadam-guda	Pungam	Mathili	23 km	Bhumia	Cultiv-ation	Minihaller	30000	20000	10000	2009-10	SGSY	4260	Mini bank
15	Kesab Bhumia	Matkam-iguda	Pungam	Mathili	15 km	Bhumia	Agr. labour	Minihaller	30000	20000	10000	2009-10	SGSY	1184 024260	SBI Pungam
16	Hadi Kirsani	Muduli-pada	Mucul-ipada	Khairput	5 km	Bonda	Agr. labour	Poultry	30000	20000	10000	2006-07	BDA	with bank	UGB Pungam
17	Sania Kirsani	Phusur-uguda	Kadam-guda	Khairput	14 km	Bonda	Agr. labour	Carpentry	12000	6000	6000	2005-06	BDA	not shown	UGB Khairput
18	Ram Muduli	Andra-hall	Andrahall	Khairput	12 km	Bonda	Agr. labour	S. Business	12000	6000	6000	2000-01	BDA	missed	UGB Khairput
19	Not found	Andra-hall	Andrahall	Khairput	27 km	Bonda		K. Shop							

(contd.)

(*contd.*)

Sl. No.	*Name of the Beneficiaries*	*Loan Disbursed*	*Subsidy disbursed*	*Scheme grounded or not*	*Unit grounded by*		*Monthly Income*	*Bank Loan repaid*	*Follow-up action by Bank*	*Follow up action by implementing Agency*	*Amount Saving*	*Annual Income from other sources*	*Annual Expenditure per Annum*	*Balance amount, if any*	*Financial Condition*	
					On Will	*By Force*									*Before financial asistance*	*After financial asistance*
1	**2**	**17**	**18**	**19**	**20**	**21**	**22**	**23**	**24**	**25**	**26**	**27**	**28**	**29**	**30**	**31**
10	Sanukhila	10000	10000	No	Own will		700		Nil	Nil		10000	14000	Nil	Weak	Good
11	Sidheswar Kuradi	10000	10000	No	Own will		800		Nil	Nil		15000	15000	Nil	Weak	Weak
12	Budra Poraja	40000	10000	No	Own will		1000		Nil	Nil		8600	18000	Nil	Weak	Weak
13	Damu Bbhumia	35000	10000	Grouned	Own will				Nil	Nil		15000	17430	Nil	Weak	Weak
14	Rama Patataka	20000	10000	Grouned	Own will		800		Nil	Nil		15500	16000	Nil	Weak	Not changed
15	Kesab Bhumia	20000	10000	Grouned	Own will		900	1000	Nil	Nil		20000	19000	NIl	Weak	Not changed
16	Hadi Kirsani	20000	10000	Grouned	Own will		500	1500	Nil	Nil	1000	18000	23000	Nil	Weak	Not changed
17	Sania Kirsani	6000	6000	No	Own will	-	1000		Nil	Nil		17000	18000	Nil	Weak	Improved
18	Ram Muduli	6000	6000	No	Own will		500		Nil	Nil		6000	10000	Nil	Weak	Not changed
19	Not found								Nil	Nil					Weak	Not changed

(*contd.*)

(contd.)

Sl. No.	*Name of the Beneficiaries*	*Village*	*GP*	*Block*	*Distance from Block H.G.*	*Caste*	*Occupation*	*Name of the Scheme*	*Unit Cost*	*Loan*	*Subsidy*	*Year*	*Name of the scheme*	*S.B. A/c No.*	*Bank*
1	**2**	**3**	**4**	**5**	**6**	**7**	**8**	**9**	**10**	**11**	**12**	**13**	**14**	**15**	**16**
20	Rama Kirsani	Mudulipada	Mudulipada	Khairput	18 km	Bonda	Cultivation	Veg. cult	12000	6000	6000	1998-99	ITDA	Missed	UGB Khairput
21	Basandra Balaram	Kumbhari	Kumbhari	N. Patna	10 km	K. Dora	Cultivation	S. business	12000	6000	6000	2001-02	SGSY	Missed	UGB N. Patna
22	Bali Sirka	Siriguda	Kumbhari	N. Patna	15 km	Kandha	Cultivation	S. business	12000	6000	6000	2001-02	ITDA	Not shown	UGB N.Patna
23	Not found	Palaput	N. Patna	N. Patna	5 km										
24	Sirka Nari	Odiapentha	N. Patna	N. Patna	4 km	Kandha	Cultivation	S. business	12000	6000	6000	2003-04	SGSY	Pass book missed	UGB N. Patna

(contd.)

(*contd.*)

Sl. No.	*Name of the Beneficiaries*	*Loan Disbursed*	*Subsidy disbursed*	*Scheme grounded or not*	*Unit grounded by*		*Monthly Income*	*Bank Loan repaid*	*Follow-up action by Bank*	*Follow up action by implementing Agency*	*Amount Saving*	*Annual Income from other sources*	*Annual Expenditure per Annum*	*Balance amount, if any*	*Financial Condition*	
					On Will	*By Force*									*Before financial asistance*	*After financial asistance*
1	**2**	**17**	**18**	**19**	**20**	**21**	**22**	**23**	**24**	**25**	**26**	**27**	**28**	**29**	**30**	**31**
20	Rama Kirsani	6000	6000	No	Own will		600		Nil	Nil		17500	18000	Nil	Weak	Not changed
21	Basandra Balaram	6000	6000	Grouned	Own will		700	700	Nil	Nil		14000	15000	Nil	Weak	Not changed
22	Bali Sirka	6000	6000	Grouned	Own will		800		Nil	Nil		15000	16000	Nil	Weak	Not changed
23	Not found			No					Nil	Nil						
24	Sirka Nari	6000	6000	No	Own will		900	100	Nil	Nil		16000	18000	Nil	Weak	Not changed

and grounding of units have been examined. Besides the Bankers and the implementing agencies were also covered in the primary investigation process. The findings have been tabulated in Table 4.9.

4.7.3 *Evaluation Study*

The evaluation study revealed that tribal beneficiaries have been benefited from different schemes such as Integrated Tribal Development Agency (ITDA), Odisha State Finance Development Corporation (OSFDC) and Swarozgar Swarna Jayanti Yojana (SGSY).

4.7.3.1 *Occupation*

It is found from field study that the main occupation of the beneficiaries are labour and cultivation. Their economic condition is not so sound and all of them are coming under BPL category (Column No. 8 of Table 4.9).

4.7.3.2 *Units Financed*

Column No. 9 indicates that beneficiaries of Sl. No. 1 and 3, are financed for installation of tea stall, who have been financed by Utkal Grameen Bank, Digapur under SGSY Scheme in the year 2004-05 and 2005-06 respectively. Sl. Nos. 4, 5, 6, 10, 11, 18, 21, 22 and 24 were financed for small business, Sl. Nos. 7, 8, and 20 got finance for grounding of vegetable cultivation, Sl. Nos. 12,13,14 and 15 were financed for mini haller, Sl. No. 16 were financed for poultry farming, Sl. No. 17 for Carpentry and Sl. No. 19 for Kirana Shop. These beneficiaries were financed from their local bank from 1998-99 to 2009-10 respectively, which has been reflected in column Nos. 9 and 16.

4.7.3.3 *Loan and Subsidy Component*

It is found that loan sanctioned in favour of these beneficiaries varied from Rs. 6000 to Rs. 30000 and financed by financing institutions of the locality. Further, the subsidy amount of Rs. 6000 to Rs. 10000 has been paid to the bank concerned by the Bonda Development Agency. Integrated Tribal Development Agency and District Rural Development Agency. (Column Nos. 10, 11 and 12).

4.7.3.4 *Loan Account*

It is reported by the beneficiaries of Sl. Nos. 3, 5, 13, 14 and 16 that the loan accounts are with the financing institutions. They have not received their loan account from banks. Sl. Nos. 7 and 22 have lost their loan account pass book that is why the detailed position of loan has not been properly assessed.

4.7.3.5 *Unit Grounding*

Grounding of unit is an important aspect of the income generating schemes. But the primary investigation revealed that Sl. Nos. 1, 5, 6, 7,10, 11, 12, 17, 18, 20 and 24 have not grounded the units. Out of those beneficiaries Sl. Nos. 3, 4, 8, 13, 14, 15 and 16 have grounded their units which has been reflected in Column No. 19 of Table 4.9. Asked about the problems of non-grounding of the units, they reported that loan sanctioned for them has not been disbursed fully, even it has been disbursed at fag end of financial year, so they failed to ground the units. It was also found that the beneficiaries who have grounded their units are unable to manage them properly.

4.7.3.6 *Modes of Selection, Joint Verification and Training*

It is reported by the beneficiaries that before selection of beneficiaries joint verification by sponsoring agency and financial institution has not been done. Interested beneficiaries have approached to the sponsoring agency and their names have been sponsored for finance. Before grounding the unit proper training has not been imparted to the beneficiaries, as a result of which the units have not been grounded successfully.

4.7.3.7 *Income of the Beneficiaries after Receiving Finance*

It has been noted in the field that the income level and standard of living of the beneficiaries have not changed. Rather it has been noted that after receiving finance, the beneficiaries have spent the money for meeting with their personal wants and the money has not been utilised for the purpose for which they have received the loans with subsidy. Only four beneficiaries have fruitfully utilised the loan and there has been a visible change in their living standard.

4.7.3.8 *Recovery Position*

The loan received and recovery position has been indicated at Column Nos. 17 and 23 of Table 4.9. It is found that the beneficiaries at Sl. No. 6, 8, 15, 16, 21 and 24 have repaid Rs. 7,000, Rs. 10,000, Rs. 1000, Rs. 1500, Rs. 700 and Rs. 900 respectively as against the loan amount of Rs. 10,000. Thus, it is seen that Sl. Nos. 1, 3, 4, 5, 7, 9, 10, 11, 12, 13, 14, 17, 18, 20 and 22 beneficiaries have not repaid the loan taken.

It may be noted that each of the beneficiaries have received a subsidy of Rs. 10,000. But due to non-utilisation of the loan properly they have not improved their standard of living. Until the beneficiaries are made aware of the advantage they can get out of the loan with 100 per cent subsidy and properly trained about the benefit they will get out of the investment, and these projects cannot be successful.

4.7.3.9 *Follow up Action Taken*

It was found in the field that neither the sponsoring agency nor the financial institutions have made proper and timely supervision for grounding the investment units. The sponsoring agency should have taken care to advise and educate the beneficiaries on the project. Without proper motivation and supervision at the initial stage of grounding a unit, the project generally fails. Hence, it is necessary on the part of implementing agency to ensure proper supervision of a unit that is going to be grounded.

4.7.3.10 *Personal Saving of Beneficiaries*

During the course of primary investigation it is reported by the respondents that Sl. Nos. 8 and 16 beneficiaries have deposited Rs. 600 and Rs. 1000 only in their SB account respectively. Excepting them none of the beneficiaries has saving in their saving accounts. The detailed survey report has been reflected in Column No. 26 of Table 4.9.

4.7.3.11 *Approximate Annual Income*

Column No. 27 indicates that the annual income of the beneficiaries are not more than Rs. 20000 per annum. In comparison to their expenditure, the annual income of the beneficiaries are lower and they often depend upon individual borrowing.

4.7.4 ***Findings***

It is very unfortunate to note that the beneficiaries have not been motivated properly either by the sponsoring authorities or the financial institutions. Without following the guidelines issued by the Central and State Governments, the implementing agencies disburse the loans to achieve the target. Hence, in spite of the efforts taken at the Government level, the people of the study area still suffer from poverty and food in security.

Hence, it is desirable on the part of the implementing agency to select honest and capable beneficiaries who can use the loan amount efficiently and can improve their standard of living. Until and unless every care is taken to invest the money fruitfully by the beneficiaries, development of the tribals and other weaker sections of the society cannot be made possible and practicable.

The primary information collected from different revenue villages of Khairput, Mathili and Kudumuluguma Block of Malkangiri district and Narayanapatna, Baipariguda and Kundra Block of the Koraput district has been evaluated and it was found that many of the beneficiaries have started the grounding of the schemes and discontinued in the mid time. Further, they have not shown their Saving Bank account as well as reported that the banks have not provided the loan account pass book to them for which no proper position of recovery of loan has been assessed. Actually loan has not been fully disbursed to the beneficiaries. During the interaction with the beneficiaries, it is reported that they have not received the loan in proper time. The loan amount disbursed was not sufficient to ground the units. No training has been imparted to the beneficiaries for successful grounding of the units. None of the concerned official and financial institutions have taken any steps for successful grounding of the units.

During the course of primary investigation, the welfare extension officer or special officer of micro projects were present. When they were asked about the reasons of the failure of the projects they simply replied that they are overburdened with the workload and are not able to give their personal attention in the matter.

These findings have an important policy implication. The extension officers should be entrusted with limited workloads and they should be made responsible if a beneficiary cannot come up successfully in his project.

4.7.5 *Lacunas of the Schemes*

The primary investigation on income generating schemes conducted in Koraput and Malkangiri districts has indicated the following lacuna in the implementation of income generating schemes:

1. No training has been imparted to the beneficiaries before and after grounding the unit. As a matter of fact beneficiaries are unable to implement the schemes in a successful manner.
2. Joint verification has not been physically conducted by the line department and financial institution as well as the programme implementing agency.
3. Without evaluation/selection of the beneficiaries loan has been sanctioned in the fag end of the financial year to achieve the target set by the government.
4. Unit cost sanctioned by the financing institution has not been disbursed fully and timely resulting in failure of the projects.
5. Evaluation and monitoring system by the implementing agency and finance institution are weak.
6. Beneficiaries are taking loan for a particular purpose but spending the same in another way.
7. Repayment position of beneficiaries is very poor.
8. Target oriented programmes without taking into account the need of the people generally fails.
9. Regular recovery camps by the financial institutions are not organized.

4.7.6 *Prospect of the Scheme*

Income generating schemes are mainly implemented with an expectation to raise the living standard of the poorest of the poor people. The Sampurna Gramin Rozgar Yojana (SGRY) was started with merger of Employment Assurance Programme (EAS) and Jawahar Gramin Samruddhi Yojana (JGSY) with effect from 25th September, 2001. SGRY expected to take care of food security and additional wage employment to the poorer sections of the people likewise the Swarna Jayanti Gram Swarozgar Yojana was implemented from 1st April, 1999 after restructuring erstwhile IRDP, TRYSEM, SITRA, GKY and MWS. The basic objective of the schemes was to bring assisted poor families (Swarozgary) above the poverty line through provision of mix of bank credit and subsidy. National Rural Employment Guarantee Act (NREGA) was implemented to enhance livelihood security in vulnerable area by providing at least 100 days of guaranteed wage employment in a financial years to every household. This work guarantee can also serve other objectives of generating productive assets, protecting the environment, empowering rural women by reducing rural-urban migration and fostering social equality among others. Besides all these programmes, the bank linkage credit and subsidy income generating schemes has its impact upon the amelioration of poverty among the SCs and STs poor people. Many of the Scheduled Caste and Scheduled Tribe beneficiaries grounded the unit properly after getting the bank loan and are able to cross the poverty line. Hence, it is necessary that these programmes are to be implemented in a proper way.

4.7.7 *Conclusion*

In order to eradicate the poverty among the tribes various bankable income generating schemes have been introduced by the Government in the Centre and the State. The tribal Sub-plan was launched during Fifth Five Year Plan. 21 Integrated Tribal Development Agency and 17 PTG projects have been established. In addition, the prgramme of Modified Area Development Approach and Dispersal Tribal belt were identified for their economic development. Different income generating schemes are being implemented for the purpose. The implementing agency is responsible for providing subsidy linkage with bank loan to the SCs & STs beneficiaries. In this regards several schemes and programmes such as IRDP, SGSY, ITDA, MADA and OSFDC are being implemented for income generating schemes for economic upliftment of the tribal. During the field investigations in the study area, it is observed that due to some lapses proper grounding of the units is far from the beneficiaries. Further it is found that the unit cost meant for the schemes are not being fully disbursed among the beneficiaries.

Even those amount are disbursed to them are not in time. The selection procedure is not being properly adopted by the sponsoring agency and financing institutions. Joint verification is not being physically conducted. No training are being imparted to the beneficiaries before and after finance, follow up action by the implementing agency and recovery camps by the financial institutions are not done in time.

Therefore, it is suggested that the guidelines for the implementation of income generating schemes are to be strictly followed to achieve the objectives of these schemes.

4.8 Evaluation Study on Indira Awas Yojana

4.8.1 *Objective*

Housing is one of the basic requirements for human survival. For a normal citizen owning a house provides significant economic and social security and status in the society. For a shelterless person, a house brings about a profound social change in his existences endowing him with an identity, thus integrating him with his immediate social environment. The genesis of the Indira Awas Yojana (IAY) can be traced to the programmes of rural employment, which started in the early 1980 and Rural Landless Employment Guarantee Programme (RLEGP) which began in 1983. There was, however, no uniform policy for rural housing in the states. For instance some states permitted only part of the construction cost to be borne from (RLEGP) funds and the balance was to be met by beneficiaries from their saving or loans. On the other hand, other states permitted the entire expenditure to be borne from NREP/RLEGP funds. While some states allowed construction of only dwelling, others permitted renovation of existing houses of beneficiaries. As per announcement made by the Government of India in June 1985, a part of the RLEGP funds was earmarked for the construction of houses for SC & STs and freed bonded labourers. As a result, Indira Awas Yojana (IAY) was launched during 1985-86 as a sub-scheme of RLEGP. I.A.Y. thereafter continued as a Sub-Scheme of Jawahar Rozgar Yojana (JRY). Since its launching in April 1989, six per cent of the total JRY funds were allocated for implementation of IAY. Then it was extended to cover households below the poverty line Non-Scheduled Castes and Non-Scheduled Tribes families in the rural area. Simultaneously, the allocation of funds for implementing the scheme was raised from 6 per cent to 10 per cent of the total resources available under JRY at the national level, subject to the condition that the beneficiaries to Non-Scheduled Castes and Non-Scheduled Tribes poor should not exceed 4 per cent of the total JRY. Indira Awas Yojana was de-linked from JRY and made an independent scheme with effect from 1st

January, 1996. Since 1999-2000, a number of initiatives have been taken to improve the Rural Housing (RH) programme by making provision for upgradation of unserviceable *Kacha* houses and by providing credit with subsidy for helping the poor. Emphasis has also been laid on use of cost effective resistant and environment friendly technologies in rural housing programmes. The main objective of the Indira Awas Yojana is primarily to help construction/upgradation of dwelling units of members of Scheduled Castes and Scheduled Tribes, freed bonded labourers and others below poverty line non-SC & ST rural households by providing them a lump sum financial assistance. Since inception of the scheme, Scheduled Tribe and Scheduled Caste beneficiaries have been associated and provided IAY houses. Hence, it is necessary to evaluate the project implemented by the government from time to time to examine how the poor tribal people are taking its advantages, whether the beneficiaries are being selected in a statutory mode or not and whether the houses are constructed in a proper manner. Therefore, this evaluation study has been taken up in the Koraput and Malkangiri district in a random sampling basis.

Scholar investigating on IAY in the study area

Scholar investigation on IAY in the study area

4.8.2 *Data Collection*

Primary data has been collected from the 24 beneficiaries from 24 revenue villages of Narayanapatna, Baipariguda and Kundra block of Koraput district and Mathili, Kudumuluguma and Khairput block of the Malkangiri district under random sampling basis. In this connection, 24 beneficiaries along with their family members have been interacted and the findings collected from them on the selection process of beneficiaries, mode of construction of Indira Awas, and method of release of instalments have been indicated in Table 4.10.

4.8.3 *Evaluation Study*

Primary data from the study area of Koraput and Malkangiri district has been collected. During the course of primary investigation, 24 beneficiaries from 24 villages were examined about the availing the houses under Indira Awas Yojana and evaluated, the findings which has been reflected in Column Nos. 2, 3, 4, and 5 of Table 4.10. It is reported by the respondent that, beneficiaries are generally selected in the Palli Sabha and Gram Sabha concerned. No beneficiaries has been recommended (Column Nos. 6 and 7) but it is further investigated that during the course of Palli Sabha and

Gram Sabha due to influence of political people some beneficiaries are being selected in the Palli Sabha. Poor people those who do not raise their voice in the meeting are left out. Beneficiaries under IAY scheme for the period of 2000-01 to 2009-10 of the study areas have been examined and evaluated (Column No. 8). During the period under investigation, the unit cost of the IYA was Rs. 22,000 to Rs. 35,000. As regards the construction works of IAY it was found that Sl. Nos. 1, 3, 4, 7, 14, 15, 19, 23 and 24 have constructed IAY houses without entrusting to local contractor. Excepting these beneficiaries others have entrusted local contractors for construction of their IAY houses (Sl. Nos. 2, 5, 6, 8, 9, 10, 11, 12, 13, 16, 17, 18, 20, 21 and 22), it is found that house under the scheme of Sri Kedriki Sisa of village Andrahall on the Bonda hill has constructed concrete slabs. (Column 12) and the roof of other beneficiaries have been done with A.C. sheet which is indicated in Column No. 13. Further it is assessed that there is single door provision in the IAY houses. An evaluation of the present condition of the houses in the study area and found that house of Mangali Minarbalia of village Siribeda under Parkanmala G.P., Sr. Bisnath Kirsani of village Kadamguda, Budu Muduli of village Mudulipada, and Subash Soura of village Jantaput are in very weak condition which are in an uninhabitable condition. Except these houses, others are in good and habitable dwelling condition. Asked about the duration of the construction of the houses to the respondents it was reported that duration of construction of the IAY houses is 6 months to one year. Further it is ascertained that where the contractors are engaged for construction of IAY houses they are taking more time to complete the construction work. From field verification it is found that the beneficiaries have constructed 1 room with AC sheet roof having one door. There is no smokeless *Chulha* and toilet facilities in these IAY houses. Further, it has been reported that the existing rate of unit cost for construction of IAY is not enough (Column Nos. 17, 18. 19 and 20).

The primary data collected from different villages of Koraput and Malkangiri district indicated that the IAY beneficiaries have been allotted the IAY houses without sanitation system. Some of the houses have not been completed since long. The contractors engaged for execution of the work have not taken any step to complete the IAY houses. The houses are lying incomplete for years together. The primary facilities like sanitation and smokeless *Chulha* which are highly essential are not being found in such as IAY houses. During the course of investigation, it came to light that maximum number of beneficiaries are ignorant about the cost of their house. The scholar discussed about the incomplete Indira Awas Yojana houses and it was found that, after receipt of the payment from the beneficiaries, the contractors have left the house incomplete. As the work order is being issued by the name of the beneficiaries by the implementing agency and payment are being made accordingly, all responsibilities to construct the IAY house goes to beneficiaries concerned. But when the contractors are engaged by the beneficiaries they are taking their payment leaving the construction work to the beneficiaries. Subsequently, with the increase in the rate of labour and materials, the sanctioned amount is not enough to complete the houses allotted in favour of the beneficiaries.

4.8.4 *Broad Implications*

Indira Awas Yojana was launched during the year 1985-86 as a sub-scheme of rural landless employment guarantee programme (RLEGP) and continued as a sub-plan of Jawahar Rozgar Yojana since it is launching from April 1989. It has been delinked from the JRY with effect from January 1, 1996 with an objective to provide houses to the members of Scheduled Tribes, freed bonded labourers as well as non-SCs/STs belonging to BPL category. As per the provision contained in the Government Guideline, 60 per cent of this total IAY allocation during the financial year should be utilized for construction/upgradation of dwelling units for SC/ST/ BPL holder. Further, 3 per cent of IAY funds have been preserved for the physically and mentally challenged persons, 15 per cent of the Physical target have been earmarked for the BPL, minority communities in area as indicated by the ministry. As a result of which the Scheduled Caste and Scheduled Tribe, Non-SC/ST, minority, BPL Category and mentally and physically challenged person of the society are provided houses as per the government norm and conditions and emancipated themselves from home steadless. Subsequently, this scheme has been extended to the Scheduled Tribe beneficiaries under Forest Rights Act. Those tribal beneficiaries have provided Right of Records under the provision of the Act.

4.8.5 *Lacuna of the Scheme*

Though the Indira Awas Yojana is a holistic scheme for the beneficiaries living below poverty line and specially the Scheduled Caste and Scheduled Tribe people and being implemented since long still there are a number of defects noted during the course of investigation in the study area:

1. Only a single roomed house is provided to the beneficiaries which is very difficult to accommodate a family with more than two members.
2. A sum of Rs. 45000 (Rupees Forty Five Thousand) only is not enough to construct a IAY house in complete manner. Though the cost of IAY houses has been raised from Rs. 35000 to Rs. 45000 and now the cost of the said house is enhanced up to

Rs. 75000 still it is not enough to compete with the present market rate of materials and labour.

3. There is a provision to deduct Rs. 600 (Rupees Six Hundred) only for construction of latrine and similarly Rs. 100 (Rupees One hundred only) for smokeless *Chulha* which further limits the amount for construction.
4. Communication gap between the beneficiaries and implementing agency is an imporatant factor towards the construction of IAY house.
5. The IAY houses are being constructed in a scattered manner according to the space available for the beneficiaries. The limited space for construction limits the construction of other facilities, i.e. toilets and kitchen garden.
6. Politically influenced beneficiaries are taking advantages to get the IAY houses.
7. Beneficiaries under the schemes are to be selected in the Palli Sabha and Gram Sabha, but it is not conducted in a fair manner. The attendance of the villagers in the meeting is very poor so that they are not able to submit their claim in the Palli Sabha. Those who raise their voice in the meeting are taking the advantage of the scheme but the actual beneficiaries are being deprived of this benefit.
8. The houses constructed by the beneficiaries entrusting them to local contractors remain incomplete.

4.8.6 *Prospect of the Scheme*

The implementation of the Indira Awas Yojana by the Central as well as State Governments, has benefited the BPL category, homesteadless people. As there is a earmarked reservation system for the Scheduled Caste and Scheduled Tribe people as well as non-SCs & STs, minorities and physically challenged person of the society they are getting houses under the scheme as per the ratio provision contained in the Government guideline. So far as the Koraput reign is concerned, it is coming under Fifth Schedule area. Maximum Scheduled Tribe people are residing and the beneficiaries under tribal group have been allotted IAY houses. For the implementation of the IAY houses many of the homesteadless people are getting the housing facility. Poor people affected from natural calamity are availing the housing facility on a priority basis. Under the provision of the scheme Scheduled Tribe people are getting dwelling houses. Every year a target for construction of Indira Awas Yojana houses are being allotted to a blocks and in turn it is divided on Gram Panchayat basis. The Gram Panchayat again distribute the same revenue village-wise according to the ratio contained in the provision of the Indira Awas Yojana.

Table 4.10: Indira Awas Yojana

Sl. No.	Name of the Beneficiaries	Village	GP	Block	Type of selection		Year of sanction	Sanction Amount	House Constructed by	
					Palli Sabha	Recom-mendation			Own	Contractor
1	2	3	4	5	6	7	8	9	10	11
1	Krushna Bhumia	Kadamguda	Pangam	Mathili	Palli Sabha	Nil	2001-02	22000	Own	
2	Srikar Bhumia	Pangam	Pangam	Mathili	Palli Sabha		2000-01	22000		Contractor
3	Padmanabha Dora	Ambaguda	Ambaguda	Mathili	Palli Sabha	Nil	2005-06	22000	Own	
4	Kesab Bhumia	Matkamiguda	Ambaguda	Mathili	Palli Sabha	Nil	2003-04	22000	Own	
5	Samala Dora	Kandel	Somnathpur	Kudumuluguma	Palli Sabha	Nil	2009-10	35000		Contractor
6	Mangliminarbalia	Siripeta	Parkanmala	Kudumuluguma	Palli Sabha	Nil	2002-03	22000		Contractor
7	Lachhma Muduli	Sindhiguda	Parkanmala	Kudumuluguma	Palli Sabha	Nil	2009-10	35000	Own	
8	Jagat Khila	Pilakusum	Somnathpur	Kudumuluguma	Palli Sabha	Nil	2003-04	22000		Contractor
9	Bisnath Kirsani	Kadamguda	Kadamguda	Khairput	Palli Sabha	Nil	2001-02	22000		Contractor
10	Sukra Kirsani	Pusuguda	Kadamguda	Khairput	Palli Sabha	Nil	2001-02	22000		Contractor
11	Budu Muduli	Mudulipada	Mudulipada	Khairput	Palli Sabha	Nil	2008-09	22000		Contractor
12	Kedriki Sisa	Andrahal	Andrahal	Khairput	Palli Sabha	Nil	2009-10	35000		Contractor
13	Subash Soura	Jantaput	Masigan	Kundra	Palli Sabha	Nil	2006-07	35000		Contractor
14	Bhisma/Bhumia	Massigan	Massigan	Kundra	Palli Sabha	Nil	2003-04	22000	Own	
15	Bhagaban Pujari	Kalapada	Ghumar	Kundra	Palli Sabha	Nil	2008-09	22000	Own	
16	Dasa Poraja	Paknaguda	Ghumar	Kundra	Palli Sabha	Nil	2000-01	35000		Contractor

(contd.)

(contd.)

Sl. No.	Name of the Beneficiaries	Type of Roof		No. of Doors/ Windows	Condition of House	Duration of Construction	Sanction amount sufficient or not	No. of quarters	Toiletry facility
		Slab	Ashb.						
1	**2**	**12**	**13**	**14**	**15**	**16**	**17**	**18**	**19**
1	Krushna Bhumia		A.C. sheet	1	Good	6 monts	No	1	No
2	Srikar Bhumia		Ashb.	1	Good	6 months	No	1	No
3	Padmanabha Dora		Ashb.	1	Good	8 months	No	1	No
4	Kesab Bhumia		Ashb.	1	Good	6 months	No	1	No
5	Samala Dora		Ashb.	1	Good	7 months	No	1	No
6	Manglimiaarbalia		Ashb.	1	Weak	1 year	No	1	No
7	Lachhma Muduli		Ashb.	1	Good	10 months	No	1	No
8	Jagat Khila		Ashb.	1	Good	1 year	No	1	No
9	Bisnath Kirsani		Ashb.	1	Weak	1 year	No	1	No
10	Sukra Kirsani		Ashb.	1	Good	1 year	No	1	No
11	Budu Muduli		Ashb.	1	Weak	1 year	No	1	No
12	Kedriki Sisa	Slab		1	Good	6 months	No	1	No
13	Subash Soura		Ashb.	1	Weak	1 year	No	1	No
14	Bhisma/Bhumia		Ashb.	1	Good	6 months	No	1	No
15	Bhagaban Pujari		Ashb.	1	Good	6 months	No	1	No
16	Dasa Poraja		Ashb.	1	Good	6 months	No	1	No

(contd.)

(contd.)

Sl. No.	*Name of the Beneficiaries*	*Village*	*GP*	*Block*	*Type of selection*		*Year of sanction*	*Sanction Amount*	*House Constructed by*	
					Palli Sabha	*Recom-mendation*			*Own*	*Contractor*
1	**2**	**3**	**4**	**5**	**6**	**7**	**8**	**9**	**10**	**11**
17	Daitari Bhumia	Baligan	Baligan	Baipariguda	Palli Sabha	Nil	2005-06	22000		Contractor
18	Madhu Pujari	Sindhigan	Baligan	Baipariguda	Palli Sabha	NIL	2002-03	22000		Contractor
19	Madhaba Nayak	Majhiguda	Doraguda	Baipariguda	Palli Sabha	Nil	2000-01	22000	Own	
20	Beena Pujari	Doraguda	Doraguda	Baipariguida	Palli Sabha	Nil	1999-2000	22000		Contractor
21	Sirka Rupa	Kumbhari	Kumbhari	Narayanpatna	Palli Sabha	Nil	2001-02	22000		Contractor
22	Sirka Nuris	Siribeda	Kumbhari	Narayanpatna	Palli Sabha	Nil	2000-01	22000		Contractor
23	Phania Hirika	Palaput	N.Patna	Narayanpatna	Palli Sabha	Nil	2002-03	22000	Own	
24	Mala Huika	Odiapentha	N.Patna	Narayanpatna	Palli Sabha	Nil	2001-02	22000	Own	

(contd.)

(contd.)

Sl. No.	*Name of the Beneficiaries*	*Type of Roof*		*No. of Doors/ Windows*	*Condition of House*	*Duration of Construction*	*Sanction amount sufficient or not*	*No. of quarters*	*Toiletry facility*
		Slab	*Ashb.*						
1	**2**	**12**	**13**	**14**	**15**	**16**	**17**	**18**	**19**
17	Daitari Bhumia		Ashb.	1	Good	6 months	No	1	No
18	Madhu Pujari		Ashb.	1	Good	7 months	No	1	No
19	Madhaba Nayak		Ashb.	1	Good	1 year	No	1	No
20	Beena Pujari		Ashb.	1	Good	1 year	No	1	No
21	Sirka Rupa		Ashb.	1	Good	1 year	No	1	No
22	Sirka Nuris		Ashb.	1	Good	1 year	No	1	No
23	Phania Hirika		Ashb.	1	Good	6 months	No	1	No
24	Mala Huika		Ashb.	1	Good	6 months	No	1	No

4.9 Evaluation Study on Grain Bank

4.9.1 *Objective*

Grain bank scheme has evolved with the prime aim of mobilizing and organizing the productive ability of the tribals after harvest. It is not simply a process of raising individual income of the contributors, but to help the poor and needy villagers to position themselves securely during lean season and to make them free from exorbitant rates of interest charged by traders and money-lenders etc. The community managed grain bank have been in the tribal areas. Later on Government of India have formulated the scheme of grain bank in the year 1996-97 to arrest the starvation deaths in the vulnerable area of 12 states identified by the Central Planning Committee which included the Chenchu area of Andhra Pradesh having the main objective of :

- To combat the problems of foodgrain security during the lean season.
- To avoid or reduce dependency on legal money-lender or traders for borrowing grain during the lean season at exorbitant rates of interest.
- To ensure food security during the monsoon period.

Monthly Meeting of Grain Bank Members

- To help the tribal community to break the nexus of money-lenders, traders etc.
- To promote the habit of self help among the tribals.
- To develop a system, which could be managed by community participation in sustainable manner over a long time.
- To lay the foundation for an able community base organization to look into the community needs and address the development issues in a sustainable and democratic way.

4.9.2 *Data Collection*

As per the objective of the study primary information has been collected from the study area of the Koraput and Malkangiri districts. As the grain bank are not functioning in the study villages, hence, grain banks of Kundra, Baipariguda and Jeypore blocks have been taken as samples for evaluation. Focus Group Discussion (FGD) have been taken up in different grain banks. 75 beneficiaries have been associated in the evaluation process. and the primary data so collected have been suitably tabulated in the Table 4.11. During the course of investigation on the way Mahulbhata grain bank under Bariniput G.P. of Jeypore Block has been evaluated though it is not coming under selected villages in the sample.

4.9.3 *Evaluation Study*

Grain Banks have been formed by the villagers themselves and the surplus produce of the villagers are stored in the Grain Bank during the harvest period and the needy members will take loan in the firm of Paddy, Ragi etc. for meeting with their needs. It is managed by an executive committee formed through election by the members of the grain bank. The Ministry of Tribal Welfare is also promoting the formation of grain banks through grants for construction of a godown and purchase of required quantities of grains depending on the needs of a village.

The scholar has examined the functioning of 11 Grain Banks of different villages of Baipariguda, Kundra and Jeypore blocks. It has been found that the grain bank of Tulur village of Baipariguda block promoted by the NGO SOVA is functioning better. But the members are few and it has not covered the entire village households. On the other hand, it has been found that the grain banks promoted by ITDA and run through blocks are functioning on a wider scale and doing better to meet with the needs of all the villagers.

However, it has also been found that excepting the grain banks of Tulur, Jabapadar and Mahulbhatta, the other grain banks are assisted only 10 quintals per grain bank by the implementing agency. The availability of other foodgrains is also limited. The rate of interest fixed by the executive committee varies from 20 to 30 per cent (Column No. 13 of Table 4.11). The time of collection and distribution of food stuff is October-January

Table 4.11: Detailed Information of Evaluation of Grain Bank

Sl. No.	*Name of the Grain Bank with Address*	*Total House-holds*	*No. of Family Benefited*	*No. of Executive Members*	*Year of Formation*	*Mode of Meeting*	*% of Attendance*
1	**2**	**3**	**4**	**5**	**6**	**7**	**8**
1	Beheraguda Sasya Bhandara, Vill : Beheraguda, GP: Lima	30	15		2007	Quarterly	80%
2	Beheraguda Colony Sasya Bhandara, Vill : Beheraguda, GP: Lima	19	14		2008	Quarterly	75%
3	Bandhiguda Sasya Bhandara Vill : Beheraguda GP: Lima	35	17		2010	Quarterly	85%
4	Jhiligaon Sasya Bhandara, Vill : Jhiligaon, GP: Kundra	52	14		2008	Quarterly	90%
5	Majurgola Sasya Bhandara, Vill : Majurgola, GP: Kundra	32	19		2007	Quarterly	74%
6	Bhadraguda Sasya Bhandara, Vill : Bhadraguda, GP: Kundra	19	8		2008	Quarterly	69%

(contd.)

(contd.)

Sl. No.	Name of the Grain Bank with Address	Foodgrain Assisted		Foodgrain Available		Rate of Interest	Month of Distri-bution	Month of Colle-ction	% of Repay-ment	% of Wilfull Defa-ulter	Monit-oring Agency
		Rice (Qntl.)	Ragi (Qntl.)	Rice (Qntl.)	Ragi (Qntl.)						
1	**2**	**9**	**10**	**11**	**12**	**13**	**14**	**15**	**16**	**17**	**18**
1	Beheraguda Sasya Bhandara, Vill : Beheraguda GP: Lima	5.00	-	6.50	-	20%	May to January	Dec. to January	75%	15%	SOVA NGO
2	Beheraguda Colony Sasya Bhandar, Vill : Beheraguda, GP: Lima	5.00	-	7.00	-	20%	May to January	Dec. to January	85%	10%	SOVA NGO
3	Bandhiguda Sasya Bhandara, Vill : Beheraguda, GP: Lima	3.00	1.00	7.00	1.50	30%	May to January	Dec. to January	95%	0%	SOVA NGO
4	Jhiligaon Sasya Bhandara, Vill : Jhiligaon, GP: Kundra	5.00	-	7.64		20%	May to January	Dec. to January	90%	5%	SOVA NGO
5	Majurgola Sasya Bhandara, Vill : Majurgola, GP: Kundra	5.00	1.00	8.50	1.00	20%	May to January	Dec. to January	95%	5%	SOVA NGO
6	Bhadraguda Sasya Bhandara, Vill : Bhadraguda, GP: Kundra	4.00	0.32	6.00	0.55	20%	May to January	Dec. to January	65%	10%	SOVA NGO

(contd.)

(contd.)

Sl. No.	Name of the Grain Bank with Address	Total House-holds	No. of Family Benefited	No. of Executive Members	Year of Formation	Mode of Meeting	% of Attendance
1	**2**	**3**	**4**	**5**	**6**	**7**	**8**
7	Heruguda Colony Sasya Bhandara, Vill: Heruguda Colony, GP: Kundra	36	22		2008	Quarterly	72%
8	Heruguda Colony Sasya Bhandara, Vill: Heruguda Colony, GP: Kundra	32	16		2009	Quarterly	70%
9	Mahulbhata GB Sasya Bhandara, Vill : Bariniput, GP: Kundra	75	65		2003	Quarterly	0%
10	Tatur GB Sasya Bhandara, Block : Boipariguda	69	69		2004	Quarterly	50%
11	Jabapadar GB Block : Assna	55	55		2004	Quarterly	10%

(contd.)

(contd.)

Sl. No.	*Name of the Grain Bank with Address*	*Foodgrain Assisted*		*Foodgrain Available*		*Rate of Interest*	*Month of Distri-bution*	*Month of Colle-ction*	*% of Repay-ment*	*% of Wilfull Defa-ulter*	*Monit-oring Agency*
		Rice (Qntl.)	*Ragi (Qntl.)*	*Rice (Qntl.)*	*Ragi (Qntl.)*						
1	**2**	**9**	**10**	**11**	**12**	**13**	**14**	**15**	**16**	**17**	**18**
7	Heruguda Colony Sasya Bhandara, Vill: Heruguda Colony, GP: Kundra	5.00	1.00	10.00	2.50	20%	May to January	Dec. to January	95%	5%	SOVA NGO
8	Herududa Colony Sasya Bhandara, Vill: Heruguda Colony GP: Kundra	4.00	1.00	5.00	1.00	30%	May to January	Dec. to January	60%	15%	SOVA NGO
9	Mahulbhata GB Sasya Bhandara, Vill : Bariniput, GP: Kundra	50.00	10.00	-	-	20%	May to January	Dec. to January	0%	0%	SOVA NGO
10	Tatur GB Sasya Bhandara, Block : Boipariguda	50.00	10.00	-	-	20%	May to January	Dec. to January	5%	90%	SOVA NGO
11	Jabapadar GB Block : Assna	30.00	-	-	-	20%	May to January	Dec. to January	0%	0%	SOVA NGO

and May-June respectively (Col. 15). An interaction with the executive committee members about the rate of recovery is poor in respect of old grain banks and the newly formed grain banks are functioning better than the old ones.

4.10 Evaluation on Tribal Women SHG

4.10.1 *Objective*

Women in most societies are subject to discrimination. The U.N. convention makes it binding on the consenting nations of world to take corrective measures to have gender equality and elimination of violence against women as well as to give women equal property rights, opportunities in education, access to health care, equal work opportunities and wages and costumes that are derogatory to women. The formation of women self help groups have emerged since the seventies in Bangladesh and since the early nineties in India predominantly in the southern states. The groups typically have a membership of between five and twenty members are informal association of women. Women generally face several traumas in life by virtue of their second status in society. The culture of science that is prevalent among this suffering are manifold. There are social taboo against women to express their sorrow or narrate their household problems to the outsider. Self help groups have emerged as support group to bring about women solidarity in facing all kind of problems in their domestic environment. This has led to the increasing empowerment of women. Further, self help groups have emerged as a means of providing poor people with the credit that, they need to emerge from poverty. These groups are formed to help women to meet with their needs through friendly credit.

Group discussion of Tribal Women SHG

Group discussion in Bonda women SHG

Self help group emerged in India by MYRADA in the year 1984-85 and initially functioned as credit management group. In 1987, NABARD sanctioned a group to MYRADA for the institutional capacity building of the self help group saving. In fact several NGOs notably PRADHAN and Dhan Foundation are working in Rajasthan and Tamil Nadu realized that the IRDP system of provision for credit to the poor was making them run to the banks. Self help groups were also set up in Andhra Pradesh in 1992. It started a total literacy campaign in Nellore district which led to the anti-arrack movement. In Maharshtra NGOs like Chaitanya and BAIF have been active in forming SHGs for over fifteen years. The Government supported programme started in twelve districts in 1994 with IFAD funding and was implemented by Women Development Corporation (MAVIM, 2003).

In Orissa, DANIDA has started the livestock development project in Koraput district in the year 1993-94. Subsequently formation of Self help group has been emerged in Laxmipur, Koraput, Jeypore and Kundra block by them in the year 1997. 137 women self help groups have been formed with a maximum of twenty members of each group and managed by them providing revolving funds and other facilities. Gradually, Self help groups have been formed by the different NGOs, Block official, ICDS project, ITDAs and Banks. Groups are being graded and associated with SGSY and ITDA programmes providing revolving funds and bank linkage in the year 1999. For overall monitoring with a objective to associate at least one woman member from each family into the self help group for women empowerment, the Government in W and CD Department in Orissa has launched Mission Shakti propaganda on 8.4.2001 to empower the women in the society.

4.10.2 *Data Collection*

Primary information on evaluation of 24 tribal women self-help groups was collected from Sri Radha SHG, Kadamguda, Maa Durga SHG, Pungam, Ma Tarinin SHG, Ambaguda, Ma Taratarini SHG of village Matkamiguda of Mathili block, Nilakantheswar SHG, Kondel, Ma Durga SHG, Siripeta, Maa Bhairabi SHG, Sindhiguda, Bhairabi SHG, Pilakusum of Kudumuluguma block, Maa Bhagabati SHG, Kadamguda, Pindapakna SHG, Pusuguda, Jhadikendu SHG, Andrahall and Mudulipada SHG of Mudulipada of Khairput block of Malkangiri district and Maa Jantamayee SHG, Jantaput, Ma Santoshi SHG, Massigan, Jhadeswari SHG, Kalapada, Jadheswari SHG, Paknapada of Kundra Block, Maa Santoshi SHG, Baligan, Gramdevta SHG, Sindhigan, Rameswari SHG, Majhiguda, Maa Kalyani SHG, Doraguda of Baipariguda Block, Maa Tulasi SHG, Kumbhari, Maa Jhanjabati SHG, Palaput of Narayanpatna Block of Koraput district. The scholar conducted evaluation on attendance of members in the meeting, mode of meeting, contribution/subscription of the members, monitoring and supervision, availability of revolving funds, records and book keeping, sustainability, capacity building training, exposure visit, decision making, grading, microcredit support, bank linkage, availing loan and subsidy, and recovery position which has been tabulated in Table 4.12.

4.10.3 *Evaluation Study*

4.10.3.1 *Formation and Size of Self Help Group*

The self help group is a group of rural poor who have volunteered to organize themselves in a group with a common purpose for eradication of poverty of the members of SHGs . They help each other to solve their problems. A person should not be member of more than one group. In this connection, it is observed that excepting 2 SHG, most of the SHG groups are homogenous in nature and their size is limited with 10 to 13 members (Colomun No. 10). On the other hand as per the SHG concept one member from each family should be the member of a SHG, but it is found that 2 to 3 members of a single family are also associated themselves in a SHG of their village. The occupation of the members is agricultural labourer and cultivation (Column No. 8 of Table 4.12).

4.10.3.2 *Mode of Meeting*

From the primary investigation it is assessed that mode of meeting vary from place to place. In some cases, the meeting of the SHGs are being conducted on a monthly basis in Malkangiri district, weekly basis meeting are being conducted in the Koraput district. Some of the SHGs are conducting their meeting on fortnightly basis. There is no standard system of conducting meeting among the SHGs. But during the verification of their records and as reported by the members, it is found that the SHGs meeting are not being conducted on a regular interval.

4.10.3.3 *Attendance of Members in the Meeting*

The attendance position of the members is very poor, some of the members are deliberately not coming to the statutory meeting. Further, it is noted that there is no penalty system adopted for absentee members and if some where adopted penalty system are not being implemented.

4.10.3.4 *Saving/Subscription of Members*

Saving of the members are an important aspect of the SHGs. Generally, SHG members start self-dependence with small saving and all members should save a fixed amount, which has been fixed by the group to build their corpus. The loan can be given for consumption purpose and other emergent needs like education, health care, social functions, repair to house etc. In this regard the group may decide to collect voluntary savings at weekly/fortnightly/monthly intervals as may be decided by its members. In this context, it is observed that all members are not regular to deposit the subscription (Col.14 of Table 4.12).

4.10.3.5 *Grading of SHGs*

The main objective of the grading exercise is to identify the weakness, if any and help the group to overcome through training and capacity building inputs so as to develop it into a good group. Grading exercise should not be questionnaire-oriented exercise where the members become passive participants. It should provide an opportunity for the members to assess their own performance in a participatory approach and the investigator assume the role of the facilitator in the process. Accordingly, the grading at the end of the 6 months of formation of SHG should be with reference to the objectives in 1st stage of the evaluation of the self help group to be taken up. Further after one year SHG should be evaluated for 2nd stages but the evaluation study revealed that out of 24 SHGs evaluated in the study area 6 SHGs have not been graded (Col. 25 of Table 4.12).

4.10.3.6 *Internal Lending*

The group starts the internal lending among the group members out of their saving. The groups develop their own lending norms and condition such as purpose, amount of interest, repayment period etc. and prioritization of loan requirement of various members. The decision to advance loans are taken in the group meeting through a participatory decision making process. But it was found, internal lending among the group members are not properly functioning.

4.10.3.7 *Decision-making*

Decision-making is an important aspect of the SHG members. Different issues are being discussed in the meeting and the decision can be taken in a democratic way. All members have equal right in the SHG. They can express their valuable view for welfare of the members and SHG. Every decision can be taken in the meeting after thorough discussion among the members. But during the primary investigation it is reported to be found that the group leaders are taking the decision as they are the influential persons of the group. In this regard all members should participate in the decision making process meeting and eaual weightage are to be given to each member of the group. Awareness among the members about decision making is also educative among them. The decision making process of the SHG has been reflected in the Col. 24 of Table 4.12.

4.10.3.8 *Activities of Group*

During the primary investigation on the Tribal women SHG in the study area, it is observed that the activities of the group are not in a group manner. Maximum members belong to cultivating families. And their activities are agriculture based. In rare cases, the activities of the members are found in dairy and business sector (Col. 18 of Table 4.12). Those group are financed under the bank credit linkage with subsidy under ITDA, OSFDC and SGSY for a particular scheme. Their activities also vary from each other. The activities are mainly individual oriented.

4.10.3.9 *Monitoring and Supervision*

As the tribal women are illiterate and ignorant about the formation and function of the SHG in the different stages, the monitoring and supervision by the programme implementing agency (PIA) play a vital role for smooth and better functioning of the women SHG specially in the tribal area. The Bankers, NGOs, Block, ICDS and community organizers under watershed development programme facilitate formation of the SHGs. It is found that the PIA are thinking that after opening the tribal women self help group their duties are over and left the SHGs are free to function as they like. Moreover, it was observed that the supervision and monitoring work has not been properly done by the programme implementing agency.

4.10.3.10 *Members' Contribution/Subscription*

From the primary investigation conducted on the self help groups in the study area it is observed that contribution of the members are different for each group. Some groups are collecting their subscription on weekly basis, some of them are collecting the same on a fortnightly basis and other groups are contributing subscription on monthly basis. It is between Rs. 10 to Rs. 100 per member. The details in this regard has been reflected in Colomun 14 of Table 4.12.

4.10.3.11 *Micro Credit Support*

During the stage of group formation, the SHG should be brought into contact with the local banks through opening of saving Bank account preferably in their service area branch. This has dual purpose. The SHG members are made aware of the opportunities and also the mode of dealing with the banks. The programme implementing agency, Bankers and the Block officials should familiarize with the SHG members and they may also explain to them about the process of graduation taking into account the full-fledged self-employment activities. Training and capacity building programmes for the SHGs in different stages of development may be organized periodically on a continuous basis .When the SHGs are provided with the revolving funds, banker should take active interest to sanction micro-credit support as per the norm and conditions contained in the SGSY guidelines. But during the primary investigation of the respondent of various SHGs in the study area, it was found that SHGs functioning without having the micro-credit support are functioning with its own funds.

4.10.3.12 *Revolving Fund*

The main objective of the revolving funds for SHG is augmentation of group corpus, enabling more members to avail the loan from the group, increase in per capita loan available to the members, imparting credit discipline and financial management skills to members and capacity building of the group. It is to be given in the form of cash credit facility. During the micro-credit stage when a group is considered eligible to be linked with the bank to receive revolving funds loan and subsidy so that it can practice micro-credit activities on a larger scale. A group may reach this stage in about six months or so after its formation. However, it may take a little longer time also, as it depends on several factors such as literacy, awareness level and socio-economic background of the members

Table 4.12: Evaluation of Tribal Woman SHG (Group Discussion)

Sl. No.	*Name of the SHG*	*Village*	*GP*	*Block*	*Dist-ance from Block H.Q.*	*Dist-ance from District H.Q.*	*Caste*	*Occu-pation*	*Date of formation*	*Size of SHG*	*Homo-genous or no*	*Cate-gory*	*Mode of meeting*	*Amount subscri-ption*	*Saving amount*	*Type of micro credit*
1	**2**	**3**	**4**	**5**	**6**	**7**	**8**	**9**	**10**	**11**	**12**	**13**	**14**	**15**	**16**	**17**
1	Sri Radha SHG	Kada-mguda	Pangam	Mathili	15 km	55 km	Bhumia	Culti-vation	10.11.2002	10	Yes	BPL	Monthly	30 per month	29067	5000
2	Ma Durga SHG	Pangam	Pangam	Mathili	8 km		Bhumia	Culti-vation	1.1.2002	13	Yes	BPL	Monthly	20 per month	15670	
3	Ma Tarini SHG	Amba-guda	Amba-guda	Mathili	6 km		Mixed	Culti-vation	1.1 2004	15	No	BPL	Monthly	40 per month	20351	
4	Ma Tarini SHG	Matkam-iguda	Amba-guda	Mathili	5 km		Bhumia	Culti-vation	26.9.2006	10	Yes	BPL	Monthly	20 per month	31250	
5	Nilakantheswar SHG	Kandel	Somna-thpur	Kudumul-uguma	7 km		Mixed	Culti-vation	4.2.2002	10	No	BPL	Monthly	10 per month	17335	
6	Maa Dongardei SHG	Siripeta	Parkan-mala	Kudumul-uguma	7 km		Mixed	Culti-vation	5.1.2003	10	No	BPL	Weekly	10 per month	25000	
7	Maa Bhairabi SHG	Sindhi-guda	Parkan-mala	Kudumul-uguma	7 km		Mixed	Culti-vation	14.1.2001	12	No	BPL	Monthly	10 per month	24000	
8	Bhagabati SHG	Pilaku-sum	Somna-thpur	Kudumul-uguma	4 km		Bhumia	Culti-vation	12.12.2006	12	Yes	BPL	Monthly	10 per month	31060	
9	Maa Bhagabati SHG	Kadam-guda	Kadam-guda	Khairput	12 km		Bonda	Culti-vation	27.1.2003	12	Yes	BPL	Monthly	10 per month	29357	
10	Pindapakhna SHG	Pusu-guda	Kadam-guda	Khairput	10 km		Bonda	Culti-vation	23.9.2003	11	Yes	BPL	Monthly	10 per month	20000	
11	Jhadikendu SHG	Andr-ahall	Andr-ahall	Khairput	11 km		Bonda	Culti-vation	2.62003	10	Yes	BPL	Monthly	20 per month	12800	
12	Mudulipada SHG	Mudul-ipada	Muduli-pada	Khairput	27 km		Bonda	Culti-vation	11.5.2005	11	Yes	BPL	Monthly	20 per month	1355	

(*contd.*)

(contd.)

Sl. No.	Name of the SHG	S.B. A/c with Bank	Activities Group	Name of PIAS	Revolving Fund	Book keeping	Capacity building training	Exposure visit	Decision making	Stage of SHG	Financed for the year	Financed under plan	Unit Cost	Loan	Subsidy	Unit grounded	Repayment
1	2	18	19	20	21	22	23	24	25	26	27	28	29	30	31	32	33
1	Sri Radha SHG	11840823039	Dairy-farming	Mission Shakti.	5000	Not updated	Not imparted	No	By leader	Second	2005-06	ITDA	400000	300000	100000	Partly	Nil
2	Ma Durga SHG	Not shown	Agri-culture	Mission Shakti.	5000	Not updated	Not imparted	No	indivi-dual	Not graded							
3	Ma Tarini SHG	5003 U.G.B.	Small business	Mission Shakti	5000	Not updated	Not imparted	No	By leader	First							
4	Ma Tarini SHG	5865 U.G.B..	Agri-culture	Mission Shakti	nil	Not updated	Not imparted	No	By leader	Not graded							
5	Nilakantheswar SHG	2435 U.G.B.	Indivi-dual	Mission Shakti	5000	Not updated	Not imparted	No	indivi-dual	second	2007-08	ITDA	300000	200000	10000	Partly	20000
6	Maa Dongardei SHG	Not shown	Indivi-dual	Mission Shakti	5000	Not updated	Not imparted	No	By leader	Not graded							
7	Maa Bhairabi SHG	Not shown	Agri-culture	Mission Shakti	15000	Not updated	Not imparted	No	indivi-dual	First							
8	Bhagabati SHG	31365 U.G.B.	Indivi-dual	Mission Shakti	5000	Not updated	Not imparted	No	By leader	Not graded							
9	Maa Bhagabati SHG	3021 U.G.B..	Agri-culture	Mission Shakti	5000	Not updated	Not imparted	No	By leader	First							
10	Pindapakhna SHG	30370 U.G.B.	Agri-culture	Block office	5000	Not updated	Not imparted	No	By leader	Second							
11	Jhadikendu SHG	1972 Mini B..	Agri-culture	BDA	5000	Not updated	Not imparted	No	By leader	Second	2007-08	BDA	280000	180000	100000	Partly	12578
12	Mudulipada SHG	Not shown	NTPC	BDA	5000	Not updated	Not imparted	No	By leader	Second	2007-08	BDA	300000	190000	110000	Partly	17575

(contd.)

(contd.)

Sl. No.	Name of the SHG	Village	GP	Block	Distance from Block H.Q.	Distance from District H.Q.	Caste	Occupation	Date of formation	Size of SHG	Homogenous or no	Category	Mode of meeting	Amount of subscription	Saving amount	Type of micro credit
1	2	3	4	5	6	7	8	9	10	11	12	13	14	15	16	17
13	Jantamayee SHG	Jantaput	Massigan	Kundra	14 km		Mixed	Cultivation	1.8.2000	17	No	BPL	Weekly	10 per month	17912	
14	Maa Santoshi SHG	Massigan	Massigan	Kundra	17 km		Bhumia	Cultivation	11.2.2000	20	Yes	BPL	Weekly	10 per month	41235	
15	Jhadeswaree SHG	Kalapada	Ghumar	Kundra	15 km		Bhumia	Cultivation	24.5.2006	12	Yes	BPL	Weekly	30 per month	37215	
16	Jhadeswaree SHG	Paknaguda	Ghumar	Kundra	30 km		Bhumia	Cultivation	24.5.1999	12	Yes	BPL	Weekly	300 per month	37215	
17	Maa Santosi SHG	Baligan	Baligan	Baipariguda	25 km		Bhumia	Cultivation	3.2.2000	12	Yes	BPL	Weekly	10 per month	20000	
18	Grama Devati SHG	Sindhigan	Baligan	Baipariguda	12 km		Bhumia	Cultivation	1.5.2005	13	Yes	BPL	Weekly	10 per month	30000	
19	Rameswaree SHG	Majhiguda	Doraguda	Baipariguda	23 km		Bhumia	Cultivation	5.92007	20	Yes	BPL	Weekly	10 per month	Not shown	
20	Maa Kalyanee SHG	Doraguda	Doraguda	Baipariguida	8 km		Bhumia	Cultivation	20.2.2001	12	Yes	BPL	Monthly	100 per month	Not shown	
21	Maa Tulasi SHG	Kumbhari	Kumbhari	Narayanpatna	12 km		Kandha	Ag. labour	1.5.2000	13	Yes	BPL	Monthly	30 per month	25000	
22	Not found	Siribeda	Kumbhari	Narayanpatna	10 km		NA		NA	NA	No	BPL	NA		NA	NA
23	Maa Jhanjabati SHG	Palaput	N. Patna	Narayanpatna	3 km		Kandha	Ag. labour	10.3.2000	12	Yes	BPL	Monthly	50 per month	27300	
24	Not found	Odiapetha	N. Patna	Narayanpatna	4 km	NA	NA	NA	NA	NA	NA	NA	NA	NA	NA	NA

(contd.)

(contd.)

Sl. No.	Name of the SHG	S.B. A/c with Bank	Activities Group	Name of PIAS	Revolving Fund	Book keeping	Capacity building training	Exposure visit	Decision making	Stage of SHG	Financed for the year	Financed under plan	Unit Cost	Loan	Subsidy	Unit grounded	Repayment
1	**2**	**18**	**19**	**20**	**21**	**22**	**23**	**24**	**25**	**26**	**27**	**28**	**29**	**30**	**31**	**32**	**33**
13	Jantamayee SHG	1/48 U.G.B.	Agri-culture	Mission Shakti.	12000	Not updated	Not imparted	No	By leader	Second	2006-07	SGSY	400000	275000	125000	Grounded	17372
14	Maa Santoshi SHG	Left with bank	Agri-culture	Mission Shakti	17000	Not updated	Not imparted	No	By leader	Second	2007-08	ITDA	300000	175000	125000	Partly	19750
15	Jhadeswaree SHG	3519U.G.B.	Agri-culture	Mission Shakti	10000	Not updated	Not imparted	No	By leader	Second	2007-08	SGSY	300000	180000	120000	Grounded	15400
16	Jhadeswaree SHG	35/9 U.G.B.	Agri-culture	Mission Shakti	10000	Not updated	Not imparted	No	By leader	Second	2005-06	SGSY	418000	318000	100000	Grounded	20350
17	Maa Santosi SHG	Not Shown	Agri-culture	Mission Shakti	10000	Not updated	Not imparted	No	By leader	First							
18	Grama Devati SHG	Not Shown	Agri-culture	Mission Shakti	15000	Not updated	Not imparted	No	Individual	First							
19	Rameswaree SHG	With Bank	Agri-culture	ICDS	0000	Not updated	Not imparted	No	By leader	First							
20	Maa Kalyanee SHG	With Bank	Agri-culture	Mission Shakti	10000	Not updated	Not imparted	No	By leader	First							
21	Maa Tulasi SHG	With Bank	Agri-culture	ICDS	10000	Not updated	Not imparted	No	By leader	Not graded	2006-07	SGSY	300000	180000	120000	Grounded	22500
22	Not found	NA	NA	NA	NA	NA	NA	NA	NA	NA.							
23	Maa Jhanjabati SHG	With bank	Agri-culture	ICDS	10000	Not updated	Not imparted		By leader	Second							
24	Not found	NA	NA	NA	NA	NA	NA	No	NA	NA	NA	NA	NA	NA	NA	NA	NA

and the skills of the facilitator agency. In this context, some of the group, have not been graded in time so that the Groups are being deprived of from revolving funds only they are having the contribution funds of their members (Col. 20 of Table 4.12)

4.10.3.13 *Capacity Building and Training*

During the focus group discussion among the women members of the SHGs in the study area of Malkangiri and Koraput districts, it was observed that the training and capacity building input is highly educative to the members of the SHG for their all-round development and develop into good groups. But none of the group under the study area have got any capacity building training by the programme implementing agency or by any other agency (Col. 22 of Table 4.12).

4.10.3.14 *Record Keeping*

The records including cash book, meeting book and individual pass book and other records relating to the SHG are to be meticulously maintained by the group. So that the details report such as regular conducting of meeting, participatory decision making, regular saving, systematic assessment of credit need of members, internal loaning to members, payment and enforcement of financial discipline in the group can be kept in a disciplinary manner. But during the primary investigation on functioning of SHG, it was found that book keeping system of the SHGs is not up to the mark. As the president and secretary of the groups are illiterate and ignorant, the book writer playing the vital role towards booking system. They are writing the meeting proceeding and other relevant records in a very irregular manner. Some of the groups were not maintaining the records since last 6 months to years together. None of the members of the SHGs are having their individual Pass book account, and they were unable to express about their saving (Col. 21 of Table 4.12).

4.10.3.15 *Exposure Visits of Member*

During the interaction among the SHG members, it was found that no exposure visit has been organized for them or by the programme implementing agency. In this regard, all the members are ignorant about the exposure visit. Though the exposure visit is an important aspect to gain knowledge from different fields from different places. Still the SHGs of this village are in dark condition about the same (Col. 23 of Table 4.12).

4.10.3.16 *Awareness about Schemes and Programme*

During the course of discussion, it is revealed that awareness regarding schemes and programme is required among the SHG members. From the primary investigation it was observed that SHG members are ignorant about the various schemes and programmes implemented by government from time to time. Asked about the formation, function, sanctioning of loan and microcredit support as well as the provision of availing subsidy, it was found that the SHG members were not that much aware which would enable them to express about the merits and demerits of different schemes and programmes meant for the tribal development.

4.10.3.17 *Mode of Leadership*

As per the guideline of the functioning of SHG leadership should be changed in every 6 months, so that all members of the group will get the chance to became a leader of their SHG and they will be acquainted with the banking and leadership process. But during the investigation process, it was observed that the groups are being dominated by some of the influential members. Leadership are not changing for years together. The absence of the scope for change of leadership has resulted in making other members ignorant about the management of SHGs.

4.11 Evaluation study on Public Distribution System

4.11.1 ***Objective***

The objective of Government of India's food security policy are to ensure adequacy or sufficiency in supply of foodgrains and distribution of foodgrains at an affordable price. The public distribution system (PDS) which continues to exist in India since the Second World War, attempts to meet the twin objectives. Public distribution system (PDS) is an Indian food security system established by the Government of India under Ministry of Consumer Affairs. Food and public distribution are managed jointly with State Government and Government of India. It distributes subsidized food and noon food items to poor people of India, major commodities which are distributed include staple foodgrains, such as wheat, rice, sugar and kerosene, through a network of public distribution system (also known as Ration shops) established in several states across the country. Food corporations, the Government owned corporation, procures, maintains stock of foodgrains for the public distribution system. To meet the consumption needs of the poor as of date there are about 4.99 lakh Fair Price Shops (FPSs) working across India (website Public Distribution System, 2010).

Scholar is interacting with the PDS beneficiaries

PDS is operated under the joint responsibility of the Central and the State Governments. The State Government has assumed the responsibility of identification of families below the poverty line, issue of Ration Cards and supervision of the functioning of PDS. States/UTs also distribute additional items of mass consumption through the PDS outlets such as pulses, edible oils, Iodized salt, spices etc.

The Revamped Public Distribution System (RPDS) was launched in June 1992 with a view to strengthen and streamline the PDS as well as to improve its reach in the far-flung, hilly remote and inaccessible areas where a substantial section of the poor resides. It covered 1775 blocks wherein area specific programmes, such as drought prone areas programme (DPAP), Integrated Tribal Development Project (ITDP), Desert Development Programme (DDP) and certain Designated Hill Areas (DHA) identified in consultation with State Governments for special focus, with States. With respect to improvement of the PDS infrastructure foodgrain for distribution in RPDS areas were issued to the States at 50 paisa below the central issue price. One beneficiary can purchase 20 kgs. per card at subsidized price.

In June 1997, the Government of India launched the targeted public distribution system (TPDS) with focus on the poor. Under the TPDS states are required to formulate and implement foolproof arrangements for identification of the poor for delivery of foodgrains and for its distribution in a transparent and accountable manner at the FPS level. The scheme was introduced for benefit of about 6 crore poor families. The Identification of the poor under the schemes is done by the States as per statewise poverty estimate of the Planning Commission for 1993-94. Keeping in view the consensus on increasing the allocation of foodgrains to BPL families and to achieve of better target the food subsidy, Government of India increased the allocation to BPL families from 10 kg to 20 kg of foodgrain per family per month. Since 1997, the scale of the BPL families has been gradually increased from 10 kg to 35 kg The scale of issue of BPL families was increased from 10 kg to 20 kg per family per month with effect from 1.4.2000. The allocation of foodgrains for BPL family was increased from 20 kg to 25 kg per family per month with effect from July 2001. Initially, the Antyodaya family were provided 25 kg of foodgrains per month at the time of launching of the scheme in December 2000. The scale of issue of foodgrains under APL/BPL/AAY house hold has been revised to 35 kg per month. Table 4.13 indicates the detailed position of blockwise BPL families of Koraput district.

Table 4:13: Blockwise BPL families of the Koraput District

Sl. No.	*Name of the district*	*Name of the block*	*No. of BPL families*	*Remark*
1	Koraput	Jeypore	19257	
2	Koraput	Boriguma	19217	
3	Koraput	Kotpad	16303	
4	Koraput	Baipariguda	17258	
5	Koraput	Kundra	11575	
6	Koraput	Koraput	10301	
7	Koraput	Semiliguda	11374	
8	Koraput	Potangi	12063	
9	Koraput	Nandapur	15960	
10	Koraput	Lamtaput	10996	
11	Koraput	Dasmantpur	15095	
12	Koraput	Laxmipur	11290	
13	Koraput	Narayanpatna	7577	
14	Koraput	Bandhugan	10354	

Source: Civil Supply Office, Koraput, Jeypore.

Table 4.14: Urban BPL family

Sl. No.	*Name of the district*	*Name of Urban area*	*Nos. of BPL Families*	*Remarks*
1	Koraput	Jeypore Muncipality	7953	
2	Koraput	Kotpad NAC	2420	
3	Koraput	Sunabeda NAC	8503	
4	Koraput	Koraput NAC	4424	
	Total		23000	

Source : Civil Supply Office, Koraput, Jeypore, 2014.

4.11.2 *Data Collection*

The study covered 2 districts, i.e., Koraput and Malkangiri districts selected 3 Blocks from each district out of which 12 Gram panchayats and 24 villages has been taken up at random sampling basis. 24 beneficiaries belonging to BPL and AAY household has been evaluated. Besides the beneficiaries, the foodgrain distributing agency such as Panchayat Executive Officers and Sarapanchas were also associated in the evaluation study to generate the relevant data both from primary and secondary sources for testing the hypothesis. The sample survey was conducted in 24 villages and 12 Gram panchayats headquarters. During the primary investigation, 121 tribal households have been covered on the public distribution system, out of which 24 beneficiaries were under BPL and AAY, the rest 97 tribal households having ration cards were evaluated and suitably tabulated in Tables 4.13 and 4.14.

4.11.3 *Evaluation Study*

On public distribution system, the evaluation work has been conducted in the study area of Malkangiri and Koraput district. From the primary evaluation 24 beneficiaries under BPL, AAY and AY schemes have been done and it was found that the beneficiaries are taking the advantages of the public distribution system as per scale of foodgrains meant for them from their respective Gram Panchayat Office. It is observed that the public distribution system at Gram Panchayat level is better functioning than the private fair price shop. BPL houses from different villages of respective gram panachayts are entitled to get the foodgrains from their Gram Panchayat Office, at the rate of Rs. 2 per kg for Rice, Rs. 15 per litre of kerosene, Rs. 13.50 per kg of sugar, and Rs. 7 per kg for wheat. Besides afore mentioned households from 24 villages of Koraput and Malkangiri districts other 97 poor tribal household ration cards were also associated in the primary evaluation process and it was found that the households having without cards are not allowed to get the foodgrains under the public distribution system.

During the interaction among the Panchayat Executive Officers and G.R.S. as well as the Sarpanch concerned of the respective GP under the study areas it was reported that quantity of foodgrains has been fixed up as per the cards available or allotted in the different villages of the Gram Panchayat, and they procured that quantity of foodgrains from FCI/Storage Agents on monthly basis and distributed the essential commodities among the card holders family in the respective villages.

It was also observed that a number of poor tribal families have been deprived of getting the ration card. On enquiry it was found that the BPL cards have been supplied as per 1997 BPL Census. No new cards have been supplied since then.

It was also reported that there is a shortage of foodgrains in every bag. In a bag of 50 kgs of rice/sugar it is found that there is a shortage of 2 kg to 4 kg in every bag. This situation compels the PEOS/GRS to reduce the supply of rice/sugar by ½ kg to 1 kg for every card holder.

Further it is reported that sufficient funds are not available with Gram Panchayat to procure the foodgrains and other necessary commodities within the specific time. So the Gram Panchayat is unable to distribute the foodgrains and other necessary commodities within stipulated period, in turn the beneficiaries are deprived of the benefits from the PDS.

The public distribution system is guided on ration card basis. It is not depending on the family size basis for which every household having the card are entitled to get same quantity of foodgrains and other essential commodities. Even a household having a single member is getting equal quantity of foodgrains as household having 10 members of the family. This situation need to be rationalized as far as possible and practicable.

Some of the beneficiaries have mortgaged their ration cards to the ration shop keeper for a little amount of money. Some of them are selling the food stuff with a minimum rate for money. Further it is observed that in some cases, the BPL cards has been provided to the rich households who are not eligible to avail the benefit. The BPL cards of the households those who are economically sound should be cancelled. Every year physical verification of BPL cards should be made and the cards with economically sound families are to be cancelled. However, due to political reasons this is not done.

Table 4.15: Evaluation of Public Distribution System

Sl. No.	*Name of the Beneficiaries*	*Village*	*GP*	*Block*	*Distance from Block H.Q.*	*Caste*	*Occupation*	*Category*				*Monthly kota of Rice*	*Rate per kg*
								BPL	*APL*	*AY*	*AAY*		
1	**2**	**3**	**4**	**5**	**6**	**7**	**8**	**9**	**10**	**11**	**12**	**13**	**14**
1	Padma Bhumia	Ambaguda	Ambaguda	Mathili	6 km	Bhumia	Cultivation	BPL				25 kg	Rs. 2
2	Umakanta Nayak	Kadamguda	Pungam	Mathili	16 km	Bhumia	Agrl. Labour	BPL				25 kg	Rs. 2
3	Bhagaban Pujari	Matkamiguda	Ambaguda	Mathili	5 km	Bhumia	Cultivation				AAY	35 kg	Rs. 2
4	Mangaraj Bhumia	Pungam	Pungam	Mathili	8 km	Bhumia	Agrl. Labour				AAY	35 kg	Rs. 2
5	Laxmi Kanta Chalan	Kadamguda	Kadamguda	Khairput	10 km	Bonda	Agrl. Labour			AY		10 kg	Free
6	Keduki Sisa	Andrahall	Andrahall	Khairput	27 km	Bonda	Agrl. Labour				AAY	35 kg	Rs. 2
7	Mangali Sisa	Mudulipada	Mudulipada	Khairput	15 km	Bonda	Cultivation	BPL				25 kg	Rs. 2
8	Ram Sisa	Mudulipada	Mudulipada	Khairput	15 km	Bonda	Cultivation	BPL				25 kg	Rs. 2
9	Sama Dora	Pilakusum	Somnathpur	Kudum-uluguma	15 km	Bhumia	Cultivation	BPL				25 kg	Rs. 2

(contd.)

(contd.)

Sl. No.	Name of the Beneficiaries	Free / Sub-sidy	Rice distribution centre	Sugar quota pm	Rate of suger per kg	K. oil per family	Avail-ability	Rate per litre	Whether the food stuff distributed		Whe-ther the food- stuff distri-buted by Govt. Age-ncy	Whether the food stuff distri-buted by Private Retailer	People Need the PD from Govt. Agency	People Need the PD from Private Retailer	Prob-lem if any
									Regu-larly	Irre-gular					
1	**2**	**15**	**16**	**17**	**18**	**19**	**20**	**21**	**22**	**23**	**24**	**25**	**26**	**27**	**28**
1	Padma Bhumia	Subsidy	G.P. Office	3 kg	Rs. 13	4 litre	Not regular	Rs. 13		Irregular	Yes	No	Yes	No	
2	Umakanta Nayak	Subsidy	G.P. Office	3 kg	Rs. 13	4 litre	Yes	Rs. 13		Irregular	Yes	No	Yes	No	
3	Bhagaban Pujari	Subsidy	G.P. Office	3 kg	Rs. 13	4 litre	Yes	Rs.13		Irregular	Yes	No	Yes	No	
4	Mangaraj Bhumia	Subsidy	G.P. Office	3 kg	Rs. 13	4 litre	Regular	Rs. 13		Irregular	Yes	No	Yes	No	
5	Laxmikanta Chalan	Free	G.P. Office	3 kg	Rs. 13	4 litre	Irreglar	Rs. 13		Regular	Yes	No	Yes	No	
6	Keduki Sisa	Subsidy	G.P. Office	3 kg	Rs. 13	4 litre	Irregular	Rs. 13		Regular	Yes	No	Yes	No	
7	Mangali Sisa	Subsidy	G.P. Office	3 kg	Rs. 13	4 litre	Irregular	Rs. 13		Regular	Yes	No	Yes	No	

(contd.)

(contd.)

Sl. No.	*Name of the Beneficiaries*	*Village*	*GP*	*Block*	*Distance from Block H.Q.*	*Caste*	*Occupation*	*Category*				*Monthly kota of Rice*	*Rate per kg*
								BPL	*APL*	*AY*	*AAY*		
1	**2**	**3**	**4**	**5**	**6**	**7**	**8**	**9**	**10**	**11**	**12**	**13**	**14**
10	Sanu Bhumia	Siripeta	Parkanmala	Kudum-uluguma	8 km	Bhumia	Cultivation	BPL				25 kg	Rs. 2
11	Budra Dora	Kombel	Somnathpur	Kudum-uluguma	20 km	Bhumia	Cultivation	BPL				25 kg	Rs. 2
12	Narsing Bhumia	Sindhiguda	Parkanmala	Kudum-uluguma	4 km	Bhumia	Cultivation	BPL				25 kg	Rs. 2
13	Narsing Pujari	Jantaput	Massigan	Kundra	18 km	Bhumia	Cultivation				AAY	35 kg	Rs. 2
14	Balaram Bhumia	Massigan	Massigan	Kundra	15 km	Bhumia	Cultivation				AAY	35 kg	Rs. 2
15	Pitabas Katia	Kalapada	Ghumar	Kundra	35 km	Bhumia	Cultivation			AY		10 kg	Free
16	Balaram Bhumia	Paknaguda	Ghumar Baligan	Kundra	36 km	Bhumia	Cultivation	BPL				25 kg	Rs. 2
17	Daimati Pujari	Baligan	Baligan	Baipari-guda	25 km	Bhumia	Cultivation	BPL				25 kg	Rs. 2/
18	Daimati Bhumia	Sindhigan	Doraguda	Baipari-guda	21 km	Bhumia	Cultivation	BPL				25 kg	Rs. 2

(contd.)

(*contd.*)

Sl. No.	*Name of the Beneficiaries*	*Free / Sub-sidy*	*Rice distribution centre*	*Sugar quota pm*	*Rate of suger per kg*	*K. oil per family*	*Avail-ability*	*Rate per litre*	*Whether the food stuff distributed*		*Whe-ther the food- stuff distri-buted by Govt. Age-ncy*	*Whether the food stuff distri-buted by Private Retailer*	*People Need the PD from Govt. Agency*	*People Need the PD from Private Retailer*	*Prob-lem if any*
									Regu-larly	*Irre-gular*					
8	Ram Sisa	Subsidy	G.P. Office	3 kg	Rs. 13	4 litre	Irregular	Rs.13		Regular	Yes	No	Yes	No	
9	Sama Dora	Subsidy	G.P. Office	3 kg	Rs. 13	4 litre	Irregular	Rs. 13.50		Irregular	Yes	No	Yes	No	
1	**i**	**15**	**16**	**17**	**18**	**19**	**20**	**21**	**22**	**23**	**24**	**25**	**26**	**27**	**28**
10	Sanu Bhumia	Subsidy	G.P. Office	3 kg	Rs. 13	4 litre	Irregular	13.5		Regular	Yes	No	Yes	No	
11	Budra Dora	Subsidy	G.P. Office	3 kg	Rs. 13	4 litre	Regular	13. 5		Regular	Yes	No	Yes	No	
12	Narsing Bhumia	Subsidy	G.P. Office	3 kg	Rs. 13	4 litre	Regular	13.5		Regular	Yes	No	Yes	No	
13	Narsing Pujari	Subsidy	G.P. Office	3 kg	Rs. 13	4 litre	Regular	13.5		Regular	Yes	No	Yes	No	
14	Balaram Bhumia	Subsidy	G.P. Office	3 kg	Rs. 13	4 litre	Regular	13.5		Regular	Yes	No	Yes	No	
15	Pitabas Katia	Free	G.P. Office	3 kg	Rs. 13	4 litre	Regular	13.5		Regular	Yes	No	Yes	No	
16	Balaram Bhumia	Subsidy	G.P. Office	3 kg	Rs. 13	4 litre	Irregular	13.5		Irregular	Yes	No	Yes	No	
17	Daimati Pujari	Subsidy	G.P. Office	3 kg	Rs. 13	4 litre	Irregular	13.5		Irregular	Yes	No	Yes	No	

(*contd.*)

(contd.)

Sl. No.	Name of the Beneficiaries	Village	GP	Block	Distance from Block H.Q.	Caste	Occupation	Category				Monthly kota of Rice	Rate per kg
								BPL	APL	AY	AAY		
1	2	3	4	5	6	7	8	9	10	11	12	13	14
19	Bati Nayak	Majhiguda	Doraguda	Baipari-guda	9 km	Bhumia	Cultivation	BPL				25 kg	Rs. 2
20	Ram Chandra Majhi	Doraguda	Doraguda	Baipari-guda	12 km	Bhumia	Cultivation				AAY	35 kg	Rs. 2
21	Puru Samaru	Kumbhari	Kumbhari	N. Patna	10 km	K. Dora	Cultivation			AY		10 kg	Free
22	Bali Sisa	Siribeda	Kumbhari	N. Patna	40 km	Kandha	Cultivation	BPL				25 kg	Rs. 2
23	Shama Minika	Odiapentha	N. Patna	N. Patna	4 km	Kandha	Cultivation	BPL				25 kg	Rs. 2
24	Huka Manda	Palaput	N. Patna	N. Patna	5 km	Kandha	Cultivation	BPL				25 kg	Rs. 2

(contd.)

(contd.)

18	Daimati Bhumia	Subsidy	G.P. Office	3 kg	Rs. 13	4 litre	Irregular	13.5		Irregular	Yes	No	Yes	No	
Sl. No.	*Name of the Beneficiaries*	*Free / Sub-sidy*	*Rice distribution centre*	*Sugar quota pm*	*Rate of suger per kg*	*K. oil per family*	*Avail-ability*	*Rate per litre*	*Whether the food stuff distributed*		*Whe-ther the food- stuff distri-buted by Govt. Age-ncy*	*Whether the food stuff distri-buted by Private Retailer*	*People Need the PD from Govt. Agency*	*People Need the PD from Private Retailer*	*Prob-lem if any*
									Regu-larly	*Irre-gular*					
1	**2**	**15**	**16**	**17**	**18**	**19**	**20**	**21**	**22**	**23**	**24**	**25**	**26**	**27**	**28**
19	Bati Nayak	Subsidy	G.P. Office	3 kg	Rs. 13	4 litre	Irregular	13.5		Irregular	Yes	No	Yes	No	
20	Ram Chandra Majhi	Subsidy	G.P. Office	3 kg	Rs. 13	4 litre	Regular	13.5		Regular	Yes	No	Yes	No	
21	Puru Samaru	Free	G.P. Office	3 kg	Rs. 13	4 litre	Regular	13.5		Irregular	Yes	No	Yes	No	
22	Bali Sisa	Subsidy	G.P. Office	3 kg	Rs. 13	4 litre	Irregular	13.5		Regular	Yes	No	Yes	No	
23	Shama Minika	Subsidy	G.P. Office	3 kg	Rs. 13	4 litre	Regular	13.5		Regular	Yes	No	Yes	No	
24	Huika Manda	Subsidy	G.P. Office	3 kg	Rs. 13	4 litre	Regular	13.5		Regular	Yes	No	No	No	

4.12 Evaluations on Water Harvesting Structure

4.12.1 *Objective*

The main objective of the construction of water harvesting structure in the tribal area is to develop waste and degraded lands, drought-prone situation, restoring ecological balance by harnessing, conserving and developing natural resources in the rural areas. Due to rapid deforestation and destruction of natural resources, the degree of rainfall has reduced. As a result tribal people who maintained their livelihood by collecting forest product from the forest and hills are losing their livelihood from the forest. Specially the tribal farmer in the rain-fed area are facing a lot of problems due to scarcity of water. In order to confront with the situation of drought prone area, Government has taken many effective steps to preserve the rain water and in turn to use the preserved water for irrigation purpose as well as to protect the groundwater level.

A Water Harvesting Structure

Water harvesting activities involves management of natural resources like soil and water along with various agronomical interventions with a focus on livelihood improvement where communities are involved in participatory planning and implementation of water harvesting programmes. Watershed development projects under various schemes such as Integrated Watershed Development Project (WDP) and Drought Prone

Area Programme (DPAP), National Watershed Development Project in Rain Fed Areas (NWDPRA), River Valley Project (RVP) are in operation. Another externally aided project funded by DFID, namely Western Orissa Rural Livelihood Project (WORLP) is currently in operation. The State Government has created Orissa Watershed Development Mission since 2000-2001. In order to ensure effective livelihood among the tribal people of Koraput region, the aforesaid watershed programmes are being implemented by the Soil Conservation Department. In addition to these, the tribal development agencies are constructing small size water harvesting structure for agronomical interventions with a focus on Tribal livelihood.

4.12.2 *Data Collection*

Primary data have been collected from the study area of the Malkangiri and Koraput district. The information has been collected from the different watershed harvesting structures constructed for the agricultural and economic development. Interaction with 5 individual beneficiaries from each watershed and Focus Group Discussion with 46 beneficiaries has been conducted in different villages of Baipariguda and Kundra blocks under Koraput district and Mathili, Kudumuluguma and Khairput block under Malkangiri district, the primary data have been tabulated in Table 4.16.

4.12.3 *Data Evaluation*

Primary information on water harvesting structure has been collected from the study area. During the course of investigation, 8 water harvesting structures have been visited and interaction has been made with the user group members. Out of 8 water harvesting structures, 1 water harvesting structure has been constructed by Bonda Development Agency and 7 water harvesting structures have been constructed by the Integrated Tribal Development Agencies concerned.

Examined the function of the Water harvesting structure among the user group members of Singbandh user group of village Matkamiguda under Mathili block, Tulaguram user group of Mudulipada under Khairput block, Gumar Paknagud, Tuloguram and Kalapada user groups under Kundra block, Pujariput user group under Jerypore block and Chandrapada user group and Panditbeda user group under Baipariguda block of Koraput district. In addition to the user group members, the officers of implementing agency have also been interacted during the course of investigation. The Special Officer, and Welfare Extension Officers, Bonda Development Agency, Khairput, Junior Engineer and Asst. Engineer ITDA, Jeypore and Koraput were interacted on the construction and functioning of the water harvesting structure. It was found that Kalapada user group and Pujariput

Table 4.16: Evaluation of Water Harvesting Structure

Sl. No.	*Village*	*GP*	*Block*	*Disrict*	*Basis of Selection*	*Implem-enting Agency*	*Year of Construction*	*Estimated cost*	*Name of the user group*
1	**2**	**3**	**4**	**5**	**6**	**7**	**8**	**9**	**10**
1	Kadamguda	Pangam	Mathili	Malkangiri	NA	NA	NA	NA	NA
2	Pangam	Pangam	Mathili	Malkangiri	NA	NA	NA	NA	NA
3	Ambaguda	Ambaguda	Mathili	Malkangiri	NA	NA	NA	NA	NA
4	Matkamiguda	Ambaguda	Mathili	Malkangiri	Officially	ITDA	2000-01	500000	Singalband User Group
5	Kandel	Somnathpur	Kudumul-uguma	Malkangiri	NA	NA	NA	NA	NA
6	Siripeta	Parkanmala	Kudumul-uguma	Malkangiri	NA	NA	NA	NA	NA
7	Sindhiguda	Parkanmala	Kudumul-uguma	Malkangiri	NA	NA	NA	NA	NA
8	Pilakusum	Somnathpur	Kudumul-uguma	Malkangiri	NA	NA	NA	NA	NA
9	Kadamguda	Kadamguda	Khairput	Malkangiri	NA	NA	NA	NA	NA
10	Pusuguda	Kadamguda	Khairput	Malkangiri	NA	NA	NA	NA	NA
11	Mudulipada	Mudulipada	Khairput	Malkangiri	Officially	BDA	2003-04	500000	Tulagram user Group

(*contd.*)

(*contd.*)

Sl. No.	*Village*	*No. of ST Farmers*	*Condition of WHS*	*Pani Panchayat formed or not*	*Mode of meeting*	*Condition of farmer before Scheme*	*Condition of farmer after Scheme*	*Area of water body*	*Present condition of Pani Panchayat*
1	**2**	**11**	**12**	**13**	**14**	**15**	**16**	**17**	**18**
1	Kadamguda	NA	NA	NA	NA	NA	NA	NA	NA
2	Pangam	NA	NA	NA	NA	NA	NA	NA	NA
3	Ambaguda	NA	NA	NA	NA	NA	NA	NA	NA
4	Matkamiguda	50	Defunct	Yes	Half yearly	As it is	No change	2 Hec.	Not functioning
5	Kandel	NA	NA	NA	NA	NA	NA	NA	NA
6	Siripeta	NA	NA	NA	NA	NA	NA	NA	NA
7	Sindhiguda	NA	NA	NA	NA	NA	NA	NA	NA
8	Pilakusum	NA	NA	NA	NA	NA	NA	NA	NA
9	Kadamguda	NA	NA	NA	NA	NA	NA	NA	NA
10	Pusuguda	NA	NA	NA	NA	NA	NA	NA	NA
11	Mudulipada	50	Partly func.	Yes	Half yearly	Same	No change	1 Hec.	Not functioning

(*contd.*)

(contd.)

Sl. No.	*Village*	*GP*	*Block*	*Disrict*	*Basis of Selection*	*Implem-enting Agency*	*Year of Construction*	*Estimated cost*	*Name of the user group*
1	**2**	**3**	**4**	**5**	**6**	**7**	**8**	**9**	**10**
12	Andrahall	Andrahall	Khairput	Malkangiri	NA	NA	NA	NA	NA
13	Jantaput	Massigan	Kundra	Koraput	Officially	ITDA	2007-08	500000	Kaliakado Check dam
14	Massigan	Massigan	Kundra	Koraput	Officially	ITDA	2008-09	400000	Field channel G. Paknaguda
15	Kalapada	Ghumar	Kundra	Koraput	Officially	ITDA	1999-2000	250000	Kalapada User Group
16	Paknaguda	Ghumar	Kundra	Koraput	Officially	ITDA	2007-08	250000	Pujariput User Group L.I. Point
17	Baligan	Baligan	Baipariguda	Koraput	Officially	ITDA	2006-07	500000	Chandra User Group
18	Sindhigan	Baligan	Baipariguda	Koraput		NA	NA	NA	NA
19	Majhiguda	Doraguda	Baipariguda	Koraput	Officially	ITDA	2006-07	500000	Panditbeda User Group
20	Doraguda	Doraguda	Baipariguda	Koraput	NA	NA	NA	NA	NA
21	Kumbhari	Kumbhari	Narayanpatna	Koraput	NA	NA	NA	NA	NA
22	Siribeda	Kumbhari	Narayanpatna	Koraput	NA	NA	NA	NA	NA
23	Palaput	N.Patna	Narayanpatna	Koraput	NA	NA	NA	NA	NA
24	Odiapentha	N.Patna	Narayanpatna	Koraput	NA	NA	NA	NA	NA

(contd.)

(contd.)

Sl. No.	*Village*	*No. of ST Farmer s*	*Condition of WHS*	*Pani Panchayat formed or not*	*Mode of meeting*	*Condition of farmer before Scheme*	*Condition of farmer after Scheme*	*Area of water body*	*Present condition of Pani Panchayat*
1	**2**	**11**	**12**	**13**	**14**	**15**	**16**	**17**	**18**
12	Andranall	NA	NA	NA	NA	NA	NA	NA	NA
13	Jantaput	50	Partly func.	Yes	Not cond.	Same	No change	1.5 Hec.	Partly functioning
14	Massigan	40	Partly func.	Yes	Not cond.	Same	No change	1.5 Hec.	Defunct
15	Kalapada	25	Not Functioning	Yes	Not cond.	Same	No change	1 Hec.	Not functioning
16	Paknaguda	25	Functioning	Yes	Half yearly	Same	No change	L I point	To be repaired
17	Baligan	50	To be repaired	Yes	Not cond.	Same	No change	1 Hec.	To be repaired
18	Sindhigan	NA	NA	NA	NA	NA	NA	NA	NA
19	Majhiguda	50	Not Functioning	Yes	Not cond.	Same	No change	1.5 Hec.	To be repaired.
20	Doraguda	NA	NA	NA	NA	NA	NA	NA	NA
21	Kumbhari	NA	NA	NA	NA	NA	NA	NA	NA
22	Siribeda	NA	NA	NA	NA	NA	NA	NA	NA
23	Palaput	NA	NA	NA	NA	NA	NA	NA	NA
24	Odiapentha	NA	NA	NA	NA	NA	NA	NA	NA

user group cover 25 Scheduled Tribe farmers and other user group cover 50 Scheduled Tribe farmers each (Column 11 of Table 4.16).

It is found that the amount at the rate of Rs. 10000 per beneficiary has been dispersed and the project cost has been estimated and sanctioned Rs. 500000 (Rupees Five lakh only) for each project except Kalapada and Pujariput (Column 9 of Table 4.16).

It was found that each watershed project is able to irrigate 50 to 60 Hectares of land of the tribal beneficiaries. But each watershed is gradually being covered up with soil and the water holding capacity of these watersheds are gradually decreasing. In this process, the watershed projects can function only for coming four to five years. The soil silting process will reduce the water level and its water holding capacity, Cols. 17 and 18 of Table 4.16 indicate this point.

As regards the functioning of user groups, it was found that Singhbandh user group of Matkamiguda, Tulagram user group of Mudulipada under Malkangiri district and Pujariput user group of Pujariput under Koraput district are conducting half yearly meeting. But other user groups are not functioning (Column 14 of Table 4.16). The users group should have met at an interval of one month to discuss about their problems.

Finally, it is investigated and observed that the Water Harvesting Structures constructed for the agricultural development of the tribal beneficiaries are not able to increase the productive capacity of land. Therefore, their economic condition have not changed. There is no provision for renovation of the water harvesting structure. Neither the implementing agency is taking care for renovation of the project nor the user group members are active to maintain the water harvesting structure in a proper manner. Understanding among the members is not cordial. Due to lack of better management, the harvesting structures have failed to achieve its goal (Columns 15, 16 and 19 of Table 4.16).

4 .13 Evaluation on Social Security Schemes

4.13.1 *Objective*

The National Old Age Pension (NOAP) scheme, State Old Age Pension Scheme (SOAT), Indira Gandhi National Old Age Pension Scheme (IGNOAP), Madhu Babu Pension Yojana (MBPY) and Odisha Disability Pension (ODP) scheme are being implemented in the Orissa. The National Old Age Pension Scheme is a 75 per cent Government of India assisted programme being implemented in the State since 15th August, 1995 for providing relief to old persons below the Poverty Line with 65 years of age or above. The pension amount has been increased from Rs. 100 to Rs. 200 with effect from 1st April, 2006. The pension amount has been further increased to Rs. 300 w.e.f. 1st April, 2012 by the State Government and the balance of Rs. 100 and 25 per cent of the rest is borne by the state.

Scholar interacting with the Social Security Beneficiaries

The Indira Gandhi Old Age Pension (IGOAP) scheme supported under National Social Assistance Programme (NSAP) with revised selection criteria is applicable to persons aged 65 and above and listed as BPL families in 2002 Survey.

Pension holders under social security schemes are waiting at GP Office

The State Old Age Pension Scheme introduced in the State since April 1975 was providing Rs. 100 per beneficiary per month to old and destitute persons of 60 years or above. This pension amount has also been increased to Rs. 300 from 1st April, 2012.

In January 2008, the state introduced Madhu Babu Pension Yojana (MBPY) by merging two pension schemes – State Old Age Pension rules, 1989 and Orissa Disability Pension Rule, 1985. All beneficiaries of these schemes are covered under MBPY since 2008. This pension amount has been increased to Rs. 300 from 1st April, 2012. Leprosy patients with visible signs of deformity and destitute widows irrespective of age whose annual income does not exceed Rs. 3200 are included under the scheme.

4.13.2 *Data Collection*

Primary data under social security schemes such as SOAP, NOAP and ODP have been collected from 24 beneficiaries of the 24 villages under study area of the Malkangiri and Koraput districts on random sampling basis. Besides these beneficiaries other 50 needy beneficiaries are being interacted. The data so collected from different villages of Mathili, Khairput and Kudumuluguma blocks of the Malkangiri district and Kundra, Baipariguda and Narayanpatna blocks of Koraput district is tabulated in Table 4.17.

4.13.3 *Data Evaluation*

During the course of primary investigation on social security schemes of 24 beneficiaries from 24 villages of Malkangiri and Koraput district which has been indicated in columns 2, 3, 4, 5 and 6 of Table 4.17. An examination of 24 beneficiaries under social security schemes out of which 14 are females and 10 are male beneficiaries (Columns. 7, 8 and 9). It was found that the main profession of the beneficiaries is cultivation and all beneficiaries are from tribal community. Further it is reported that they have been selected from Palli Sabha and Gram Sabha (Columns 10, 11 and 12). It was also found that those beneficiaries who attained the age of 65 years have been sanctioned under NOAP and beneficiaries who have reached the age of 60 are sanctioned under SOAP schemes. Widow pension is coming under SOAP. Any widow under BPL category is eligible to get Widow Pension. Though the ODP pensioner are not being covered in course of primary investigation as there is no ODP beneficiaries available in the investigated villages. However, it is reported by the Social and Educational Organizer of Kundra and Baipariguda block that any eligible beneficiary who has attained the age of at least 5 years is getting Orthopaedically Handicapped pension.

Table 4.17: Evaluation of Pension Schemes

Sl. No.	Name	Village	GP	Block	District	Sex		Age	Category of Pension	Occupation	Tribal Groups	Mode of Selection
						Male	Female					
1	2	3	4	5	6	7	8	9	10	11	12	13
1	Jaya Nayak	Kadamguda	Pangam	Mathili	Malkangiri	Male		70	NOAP	Cultivation	Bhumia	Palli Sabha
2	Chanchala Sisa	Pangam	Pangam	Mathili	Malkangiri		Female	65	SOAP	Cultivation	Bhumia	Palli Sabha
3	Mangaraj Pujari	Ambaguda	Ambaguda	Mathili	Malkangiri	Male		70	NOAP	Cultivation	Bhumia	Palli Sabha
4	Tulsi Katia	Matkamiguda	Ambaguda	Mathili	Malkangiri		Female			Ag. labour	Bhumia	Recommen-dation
5	Chanchala Hantal	Kandel	Somnathpur	Kudumu-luguma	Malkangiri		Female	65	SOAP	Labour	Bhumia	By Sarapancha
6	Sukri Pujari	Siripeta	Parkanmala	Kudumu-luguma	Malkangiri		Female	70	SOAP	Cultivation	Bhumia	By Sarapancha
7	Tulsa Khasi	Sindhiguda	Parkanmala	Kudumu-luguma	Malkangiri		Female	62	MBPY	Cultivation	Bhumia	Palli Sabha
8	Sanu Hantal	Pilakusum	Somnathpur	Kudumu-luguma	Malkangiri	Male		61	MBPY	Ag. labour	Bhumia	Palli Sabha
9	Mangali Muduli	Kadamguda	Kadamguda	Khairput	Malkangiri		Female	55	WP	Ag. labour	Bonda	Palli Sabha
10	Samari Kirsani	Pusuguda	Kadamguda	Khairput	Malkangiri		Female	70	NOAP	Ag. labour	Bonda	Palli Sabha
11	Sambari Chalan	Andrahall	Ambaguda	Khairput	Malkangiri		Female	72	NOAP	Ag. labour	Bonda	Palli Sabha
12	Sukra Batri	Mudulipada	Mudulipada	Khairput	Malkangiri	Male		66	NOAP	Cultivation	Bonda	Palli Sabha

(contd.)

(contd.)

Sl. No.	*Name*	*Size of family*	*Monthly Pension*	*Pension disbursment centre*	*Date*	*Income from Agrl.*	*Income from Animal*	*Income from wage*	*Income from Forest product*	*Income from other sources*	*Total Income*
1	**2**	**14**	**15**	**16**	**17**	**18**	**19**	**20**	**21**	**22**	23
1	Jaya Nayak	3	200	G.P. Office	15th of Month	1000	500	2000	500	2400	6400
2	Chanchala Sisa	2	200	G.P. Office	15h of Month		1000	5500	2000	2400	10900
3	Mangaraj Pujari	2	200	G.P. Office	15th of Month		1000	5500	2000	2400	10900
4	Tulsi Katia		200	G.P. Office	15th of Month		1000	4500	1000	2400	8900
5	Chanchala Hantal	2	200	G.P. Office	15th of Month	3000	1200	3000	2000	2400	10600
6	Sukri Pujari	6	200	G.P. Office	15th of Month	5000	500	6000	3000	2400	16900
7	Tulsa Khasi	9	200	G.P. Office	15th of Month	1000	3000	6000	4000	24000	16400
8	Sanu Hantal	5	200	G.P. Office	15th of Month		1000	5000	2000	24000	10400
9	Mangali Muduli	4	200	G.P. Office	15th of Month	2000	800	2600	1500	2400	9300
10	Samari Kirsani	1	200	G.P. Office	15th of Month		1000	1000	1000	2400	5400
11	Sambari Chalan	2	200	G.P. Office	15th of Month	1000	700	1000	900	2400	6000
12	Sukra Batri	5	200	G.P. Office	15th of Month	6000	1200	1500	2000	2400	10100

(contd.)

(contd.)

Sl. No.	Name	Village	G.P	Block	District	Sex		Age	Category of Pension	Occupation	Tribal Groups	Mode of Selection
						Male	Female					
1	2	3	4	5	6	7	8	9	10	11	12	13
13	Dahana Pujari	Jantaput	Masigan	Kundra	Koraput		Female	48	WP	Cultivation	Bhumia	Palli Sabha
14	Hema Minarbalia	Massigan	Massigan	Kundra	Koraput		Female	53	WP	Ag. labour	Bhumia	Palli Sabha
15	Parsu Khudupia	Kalapada	Ghumar	Kundra	Koraput	Male		65	NOAP	Labour	Bhumia	Palli Sabha
16	Budri Majhi	Paknaguda	Ghumar	Kundra	Koraput		Female	70	NOAP	Labour	Bhumia	Sarapanch
17	Barka Poraja	Baligan	Baligan	Eaipariguda	Koraput	Male		66	NOAP	Ag. labour	Bhumia	Palli Sabha
18	Jamuna Rampuria	Sindhigan	Baligan	Eaipariguda	Koraput		Female	45	WP	Cultivation	Poraj	Palli Sabha
19	Balaram Nayak	Majhiguda	Doraguda	Eaipariguda	Koraput	Male		80	NOAP	labour	Bhumia	Palli Sabha
20	Raghunath Katia	Doraguda	Doraguda	Baipariguida	Koraput	Male		65	NOAP	Cultivation	Bhumia	Palli Sabha
21	Sirka Mangali	Kumbhari	Kumbhari	Narayanpatna	Koraput		Female	50	WP	Ag. labour	Kandha	Palli Sabha
22	Sirka Sital	Siribeda	Kumbhari	Narayanpatna	Koraput		Female	45	WP	Cultivation	Kandha	Palli Sabha
23	Narayan Sirka	Palaput	N.Patna	Narayanpatna	Koraput	Male		66	NOAP	Ag. labour	Kandha	Palli Sabha
24	Sirka Dandu	Odiapentha	N.Patna	Narayanpatna	Koraput	Male		62	MBPY	Ag. labour	Kandha	Palli Sabha

(contd.)

(contd.)

Sl. No.	*Name*	*Size of family*	*Monthly Pension*	*Pension disbursment centre*	*Date*	*Income from Agrl.*	*Income from Animal*	*Income from wage*	*Income from Forest product*	*Income from other sources*	*Total Income*
1	**2**	**14**	**15**	**16**	**17**	**18**	**19**	**20**	**21**	**22**	23
13	Dahana Pujari	3	200	G.P. Office	15th of Month	3500	700	1800	800	2400	9200
14	Hema Minarbalia	4	200	G.P. Office	15th of Month	3000	900	3000	1000	2400	10300
15	Parsu Khudupia	6	200	G.P. Office	15th of Month		5000	7000		2400	14400
16	Budri Majhi	2	200	G.P. Office	15th of Month		1200	6000	1000	2400	10600
17	Barka Poraja	3	200	G.P. Office	15th of Month		2000	4000	1000	2400	9400
18	Jamuna Rampuria	4	200	G.P. Office	15th of Month	3500	800	2900	1200	2400	10800
19	Balaram Nayak		200	G.P. Office	15th of Month		1000			2400	3400
20	Raghunath Katia	1	200	G.P. Office	15th of Month	3000	700	3500	1100	2400	10700
21	Sirka Mangali	2	200	G.P. Office	15th of Month		1200	3000	1000	2400	7600
22	Sirka Sital	3	200	G.P. Office	15th of Month	400	1000	2000	1100	2400	6900
23	Narayan Sirka	4	200	G.P. Office	15th of Month		800	3000	1000	2400	7200
24	Sirka Dandu	3	200	G.P. Office	15th of Month		1200	5000	1300	2400	9900

It is found that beneficiaries under social security schemes are getting Rs. 200 per month which has been distributed on 15th of every month at gram panchayat headquarters (Columns 14, 15 and 16). Examined the annual income of the beneficiaries and it was found that maximum income of the beneficiaries was Rs. 16,900, the beneficiary-wise income has been reflected in (Columns 17, 18, 19, 20, 21 and 22 of Table 4.17). The annual income of the beneficiaries revealed that income from all sources are not sufficient for their day-to-day management throughout the year. However, the Government of Orissa, Women and Child Development Department after careful consideration have been pleased to enhance the monthly pension of the Social Security pension holders under Madhubabu Pension Yojana, Indira Gandhi National Old Age Pension, Indira Gandhi National Widow Pension and Indira Gandhi National Disabled Pension from Rs. 200 to Rs. 300 per month w.e.f. 1.4.2012 in its circular No. 6049 dated 30.3.2012. But it cannot confront the present market rate hence there is a need of enhancement of pension keeping the view of the present market rate up to Rs. 1,000 per beneficiary per month.

4.14 Evaluation Study on Non-Bankable Income Generating Schemes (Plantation programme)

4.14.1 *Objective*

To enhance the living standard among the tribal people living below poverty line Government in both Centre and State have adopted different anti-poverty programme from time to time since the First Five Year Plan. The removal of poverty has been the central concern of planning process in India. During the First three Five Year Plans (1951-66), the main emphasis of planning was to achieve higher growth in Gross National Product. During the Fourth Five Year Plan (1969-74), the approach to Planning got modified and special attention was given to alleviation of poverty particularly in rural area. During Fifth Five Year Plan, Tribal Sub-plan belt were identified in the 5th Schedule area especially the area having more than 50 per cent tribal concentration and secondly dispersed Tribal concentration has also been identified in the Sixth and Seventh Plan for all-round development of tribals. However, several anti-poverty schemes have been introduced with the bank loan but the economic development of tribes is far from expectations. Loan component sanctioned in favour of the tribal beneficiaries are not being properly and fully disbursed to the beneficiaries as a result of which the tribal beneficiaries were in a trouble for grounding the unit meant for them. Hence, the Integrated Tribal Development Agencies have taken up the non-bankable income generating schemes and introduced the plantation programme such as cashew and mango plants under horticultural activities. The line department officers are being entrusted to give technical guideline to the tribal beneficiaries for better implementation of the programme and to create permanent assets among the tribal beneficiaries. The beneficiaries in this regard are being selected with the help of line department officials before rainy season and fruit bearing plantation programme are being taken up in the individual field of tribal beneficiaries out of their subsidy component providing input facilities.

A Plantation Site

4.14.2 *Data Collection*

Primary data on non-bankable income generating schemes such as Plantation programme implemented by the Tribal Development Agency Malkangiri, Bonda Development Agency, Khairput under Malkangiri district and Jeypore Integrated Tribal Development Agency and Koraput Intigrated Tribal Development Agency of Koraput were collected. During the primary field investigation, data have been collected from Sri Chandra Nayak of village Pangam, Kesab Bhumia of Matkamiguda, Some Kirsani of Kadamguda, Laxmi Jhigdi of Andarhall under Malkangiri district and Hari Pujari of Village Jantaput, Deva Bhumia, Massigan,Tularam Bhumia of Kalapada, Sanu Pujari of Baligan, Kamala Pujari of Sindhigan, Raghunath Nayak of Majhiguda and Dinabandhu Nayak of village

Doraguda under Koraput district were interacted and interviewed about the plantation programme. In addition Focus group discussion at Kadamguda and Kalapada among 40 tribal beneficiaries were conducted among the beneficiaries under the programme and the primary data collected from the study area has been tabulated in Table 4.18.

4.14.3 *Data Evaluation*

Under the non-bankable income generating schemes, 11 beneficiaries from 11 villages of study area of Malkangiri and Koraput districts and Banda Development Agency Mudulipada under Khairput block, Group discussion among Tribal beneficiaries belonging to Kadamguda and Kalapada villages of Kundra block were conducted. Integrated Tribal Development Agencies in the study area have supplemented the necessary plants and required fertilizer to tribal beneficiaries within their subsidy amount of Rs 10000 per beneficiary. The technical guidelines have been followed by the line department officers while implementing the plantation programme on the own land of the concerned beneficiaries. The investigation revealed that maximum 100 to 140 plants have been supplied to each of the beneficiaries and they have planted them maximum of 2 acres of land (Columns 15 and 18) owned by them.

It was found that an amount of Rs. 10000 (Rupees Ten Thousand) only have been spent for grounding the unit of each beneficiary (Columns 10 and 12) which were completely out of subsidy components. As regards the Survival points, it was found that the beneficiaries have taken timely proper care for the survival of the plants, their plants have survived up to 95 per cent. But the field investigation revealed that beneficiaries covered under horticultural activities by horticulture department have not taken any care for survival of the plants supplied to them. Sl. No. 9 and 13 indicates that no plant has survived in respect of two beneficiaries. Except these two beneficiaries maximum plants of other beneficiaries have survived (Column 18).

It is reported by the respondents that Sri Chandra Nayak of village Pangam is selling his fruits in the local market who is a successful beneficiary. I also found that mango and cashew plantation taken up by ITDA in the year 2005-06 are of small size and yielding capacity is low.

It was found that beneficiaries at Sl. Nos. 11, 13, 14, 15, 17, 18, 19 and 20 were earning their annual income from Rs. 1,000 to Rs. 20,000 by harvesting cashew nut. The beneficiary-wise annual income has been reflected in Column 22. From the group discussion it was learnt that they have taken the cashew plantation in the year 2001-02 and now it is as old as 9-10 years. They were applying the compost, taking inter-cropping activities in the cashew nut field hormone in time. Therefore, each

Table 4.18: Evaluation of Plantation Programme

Sl. No.	*Name of the Beneficiaries*	*Village*	*GP*	*Block*	*Distance from Block H.Q.*	*Caste*	*Occupation*	*Name of the Scheme*	*Unit Cost*	*Loan*	*Subsidy*	*Year*	*Name of Implanting Agencies*
1	**2**	**3**	**4**	**5**	**6**	**7**	**8**	**9**	**10**	**11**	**12**	**13**	**14**
1	Not found	Kadamguda	Pangam	Mathili	-	-	-	-	-	-	-	-	-
2	Chandra Nayak	Pangam	Pangam	Mathili	8 km	Bhumia	Cultivation	Plantation	10000	Nil	10000	2005-'06	ITDA
3	Kesab Bhumia	Ambaguda	Ambaguda	Mathili	5 km	Bhumia	Cultivation	Plantation	10000	Nil	10000	2005-06	ITDA
4	Not found	Matkamiguda	Ambaguda	Mathili									
5	Not found	Kandel	Somnathpur	Kudumuluguma									
6	Not found	Siripeta	Parkanmala	Kudumuluguma									
7	Not found	Sindhiguda	Parkanmala	Kudumuluguma									
8	Not found	Pilakusum	Somnathpur	Kudumuluguma									
9	Some Kirsani	Kadamguda	Kadamguda	Khairput	6 km	Bonda	Cultivation	Plantation	10000	Nil	10000	2006-07	ITDA
10	Not found	Pusuguda	Kadamguda	Khairput									
11	Laxmi Majhi	Mudulipada	Mudulipada	Khairput	27 km	Bhumia	Cultivation	Plantation	5000	Nil	5000	2006-07	BDA
12	Not found			Khairput									
13	Hari Pujari	Jantaput	Massigan	Kundra	17 km	Bhumia	Cultivation	Plantation	10000	Nil	10000	2005-06	ITDA

(*contd.*)

(contd.)

Sl. No.	Area of plant-ation	Name of plant-ation	No. of Plant supplied	No. of plant planted/ survived	Year	Unit		Yearly income	Total expen-diture	Net profit	Follow-up action by imple-menting Agency	Amount Saving	Market-ing facilities	Cond-ition of plant-ation
						On will	By force							
1	**15**	**16**	**17**	**18**	**19**	**20**	**21**	**22**	**23**	**24**	**25**	**26**	**27**	**28**
1	-	-	-	-	-	-	-	-	-	-	-	-	-	-
2	2 Ac	Mango	100	100	2005-06	On will		12500	1100	11400	Nil	Nil	Local market	Good
3	2 Ac	Cashew	140	140	2005-06	On will		12000	1000	11900	Nil	Nil		
4														
5														
6														
7														
8			-											
9	2 Ac	Mango	100		2006-07	On will		4000	1000	3000	Nil	Nil	Local market	Good
10														
11	1 Ac	Cashew	70	70	2006-07	On will		5500	1000	4500	Nil	Nil	Local Market	Good
12														
13	2 Ac	Cashew	140		2005-06	On will		7000	500	6500	Nil	Nil	Local market	Good

(contd.)

(contd.)

Sl. No.	*Name of the Beneficiaries*	*Village*	*GP*	*Block*	*Distance from Block H.Q.*	*Caste*	*Occupation*	*Name of the Scheme*	*Unit Cost*	*Loan*	*Subsidy*	*Year*	*Name of Implanting Agencies*
1	**2**	**3**	**4**	**5**	**6**	**7**	**8**	**9**	**10**	**11**	**12**	**13**	**14**
14	Deba Bhumia	Massigan	Massigan	Kundra	15 km	Bhumia	Cultivation	Plantation	10000	Nil	10000	2005-6	ITDA
15	Tularam Bhumia	Kalapada	Ghumar	Kundra	30 km	Bhumia	Cultivation	Plantation	10000	Nil	10000	2006-7	ITDA
16	Not found	Paknaguda	Ghumar	Kundra									
17	Sanu Poraja	Baligan	Baligan	Baipariguda	20 km	Poraja	Cultivation	Plantation	10000	Nil	10000	2005-6	ITDA
18	Kamala Pujari	Sindhigan	Baligan	Baipariguda	9 km	Bhumia	Cultivation	Plantation	10000	Nil	10000	2005-6	ITDA
19	Raghunath Nayak	Majhiguda	Doraguda	Baipariguda	8 km	Bhumia	Cultivation	Plantation	10000	Nil	10000	2006-7	ITDA
20	Dinabandhu Nayak	Doraguda	Doraguda	Baipariguida	12 km	Bhumia	Cultivation	Plantation	10000	Nil	10000	2006-7	ITDA
21	Not found	Kumbhari	Kumbhari	Narayanpatna	12 km	Bhumia	Cultivation	Plantation	10000	Nil	10000	2006-7	ITDA
22	Not found	Siribeda	Kumbhari	Narayanpatna	12 km	Bhumia	Cultivation	Plantation	10000	Nil	10000	2006-7	ITDA
23	Not found	Palaput	N. Patna	Narayanpatna	12 km	Bhumia	Cultivation	Plantation	10000	Nil	10000	2006-7	ITDA
24	Not found	Odiapentha	N. Patna	Narayanpatna	12 km	Bhumia	Cultivation	Plantation	10000	Nil	10000	2006-7	ITDA

(contd.)

(contd.)

Sl. No.	*Area of plantation*	*Name of plantation*	*No. of Plant supplied*	*No. of plant planted/ survived*	*Year*	*Unit*		*Yealy income*	*Total expenditure*	*Net profit*	*Follow-up action by implementing Agency*	*Amount Saving*	*Marketing facilities*	*Condition of plantation*
						On will	*By force*							
1	**15**	**16**	**17**	**18**	**19**	**20**	**21**	**22**	**23**	**24**	**25**	**26**	**27**	**28**
14	2 Ac	Cashew	70	70	2005-06	On will		10000	1000	9000	Nil	Nil	Local market	Good
15	2 Ac	Cashew	140	140	2006-07	On will		10000	900	9100	Nil	Nil	Local market	Good
16														
17	2 Ac	Cashew	140	140	2005-06	On will		20000	1000	19000	Nil	Nil	Local market	Good
18	2 Ac	Cashew	140	140	2005-06	On will		15000	1000	14000	Nil	Nil	Local market	Good
19	1 Ac	Cashew	140	140	2006-07	On will		17000	800	16000	Nil	Nil	Local market	Good
20	2 Ac	Cashew	140	140	2006-07	On will		15000	950	14050	Nil	Nil	Local market	Good
21	2 Ac	Cashew	140	140	2006-07	On will		15000	950	14050	Nil	Nil	Local market	Good
22	2 Ac	Cashew	140	140	2006-07	On will		15000	950	14050	Nil	Nil	Local market	Good
23	2 Ac	Cashew	140	140	2006-07	On will		15000	950	14050	Nil	Nil	Local market	Good
24	2 Ac	Cashew	140	140	2006-07	On will		15000	950	14050	Nil	Nil	Local market	Good

beneficiary is getting the annual income of Rs. 15000 to 20000 per annum. A discussion about supervision by implementing agency revealed that there is neither the follow-up action conducted by the implementing agency nor by the line department official. It was found that the beneficiaries were not taking primary care of cashew plantation. Therefore, the yielding capacity of fruits of cashew plants has reduced. But when they care properly, the yielding capacity become more. Asked regarding personal saving of the respondents and reported that, they have no habit of saving among the beneficiaries. Further observed that the amount earned from the cashew nut is not sufficient for their family management. Hence, they have not saved any amount for their future.

4.14.4 *Findings*

From the primary investigation on the non-bankable income generating scheme, it is found that beneficiaries among the tribal group have been encouraged to take up cashew and mango plantation on their own land. Beneficiaries for the period of 2001-02 to 2006-07 were investigated from the study area. However, in comparison to income generating schemes under bankable sector it is better than bankable norms. In the non-bankable sector plantation programme are being taken so that at least some long term assets would be created for the beneficiaries. If they failed to earn for this year then they can be able to earn money from next year. But in the bankable sector beneficiaries are not able to ground the unit and no assets are being created like plantation programme. From the primary investigation, it is learnt that the beneficiaries under the scheme are not able to save as they are not aware about their future planning. Further, it was found that they have not been imparted training either by the line department or by the implementing agency.

5
Summary and Suggestions

5.1 Summary

In order to tackle with the various tribal problems, a number of tribal development schemes and programmes have been formulated and adopted by the government from time to time during last eleven five year plan periods. A series of schemes and programmes are being implemented for elimination of various forms of tribal exploitation and increase the level of living of the tribals. Different income generating schemes are being introduced in the study area and implemented through the implementing agencies such as Integrated Tribal Development Agencies, Koraput, Jeypore and Malkangiri. Further, effort have been made for the development of Banda in Banda Development Agency at Mudulipada under Khairput block and Didaji in Didayee Development Agency at Kudumuluguma block for upliftment of primitive tribal groups inhabiting in Malkangiri district. Besides Orissa Scheduled Caste Finance Development Corporation Ltd. has been established for the economic development of Scheduled Castes and Scheduled Tribes. Odisha Tribal Empowerment & Livelihood Programme has been introduced for sustainability of livelihood of tribals in rural area. Integrated Rural Development Programme (IRDP) and Swarna Jayanty Gramya Swa-Rojgar Yojana were implemented for elimination of poverty among the people living below poverty line with special attention to tribes. For educational development of tribal students various residential schools have been established with lodging and boarding facilities. During the Eighth Five Year Plan, the historical landmark steps has been taken for the political empowerment among the tribal community to implement the PESA Act, 1996. Under the provision of this Act, the head of the Gram Panchayat, Panchayat Samiti and Zilla Parisad will be from the tribal community. So that in the 5th scheduled area Sarapanchas, Panchayat Samiti Chairman and President Zilla Parishad post are reserved for Scheduled Tribe. So it is necessary to examine how they are exercising their powers and how the beneficiaries among the tribal groups are taking advantages of different anti-poverty schemes and project implemented by the Government from time to time. The educational institutions opened and functioning of residential schools with various facilities were evaluated in the study area and found the lacuna have been discussed in the Chapter 4 of this book. Educational facilities and supply of amenities to the boarders, women education and the extent of its success has been examined. Regarding implementation of income generating schemes tribal beneficiaries benefited in different schemes in the study area has been examined. Food security system in the study area of the Koraput and Malkangiri districts, especially the functioning of grain banks adopted by the Government and Non-Governmental Organizations have been examined, group discussions on functioning of tribal Self Help Groups have been conducted and discussed in Chapter 4 of this book. Detailed discussion on social security such as Indira Gandhi National Old Age Pension (IGNOAP), Madhu Babu Pension Yojana (MBPY), Odisha Disabled Pension and National Family Benefits Schemes have been made in this study. Implementation of Public Distribution System (PDS) plays a vital role in the food security of the tribal areas. Beneficiaries from the public distribution system are also interacted and the functioning system of the scheme have been dealt. As the study area of Koraput region is hilly and inaccessible, the irrigation potentiality is less than the plain area. So different departments have given effort for construction of water harvesting structures. Even the functioning of watershed mission has been discussed. In this regard, some water harvesting structure constructed by the Integrated Tribal Development Agencies and Bonda Development Agency have been evaluated and discussed in this book.

In the earlier two plans, the strategy of tribal development was formulated in a piecemeal manner. During the Third Plan period four Special Multi-purpose Tribal Development (SMPT) Blocks were established in the State out of 43 established in the country. These blocks were established with a view to bring about rapid improvement in the socio-economic standards of the tribals. The limited number of programmes introduced in most of these blocks did not even reflect the specific needs of the tribals residing therein.

A new mode of strategy was launched in the Fourth Plan period with the establishment of two projects in the State known as Tribal Development Agencies. The main objective of the programme was to bring up the tribal population by fostering their economic development. The core economic programmes pursued by these projects comprised all aspects of agricultural development, encouragement of agro and forest based industries, strengthening of co-operative societies and the like.

The concept of Tribal Sub-Plan was evolved and adopted during the Fifth Five Year Plan. The Tribal Sub-Plan had twin objectives of accelerated socio-economic development of tribals and their protection against various forms of exploitation. Areas having more than 50 per cent tribal concentration were identified and twenty one Integrated Tribal Development Agencies were formed in the State. In addition, six micro projects were formed for development of Primitive Tribal Pockets. At present, 17 Micro Projects are functioning in the State out of which four Primitive Tribal Groups are in undivided Koraput district.

During the Sixth Plan period area with population of 10,000 or more of which more than 50 per cent of the population are tribal concentrated have been covered under "Modified Area Development Approach". In the Seventh Plan, this has been further extended to the areas with total population of 5000 and with more than 50 per cent Tribal Concentration under the cluster approach.

Dispersed Tribal Development Programme (DTDP) is being implemented by Odisha Scheduled Castes and Scheduled Tribes Development Finance Corporation for the benefit of tribal families living outside the above project areas.

In the Seventh Plan period, the emphasis was laid on economic and educational development. At the national level two Institutes were established in 1989: (a) Tribal Co-operative Marketing Federation (TRIFED), and (b) National ST & SC Finance and Development Corporation (NSTFDC).

During the Eighth Five Year Plan, educational development again received priority. The Residential Ashram schools and scholarships were increased. During the Ninth Five Year Plan, a massive effort was taken up for all-round development of STs through integrated plan.

It also focused on tribal empowerment through effective implementation of PESA in Scheduled Areas as well as raising the level of administration in scheduled areas.

In the Tenth Five Year Plan, the programmes of child and women development, irrigation, measures to improve income of tribals from forest produce and development of forest villages were given more emphasis.

The Eleventh Plan was a paradigm shift with respect to the overall empowerment of the tribal people keeping the issues related to Governance at the Centre (Awais and Khan, 2014).

Indian constitutional system provides social, economical, political justice and equality of status of all citizens of India. But, it is necessary to examine that whether the tribal people are availing the Constitutional safeguards or not. The protection of Civil Rights Act, 1955, Scheduled Caste & Scheduled Tribe Prevention of Atrocities Act,1989, Land Alienation Regulation 2 of 1956, Orissa Land Revenue Rule 22, 23 & 23(a), Bonded Labour Abolition Act, 1976, Money-lender Act, 1968,

Panchayat Extension to Scheduled Area Act, 1996, Prevention of Atrocities Rules1995, Forest Rights Act, 2006 etc. have been enacted and implemented for the constitutional safeguard of tribes. Despite all these efforts made by Government in both Centre and State, the socio-economic and political as well as educational development of the tribes are not up to expectation. Hence, the evaluation on various schemes and prorgamme implemented for the all-round development of the tribal was necessary. That is why under the random sampling basis Kundra, Baipariguda and Narayanapatna block of Koraput district and Mathili, Kudumuluguma and Khairput blocks of Malkangiri district were selected. Two gram panchayats from each block and two revenue villages from each gram panchayat were selected for case study. Besides all these case study area, one grain bank, one water harvesting structure (L.I. point) have been associated during the course of primary investigation. Primary data on various anti-poverty programmes both bankable and non-bankable schemes, social security schemes, functioning of grain bank in study area, management of water harvesting structure, educational institutions, residential school and hostel management, provision of pre-matric scholarship, public distribution system, functioning of people representative institutions and tribal women Self Help Group and Indira Awas Yojana were evaluated. In addition, the individual interaction with beneficiary, group discussion on functioning of the above programmes were examined. In this connection, 1362 respondents from different schemes implemented for the all-round development of tribes in the study area were interacted to evaluate the success and failure of the programmes cited above. After careful interaction with the respondents and field visit, primary data and secondary data collected from different sources have been tabulated and evaluated. The findings of functioning, prospect and retrospect, objective and implementation of different schemes and programmes in the study area has been given in Chapter 4 of this book and scheme-wise valuable suggestions have been suggested in Chapter 5 for better and successful implementation of the different schemes and programmes adopted by the government from time to time for all-round tribal development.

5.2 Suggestions and Recommendation for Educational Institutions

Since independence several efforts have been taken by the government for the educational development of the Tribal students. In order to attract the students towards school and education, mid-day meal programme has been implemented, which has subsequently enabled to arrest the drop-out position of students. A number of residential schools with boarding facilities have been opened in the tribal areas for strengthening of education among the tribal students. Special educational complexes have been established for the primitive tribal groups for educational development of the tribal communities of Bonda and Didayee. But there are some lacunas which have been identified during primary investigation on functioning of educational institutions. That is why some valuable suggestions have been offered in the following manner to make the programme more effective for the educational development system of the tribal students. That,

1. Sufficient teaching staff should be posted as per the norms fixed by the School and Mass Education Department so that educational standard can be improved.
2. Subject teachers are to be posted in case of High school. It is observed that Upgraded High schools are running with the primary school teachers who may not be able to teach the high school standard students. In such schools, the enrolment of students without teacher is meaningless. Therefore, posting of subject teacher in high school standard is highly essential.
3. Infrastructural development are to be made, kitchen room for mid- day meals, Additional Class Rooms are to be constructed as per the requirement of students, toilet facility are to be set up separately for boys and girls, boundry wall and playground also need to be constructed in each and every school. Within the study area, it is found that no playground is available in the schools. For the physical training or development of the pupils playground facilities are to be created in each educational institution.
4. Green vegetable need to be planted with the help of the student in the gardening class, cleanness of school campus has to be maintained properly.
5. Bench and table should be provided to the school as per the requirement of the students.
6. Exact requirement of the books are to be provided by the Head Master concerned to book supply agency sufficiently in advance every year, and the book supply agency should supply the required number of books in the first week of the month of academic session to enable all the students to get their book in time.
7. Notebooks and writing materials are to be supplied to the pupils especially in residential schools.
8. Library and reading room for the pupils are to be provided.
9. After reading the daily newspapers, important news should be explained by the students on rotation basis during completion of their prayer classes.
10. Debate competition among the students should be conducted in each month in order to improve the oratory ability and removal of stage fear.

11. Seminar classes are to be organized within their topic to improve the knowledge of students.
12. The inspecting authority should visit the educational institution at least once in a month.
13. According to the action plan, teaching as per syllabus are to be completed physically.
14. The Head Master should inspect within each fortnight subject teacher-wise whether the teacher concerned completed his course accordingly or not.
15. Remedial classes to be taken up regularly for the weak students.
16. In the schools situated in the hilly area it is found that teacher are not regular. In this connection, teachers should regularly attend the schools for better education.

The main purpose of the academic management is to evaluate and determine the effectiveness of the teaching learning process which provides valuable feedback to both teachers and pupils for improving their performance. Evaluation in curricular areas has to be continued from the beginning of the academic session. In this regard, the following academic measures can be taken.

5.2.1 *Morning Assembly*

1. The prayer of the students should be of unique nature and they should perform each prayer each day, and in case of primary stage 2 students of class IV & V respectively should sing the prayer on rotation basis in their prayer classes. This will enable the students to understand the prayer and every student will better participate in the prayer.
2. Newspaper reading on important news by the students on rotation basis has to be ensured.
3. One quiz question booklet is to be prepared and the students are to answer them. This practice will help the students to improve their general knowledge.
4. Students can be encouraged to write thought of today on the Notice Board on rotation basis. This will improve their involvement in the school activities and improve their knowledge.
5. During the school hour both the teacher and students are to be in uniform.
6. Each subject teacher should prepare lesson plan for his subject by the end of June and get it approved by the Head Master after discussion in teachers meeting.

7. Class routine and subject allotment to the teachers for each class should be finalized before 15th April of every year in the teachers meeting under the guidance of Head Master.
8. Monthly review meeting of teachers on progress of academic activities should be undertaken by the Head Master in every month and these need to be duly recorded in the monthly review meeting register, problems of students in understanding the subject and remedial measures need to be worked out. Performance of students on monthly evaluation test are to be taken up by the subject teacher for each class.
9. Remedial coaching classes for the slow learners and supervision classes for others should be conducted.
10. Home assignments and answer notebook should be evaluated and corrected by the teacher concerned on a regular manner making no lapses of time, so that students will be able to know his/her mistake.
11. Students excelling in different activities such as academic, sports, quiz and other competition should be recognized with award of prizes.
12. The TLM dictionaries, Map and chart should be displayed with achievements of students in prominent places of the school for creating competitive bent of mind among the students.
13. Unit test are to be conducted in mandatory basis along with cumulative Tests such as pre-test/half yearly and pre-board test/ annual examination. This will enable the students to be abreast with their subject. Examination in classes IX and X are to be meticulously taken up.
14. All unit tests are to be conducted in the last week of the stipulated month preferably in the 1st period in each subject. Since there are eight subjects and six working days in a week, the Head Master will decide two tests for subjects in any other day or days of the week.
15. Unit tests are to be designed with the instructional objective of setting questions out of a total mark of 25 to be answered in 45 minutes.
16. In the Staff meeting the Head Master will share the result analysis report in respect of all classes irrespective of subjects and decide the further course of action to be taken for the improvement of the students in each month and record the proceedings of the discussion for implementation.
17. Inspecting and supervising authorities such as WEOs, S.I. of schools, D.I. of Schools, C.I. of schools/BEO/CRCC/BRCC, DEO, ADWO and DWO are to monitor the progress relating to

the achievement of students in respect of their jurisdiction.

18. Subject teachers of classes IX and X are to maintain separate registers to enter the marks of the unit tests to monitor the progress of the students. A register must be maintained centrally and will be placed before the Head Master for review and monitoring.
19. Performance/Assessment of the subject teachers of each school has to be made twice in a year, i.e. in December and April by the inspector of schools.

5.2.2 *Maintenance of School Environment*

(a) All teachers including the Head Masters of residential schools should reside inside the school campus to give close attention towards students for their all-round development.

(b) Sufficient accommodation facilities are to be provided to the teachers as well as to non-teaching staff.

(c) Massive plantation programme should be taken up in the school campus during the month of June in each year.

(d) Every school should have its own composite pit, medicinal garden, kitchen garden and fruit bearing garden depending upon availability of open space.

(e) All schools should display its staff position class-wise as well as sex and category-wise enrolment position of students.

(f) Time-table, school development plan, drop-out figures, if any, school final result, outstanding performance of students on both academic and non-academic (extracurricular activities) etc. need to be displayed in the prominent place of the school.

(g) One career counselling and guidance cell in each school should be opened. A teacher in charge should keep track of timing of different examinations such as Navodaya entrance, NRTS, NTS, EMRS and admission in different diploma, ITI and colleges. A career guide book also need to be maintained.

(h) Old students association should be formed in each school and a day may be earmarked for old students meet to interact with present students once in a year to share their progress and achievement.

(i) Students help line numbers to be written on the prominent place of the school/hostels.

5.2.3 *Extracurricular Activities*

1. Students of every school should participate in Science Exhibition and other cluster level and block level competitions.
2. Every school has to organize Annual Sports competition and Annual Day function Each school should organize celebration of

important days of the national importance, picnics and also invite eminent persons of the area to give talk and interact with the students.

3. Important News—Headlines based on Science, Games, and Literature and of educative importance at State and national level may be read out in the prayer classes by the students/monitors on a rotation basis.
4. Quotation of the great men having moral values should be displayed on the walls of all the class rooms.
5. The School Annual Function and Annual Sports Day should be observed meticulously along with all the national days which are meant for the school students.
6. Recourse persons of the locality such as Engineers, Doctors, Poets, eminent Educationists and Environmentalists etc. should be invited to deliver talks on important topics.
7. Thought for the day should be written on the board provided where the students can read it.
8. Steps should be taken by the Head Masters/Head Mistress to open NCC/SCOUTS/ GUIDE (Girls) /JRC in schools.
9. Participation of students in Science Exhibition/Sports and games meet/cultural events should be mandatory.
10. Display respective Art and writing of the student on the board.
11. Exposures visit/Study-Tours/Excursion to the places of importance should be arranged at least once in a year for the students with permission from the competent authority.

5.2.4 *Maintenance of Records*

The following registers need to be maintained for the smooth management of Schools:

1. Admission Register of school.
2. School History Book.
3. Visitors Book.
4. Main Cash Book and mess cash book.
5. Receipt book.
6. Voucher guard file.
7. Class-wise attendance registers.
8. Daily stock and consumption register for MDM.
9. Store book.
10. School meeting register.
11. Register for purchase of food materials.
12. Attendance registers for teaching and non-teaching staff.

13. School Cabinet Register.
14. Unit Test Result Register.
15. Sports and Game Register.
16. Annual Result Register.
17. T.C. Book.

5.2.5 *Infrastructure Developments*

For the smooth management of the students the following steps should be taken meticulously:

(i) Cost-effective *Chulha* or smokeless *Chulha* are to be used for cooking purpose.
(ii) Class room should be constructed as per the requirement of the school.
(iii) Boundary walls has to be constructed in all schools.
(iv) Toilet for boys and girls to be constructed separately and its proper maintenance has to be ensured.
(v) Water facility with overhead tank, to be supplied to all schools.
(vi) Sufficient bench and desk are to be supplied to the school as per their requirement.
(vii) Electricity facility should be provided to the educational institutions.

5.3 Suggestions and Recommendation on PRI Members

Since time immemorial tribal communities are having their own panchayat. But after introduction of the PESA Act, 1996, role of tribal PRI members have changed. There is a scope of tribal members to exercise their power as PRI members in the Gram Panchayat, Panchayat Samiti and Zilla Parishad in the three tier system of Panchayati Raj. After careful evaluation on the powers, functions of the PRI members in the study area, the following limitations have been observed.

The field investigation made in the study area revealed that the PRI members are unable to implement the schemes and programmes meant for development of tribals in their area. The newly elected panchayat members are not aware of their duties and powers. In the Palli Sabha, all the members of the village do not attend the meeting. The Sarpanch and Ward Member of the village do not give notice for the Palli Sabha as per the rules. Only few members attend the meeting. The Sarpanch and the concerned Ward Members while making the list of beneficiaries select their friends, relatives and party members even if they are not eligible to receive the benefit.

Hence, the houses under IAY, benefits under social welfare programmes etc. are given to persons who are not eligible to receive the benefit.

Hence, the following suggestions/recommendations are to be followed to improve the functioning of the statutory panchayat:

1. Awareness has to be created among the SC/ST PRI members on PESA Act, 1996 to enable them to take proper advantage of the provisions of the Act.
2. Minimum educational qualification need to be fixed for the post of Sarapanchs, Samiti members, Z.P. Members and Chairman of the Block. Qualified members can better understand their powers and functions as well as their duties and responsibilities.
3. All concerned should be informed to attend the Palli Sabha and they should submit their claim impartially in the meeting. It is seen that villagers are not serious in attending the meeting. Even sometimes it is observed that without having Palli Sabha different proposals are being approved taking signature from the people. In this regard villagers should be informed before a fortnight and maximum number of members should attend the meeting, so that the proper claims of the people will be submitted and approved in the Palli Sabha.
4. The entire proposal passed by the concerned Palli Sabha should be submitted in the Grama Sabha and all the proposals should be approved by the Grama Sabha on priority basis.
5. All Ward Members, Sarapanch and Samiti members have to attend their respective Grama Sabha meeting. But it has been found that the percentage of attendance of Grama Sabha members is 45 to 50 per cent and for female members it is below 35 to 40 per cent. About 60 per cent male members and 70 per cent female members have no idea about the powers and functions of Palli Sabha. It is the prime duty of the administration to create awareness among the people on power and functions of the Palli Sabha and Gram Sabha.
6. The newly elected PRI representatives like Ward members, Sarpanchas, Samiti members, Chairman and Vice Chairman have little experience and knowledge about administrative affairs, development interventions and political functioning. In maximum cases, they are semi-literate or little literate. In most cases, the bureaucrats and the local elites are taking advantage because of their ignorance. Thus, a synergistic approach for creating mass awareness about the PESA Act. All the tribals should be developed at all levels, through government, NGOs and social activities

organizations for undertaking training programme, seminars and workshop.

7. The State Institute of Rural Development is organizing capacity building training programmes on the powers and functions of the PRI members. But these training programmes are limited and the illiterate/semi-literate persons do not attend such programme even if they attend the programme, they are not serious about it.
8. Well structured time bound training programmes should be organized for new PRI members. Sufficient funds need to be allotted for this.
9. The rules and regulations contained in the provision PESA Act, 1996 are to be translated in their regional language so that the tribal PRI members will be able to read and understand it easily.
10. Wide participation of women in decision making process need to be encouraged. Woman SHGs may be assisted to create awareness among the women members.
11. Grama Sabha should be conducted once in every quarter of a year in a democratic way without the intervention of the powerful money-lenders or politicians. There should be quorum in every meeting and the decision should be read out at the end of the meeting before obtaining the signature of the president and secretary all development issues should be discussed in the Gram Sabha.
12. All the plans and development programmes of government and NGOs should be incorporated in the block plan. All information regarding schemes development work orders and plan estimate unit cost and provisions should be made available in Gram Panchayat office.
13. Planning management of water bodies shall be entrusted to Gram Panchayats at the appropriate level.
14. The state legislature may endow panchayats with powers and authority as may be necessary to enable them to function as institution of self-government and shall contain safeguards to ensure that Panchayat Samiti or Zilla Parishad do not assume the powers and authority of village panchayat or Gram Sabha.
15. State legislature should follow the pattern of the Fifth Schedule to the Constitution while designing administrative arrangements in Zilla Parishads of Tribal areas. Efforts need to be made both by Government and NGOs to create awareness among the ST in this regard.

5.4 Suggestions and Recommendation on Hostel Management

A number of residential schools have been constructed by the Central and State Governments for attracting the Scheduled Caste and Scheduled Tribe students. A tribal boy or a girl is an economic asset to their parents. Hence, their parents were not able to spare their children for learning in educational institutions. The facilities provided by the government in the shape of free boarding, lodging, supply of uniforms, teaching learning materials and pocket money has now attracted the tribal students to read in the schools. The parents now have shown interest for these free educational opportunities in residential schools. Many tribal students have proved their merit to read in medical and engineering classes.

5.4.1 *Mess Management*

(a) For smooth management of mess and to ensure qualitative and quantitative food for the boarders, mess management committee consisting of one boarder elected from each class is to be constituted with a nominated teacher as Asst. Superintendent.

(b) As the Head Master is the Superintendent, he is responsible for smooth management and functioning of hostel.

(c) Monthly meeting of all the boarders in the hostel are to be conducted in the presence of Superintendent and Asst. Superintendent, Detailed discussion regarding mess management to be made to ensure provision of good quality food with the present provision of scholarship.

(d) A Purchase Ccommittee will be constituted by nomination of two members out of the mess committee on rotation basis and one teacher by the Superintendent.

(e) All grocery items should be purchased on fortnightly basis or monthly basis depending upon storage capacity to save the wastage of time for boarders and teacher. Only green vegetable items should be purchased twice in a week preferable during the local market day.

(f) A store log book should be maintained on day-to-day basis on issue of stored items. It should be maintained by food committee.

(g) The diet chart and other break up as per the Government guideline should be displayed prominently on the board so that it will be easier for all concerned to know about it.

(h) Individual pass books are to be opened for the students of class VI to class X and pocket money of boarders should be deposited as per the government instruction.

(i) Two pair of dress of good quality is to be supplied to the boarders during the academic session.

(j) Pocket money should be disbursed among the boarders in presence of PRI members and a Government Official (WEO, ADWO, DWO, BDO, ABDO, Special officer, PAITDA, PDDRDA, ADM, etc.

(k) Visiting/Inspecting officers should visit the schools and hostels at least once in a month under their respective jurisdiction and findings are to be reported to the district authority/higher authority.

(l) There should be a separate mess management account for 100 seated girls hostel, K.B.K. Girls hostel, High school hostel.

(m) A lady teacher should invariably be assigned the duty of Asst. Superintendent for the girls hostel. Boarders should not be left with the compassion of the cook-*cum*-attendant.

(n) Male fellows are strictly prohibited to enter into the ladies hostel after 5.30 pm or sunset.

(o) No Lady CCAs are allowed to reside in the ladies hostel campus with their husband.

(p) Ladies CCAs should reside with the ladies boarders for their safety and security.

(q) The Head Masters and Superintendents are to be directed not to allow to the boarders to meet with anybody or relatives except their parents/guardian, whose photograph have been affixed in the Hostel Admission Register. Even during holy day only their parents/guardians are to be allowed to take them from hostel obtaining their signature in the boarders leaving registers.

(r) The Boarders are to be supplied with reading and writing materials.

(s) Cosmetics are to be supplied to the girl's boarders on monthly basis out of their pocket money. In this regard, a day should be declared as the welfare day and on that day cosmetic and other necessary materials are to be distributed among the students.

(t) Soap, oil and surf are to be supplied to the girls and boys boarders out of their miscellaneous expenditure on a monthly basis.

5.4.2 *Health Management*

1. Health is wealth, without sound health nothing can be expected from a person. Hence, first of all to protect the health problems of the boarders supply of safe drinking water is to be ensured so that the boarders will not suffer from any water borne diseases.
2. Food hygiene need to be ensured.
3. Personal hygiene and sanitation has to be ensured.
4. Proper sanitary conditions are to be maintained in the hostels to protect the students from mosquito.

5. Health messages to be painted on the walls as "Swasthya Kantha" which should be updated regularly by the Head Master concerned.
6. Health check-up by Mobile Health Unit (M.H.U.) has to be ensured regularly.
7. Everyday health check-up to be conducted by the Head Master/ Superintendent during their prayer classes especially twice in a day during rainy and winter season to identify the sick boarders well in advance to avoid the unwanted health situation.
8. As the tribal parents are not much conscious about the malaria, hence blood sample of each boarder should be examined on return from vacation to detect malaria parasite and to avoid future health complicacy by the Head Master/Superintendents.
9. The Doctors, ANM/Asha worker should visit the school boys and girls hostel at least once in a fortnight.
10. All head masters and superintendents should ensure that students are using mosquito net and other amenities provided to them.
11. In order to avoid adulteration of food, the quality and quantity of food provided to the boarders need to be ensured.
12. Boarder fall sick should be immediately taken to nearby medical clinic/hospital for better treatment without making any delay instead of sending the boarders to their home.
13. During the rainy and winter day, stale food to be avoided to supply the boarders.

5.4.3 *Disbursement of Pre-matric Scholarship*

1. The drawing and disbursing officers are to be authorized to draw one month's current and two month scholarship in advance. It will be the responsibility of the drawing and disbursing officer to see that the scholarship bills are duly prepared in the prescribed form and submit it to the Treasury for drawing timely.
2. The scholarship advanced to the Asst. Superintendent of the Mess to undertake day-to-day management of the mess will be adjusted against the aquittance by the students at the end of the month.
3. The Asst. Superintendent will ensure that all the registers relating to the mess management are properly and correctly maintained up-to-date at all times. He/she will be personally held responsible if any lapses are found in these records.
4. The balance stock of commodities at the close of the month will be properly handed over and taken over by the outgoing and incoming mess managers in presence of the Students Mess Committee and the Superintendents of the institutions so that the future complicacy on availability of stock can be assessed.

5. The Total expenditure of a month and the cost of each meal will be worked out by the mess manager and placed before the mess committee by the third of the following month for necessary approval. The Mess Committee will also place income and expenditure statement before the General Body of the students in first week of every month.
6. The Head Master should identify the best Mess Manager in one academic year and arrange awarding the same boy or girl in any public meeting which will encourage the boarders to manage the mess in a fair manner.
7. The Head Master/Head Mistress should take charge for smooth management of the hostel. He/she may pass written orders, wherever any doubt or clarification is sought as per local requirement from time to time. The following action points/aspects shall be verified at the time of inspection.
8. From the primary investigation it is found that only Rs. 50 (Rupees Fifty only) remuneration is being paid to the hostel superintendents. In order to create the interest of the superintendents and to meet the travelling expenses, the remuneration of superintendent should be enhanced to Rs. 3000 (Rupees Three Thousand) per month.

5.4.4 Maintenance of Records

Record keeping is an important aspect of the management of hostel. As the Government has allotted a huge amount of pre-matric scholarship for educational development of tribal students, it is necessary to maintain different records and registers to make the accounting procedure clean. For the smooth management of mess management, the following registers to be necessarily maintained:

1. Admission Register of School.
2. Admission Register of Hostel, the Photograph of students and parents/guidance to be affixed in the Admission Register to avoid any future complicacy.
3. School/Hostel History Book.
4. Visitors' Book.
5. Outgoing and incoming register for boarders.
6. Main cash book and mess cash book.
7. Receipt book.
8. Voucher guard file.
9. Mess attendance register.
10. Hostel attendance registers.
11. Daily stock and consumption register.
12. Store book.

13. Cook-*cum*-attendant log book.
14. Hostel meeting register.
15. School meeting register.
16. Boarders leaving register.
17. Register for purchase of food materials.
18. Sick register.
19. Attendance registers for teaching and non-teaching staff.
20. Hostel Cabinet Register.
21. Sports and Game Register.
22. Quotation procurement files for purchase of food materials.
23. Amenities distribution registers.

5.4.5 *Infrastructure Developments*

A. Cost-effective *Chulha* or smokeless *Chulha* to be supplied for cooking purpose.
B. If more than one hostel is functioning in a single campus cooking should be rationalized.
C. Boundary wall of the ladies hostel to be upgraded and covered with barbed wire.
D. Toilet for boarders should be clean and maintained properly.
E. Supply of water facility with overhead tank, required number of cots, bench and desk, *dori*, inverter, and other necessary furnitures are to be ensured.
F. Hostel building as per the boarder's strength are to be constructed for the boarders.

5.4.6 *Supply of Amenities, Sanitation and Water Supply with Electricity Facility*

I. Amenities are to be provided according to the requirement of the boarders. It should be supplied in time.
II. Toilet facility is to be constructed with 10:1 ratio with continuous water supply facility. This will dissuade the boarders to go to outside for their natural calls.
III. Running water supply system has to be constructed with overhead tanks and bathing complex separately for boys and girls. One or two tube-wells available in the hostel campus is not sufficient for 100 boarders. Therefore, running water is highly essential.
IV. There should be provision of repair and maintenance of electricity system. This will enable the school administration to take up repair and replacement of bulb, choke, table light etc.

V. Where the conventional electricity is not available, solar light system to be provided

5.5 Suggestions and Recommendation on Pre-matric Scholarship

The scholarship is a holistic scheme which is encouraging the Scheduled Caste and Scheduled Tribe students for their educational development. Provision of Pre-matric scholarship can check the drop-out position of tribal students. It is observed that some parents of tribal students migrate to Andhra Pradesh for a period of 4 months to 6 months and in this period there is possibility of drop-out of tribal students. Since the residential facilities is running under the provision of Pre-matric scholarship pupils of migrant parents are residing in the residential school. However, a number of drawbacks have been observed in the implementation of the programme in the field. Hence, the following recommendations have been suggested for better implementation of the scheme.

1. The Pre-matric Scholarship for the Scheduled Caste & Scheduled Tribe students need to be enhanced for Classes VI & VII to a tune of Rs. 100 and Rs. 150 for boys and girls per month respectively. From Class VIII to X, it has to be enhanced from Rs. 200 and Rs. 250 per month per boy and girl respectively instead of the existing rate of Rs. 15, Rs. 20, Rs. 20 and Rs. 25 per student from the classes VI to X both boys and girls respectively. In case of Boarders rate of Pre-matric scholarship per month should be enhanced up to Rs. 1000 per boy boarder and Rs. 1100 per girl boarder.
2. Pre-matric scholarship should be rationalized, to avoid any discrimination among the students. When a boarder of Eklavya Model School is getting Rs. 1000 Pre-matric scholarship per month at the same time a boarder reading in residential school running under ST & SC Development Department are getting Rs. 620 to Rs. 650 per month.
3. Provision of pocket money should be implemented for both boy and girl boarders. So that both boarders can use their pocket money in their day-to-day life. They can purchase pen, pencil, note book etc. during their need.
4. Provision of dress materials should form a part of the Pre-matric scholarship and the concerned Head Master and the Superintendent should be responsible for the preparation and distribution of the dress at the beginning of the academic session. If the dress money will be with the Head Master/Superintendent he can call the tailor to the school point and prepare the dresses of the boarders according

to their exact measurement with qualitative clothes and supervision can be easy for the supervising officer.

5. In the recent diet chart prescribed by the Government in ST & SC Development Department there is no provision of hair oil, soap etc. for the bathing and washing purpose. So, the Superintendents/Head masters are facing problems to provide these necessary materials to the boarders. This provision has to be made by the Government.
6. Cost of electricity should also be separately specified within the provision of Pre-matric scholarship. This will enable the Head Master or the Superintendent to maintain the electricity system in the hostel during requirement.
7. During the Academic Session 2012-13, a provision of Book and *adhoc* grant for the students of class IX and X are being implemented by DFID for which both boy and girl boarder students are getting Rs. 1000 per annum and both boy and girl day scholar students are entitled to avail Rs. 750 per annum. But this provision is limited with the students of class IX and X. If this provision will be implemented and extended to the students from class VI to X then the Scheduled Caste and Scheduled Tribe students will be more benefited. This facility can also help to arrest drop-out problem.
8. The existing measures to improve girls' education facilities have resulted in getting good response from the women students. Hence, these programmes can be intensified so as to get more response from the parents.

5.6 Recommendation on Income Generating Schemes (IGSs) Bankable

During the Fourth Five Year Plan, special attention was given for alleviation of poverty. Special programmes were introduced for the benefit of the poor and relatively less privileged classes with the special attention to the tribals. The main object of the programme was creation of assets, skill development and creation of infrastructure as well as to take up development work in the backward areas. The evaluation made on income generating schemes on the basis of primary investigation and secondary data in Koraput and Malkangiri districts, revealed that income generating schemes implemented by the Government through programme implementing agencies are not free from lacunas. Hence, the following suggestions and recommendations have been made for successful implementation of the different income generating schemes that,

1. Beneficiaries are to be selected after joint verification of the line department officer, financial institution and implementing agency so that the needy and actual beneficiaries can be sponsored.

2. Precaution training on the schemes and project should be imparted among the beneficiaries before grounding the unit. The beneficiaries will gain some new ideas towards successful grounding of the scheme after receiving the training.
3. Whether the units are properly grounded or not should be regularly monitored and follow up action to be taken by the concerned line department as well as financial institution and implementing agency.
4. Marketing facility has to be created so that the products of beneficiaries will be sold easily.
5. Loan amount should be disbursed by the financial institution in favour of beneficiaries in time and it should be as per the requirement of the unit cost, so that he/she will be able to ground the unit successfully.
6. Careful monitoring has to be made so that the beneficiaries do not misutilise the loan amount released for the purpose.
7. Motivation has to be made among the beneficiaries to repay the loan amount, the finance institution should organize the loan recovery camps involving all related field functionaries in a regular interval.
8. Beneficiaries need to be facilitated to exposure visit to gain more knowledge about the successful grounding of the unit.
9. There is the necessity of creating awareness about the schemes and programmes in rural areas. The implementing agency should take proper care in selecting the beneficiaries taking into account the interest and skill of an entrepreneur/beneficiary. This is necessary to utilise the loan/subsidy funds properly.
10. Generally, it is observed that the Scheduled Caste and Scheduled Tribe people are addicted with countryside wine and intoxicated. In this connection they spend more money for wine and quest treatment. They are not only extravagant but also unnecessarily spend their valuable time. Hence, beneficiaries should be discouraged to take wine and extravagant spending.
11. The grounding of a unit should have proper link with the Insurance company. The beneficiaries at present are not aware about the facilities of insurance available in the income generating scheme. Immediately after purchase of cows, goatry unit or poultry unit these animals and birds need to be insured. This will enable the beneficiaries to repay the loan component even if these animals/ birds die due to some common disease.

5.7 Suggestions and Recommendation on IAY Houses

Indira Awas Yojana has been introduced by the Central Government to provide a house to the houseless people in the rural area. The ownership of a house will provide confidence to a poor person to enhance his income by accepting some work. But the scheme is not implemented properly and it has been found that the scheme is not working properly due to a number of limitations in the process of implementation.

The selection of IAY beneficiaries should be just and fair. It has been found that intelligible persons have been allotted houses under IAY and poor and needy persons are deprived. Hence, it is necessary to create awareness among the needy people to present in the Palli Sabha and make their claim. It is also the duty of the ward members to give proper notice of Palli Sabha in a village so that all the adults of the village will be present in the Palli Sabha meeting.

There are difficulties in the sanction and release of money. It has been noticed that the Sarpanch receives the instalment of grant and provides only a part of it to the beneficiaries. Hence, proper care has to be taken by the concerned officials to release the money and hand it over to the beneficiary.

IAY grants are released to the beneficiary on instalments. After the completion of the foundation work, the beneficiary has to submit a report to the BDO with a copy of the photograph of the foundation. The PEO will verify the spot and report to the BDO. This process takes a long time and the beneficiary loses its interest to run to the BDO.

Therefore, it is necessary that a beneficiary should get his second instalment and subsequent instalments within a month of his completion report of different stages of construction.

Sometimes, it has been observed that the work is entrusted to a contractor. Either the beneficiary fears to boodle with the Government grant or he is forced by the Sarpanch/PEO to give it on contract basis. This practice should be completely discouraged and the beneficiary should get the instalments in due time.

The households under IAY should normally be constructed on individual plots in the main habitation of the village. The houses can also be built on micro habitat approach or in a cluster within a habitation, so as to facilitate the development of infrastructure, such as internal roads, drains, drinking water facility and many other facilities. Care should be taken to see that the houses under IAY are located close to the villages and not far away so as to ensure safety and security, nearness to workplace and social communication.

Construction of the IAY houses should be done by the beneficiaries themselves from the very beginning. The beneficiaries may make their own arrangement for the construction and may engage mason and also contribute their family labour, even he should be given complete freedom as to the manner of construction of the house which will facilitate economy in cost.

So far the payment on construction of IAY houses is concerned, it should be made to the beneficiaries on staggered basis depending on the progress of the work. The entire money should not be paid in lump sum. As a matter of fact, misappropriation of the fund by the beneficiaries may be avoided and the IAY houses will be completed within the limited period with limited funds.

5.8 Suggestions and Recommendation on the Better Functioning of Grain Banks

Functioning of grain banks schemes helps tribal people during their urgent requirement in the lean season. Villages situated in the hilly area with natural barrier are facing acute problems for their food security especially during rainy days. In order to provide food security of tribal during lean season grain banks play a vital role among them. Field investigation on functioning of grain bank in the study area has been conducted and several reasons for non-functioning of grain banks have been detected. For better and successful implementation of grain banks in the tribal area, the following suggestions have been recommended for better and effective functioning of grain banks. That,

I. Grain banks should be opened in impassable tribal inhabited villages, where the tribal people are facing the food stuff problems in the lean season.

II. Members of grain banks are not aware about the functioning of grain bank. In this connection, efforts are to be made for creation of awareness among the beneficiaries on functioning of the grain banks and its impact on them.

III. Executive committee meetings are to be conducted regularly and discussion on functioning of grain banks are to be made in presence of all beneficiaries of grain banks.

IV. Penalty on the defaulters are to be discouraged. Adopting social pressure and repayment system are to be regular with impartial judgment among the members.

V. Storage facility is the vital point of the functioning of grain bank, where there is a good storage facility, the foodgrain will be secured. Hence, sufficient storage facility has to be created by the implementing agency.

VI. Book and records keeping will speak the functioning of the grain bank. Therefore, it should be properly maintained by the grain bank.

VII. Panchayat level/Block level grain banks are to be established by the implementing agency so as to come to the rescue of the village grain bank during difficult periods when the village grain banks will fail to come to the help of a needy person.

VIII. Frequent follow-up actions by the implementing agency are to be adopted. Experienced employee need to be posted, to ensure better functioning of grain banks. Monthly review meeting on functioning of grain banks to be taken up by the district authority.

5.9 Suggestions and Recommendation on Tribal Women SHG

Basing upon the evaluation study and on the basis of empirical data, focus group discussions, case studies and personal observations, the findings were obtained. In the light of findings, following suggestions have been made for improving effective functioning of the Tribal Women Self Help Groups in tribal areas:

1. SHGs are to be formed among homogenous members. Generally, all members of the SHG should belong to families below poverty line (BPL) families.
2. A member should not be a member of more than one group.
3. One member from a single household is to be taken as a member of SHG. There should not be more than one member from the same family.
4. An SHG normally consists of either men or women, mixed groups comprising both men and women as members of the same group are generally not preferred.
5. All members of an SHG should have a fixed amount of subscription/ saving, which may be decided by the group to build their corpus.
6. The group should meet regularly every week/fortnight or monthly intervals as per the convenience of all members. Regular meeting help the members to get closer and discuss various common problems and possible solutions. The periodicity venue and time for the meeting should be decided by the members. Attendance of members at the group meeting should be mandatory. The group should have a clear agenda for each meeting and discussion should be taken up.
7. As per the provisions, the President and Secretary should be changed in every six months for one year. This will help each member to develop leadership quality and management efficiency.
8. There should be the individual pass book for each member of a SHG, where their subscriptions are to be reflected, so that they will know about their financial position. Further, the book writer

should declare about the financial position of the members in the last part of each meeting.

9. Saving of the members should be regular and all possible steps need to be taken and awareness among the members should be created about it. This will enable a SHG to become self-dependent.
10. During the primary investigation it was observed that, Bank pass books are not found with the SHG, even they were unable to explain about their bank deposit. In this context, the bank pass book should be always remain with the SHG members instead of banks and book writer. The bankers should return the S.B. account pass book as well as the loan pass book.
11. Recovery camps should be organized by the financial institutions with the help of line department field functionaries on a regular interval to collect the loan amount from the SHGs.
12. Loan sanctioned by the Bank should be disbursed among the SHG members as per the project proposal submitted to the Bank. Timely and full loan amount disbursement is required for successful grounding of units. As a matter of fact, income generation can immediately start and enable them for repayment of loan amount.
13. As per the Swarna Jayanti Gram Swarozgar Yojana (SGSY) guideline grading of the Self Help Group (SHG) has to be made after six months of formation of SHG. It is observed in the field that grading of SHGs have not been done in the study area even after two years. Linking of Bank Credit with the SHGs can only encourage them to take up a group work.
14. Orientation training should be imparted to the SHG members to create sufficient awareness about the relation with banks and bank linkage as well as to create microcredit facilities.
15. Capacity building is an important aspect of the SHG members for making a sustainable SHG. Hence, steps should be taken to enhance capacity building of the SHG by the implementing agency by a series of training and exposure visits.

5.10 Suggestions and Recommendation on Public Distribution System (PDS)

Public Distribution System plays a vital role in any society for providing essential goods to the needy and poor people at a subsidized rate. This system helps to ensure food security and nutrition to the target group of population. However, during the field study, a number of lacuna has been found which need to be addressed through appropriate suggestions:

(1) A fresh BPL survey has to be done by reputed organization who will do the survey in a fair and impartial manner.

(2) Active and effective involvement of the PRIs should be build up in the process of identification of the poor households.

(3) The base line data generated through the proposed survey may be computerized for monitoring and regular updating.

(4) The full monthly quota of foodgrains for distribution must reach the retail outlets within the first seven days of the month.

(5) Sufficient funds should be reserved in the Gram Panchayat to procure the monthly quota at a time.

(6) Emphasis on creating infrastructure in different areas should be given priority, provision of godowns to accommodate the essential commodities be made.

(7) All possible steps must be taken to ensure that, the essential commodities meant for distribution do reach the poor and not diverted to the open market.

(8) Special godown should be constructed in the remote and hilly area keeping in view the accessibility of the place.

(9) Special public distribution outlets should be provided in the primitive tribe habitants of Bonda and Didayee of Malkangiri district.

(10) Every beneficiary households should have ration card not only to get the items but also to prove his identity.

(11) Each Block should have one foodgrain Godown to store PDS goods.

(12) An emergency stock of foodgrains has to be maintained at the fair price shop level to meet with natural calamities.

(13) Temporary ration cards should be provided to in-migration households as workers in constraction work, rituals and religious festival etc.

(14) False and bogus cards should be identified and cancelled.

(15) Special steps should be taken to create the food bank in the hilly and impassable tribal areas, so that no news of death from hunger comes and food security is provided to all.

5.11 Suggestions and Recommendation on Water Harvesting Scheme

Watershed projects help to provide irrigation facilities and improve production of foodgrains. This concept has gained momentum in recent years and has been able to increase the production of foodgrains in hilly and inaccessible areas.

1. There should be the provision for renovation of the water harvesting structure by the implementing agencies. So that during the need repair and maintenance can be done to get the structure ever functional.

2. As the members of user group are homogenous, there should be a cordial relation among the members and monthly meeting on functioning and the present condition of the Water Harvesting Structure need to be conducted in a regular manner. Steps need to be taken for improvement of the project and improvement of the production capacity of the user group farmers etc. have to be discussed on monthly basis.
3. Revolving funds should be created among the members of user group and it should be deposited in the Saving Bank account of the group. This will help to the user group towards the maintenance of the water harvesting structure.
4. Follow-up action should be ensured by the implementing agency and administrative as well as technical guidelines are to be given from time to time.
5. Line Department Officers like Agriculture and Horticulture should pay regular visits the user group and technical guidelines to be given to user group farmers.
6. Market facility has to be created, so that all production of the user group will be sold easily.
7. Size of catchment area of the Water Harvesting Structure should be enhanced up to minimum of 4 hectors. The water containing capacity has to be enhanced to store the rain water and to irrigate lands when required.
8. Meeting Register has to be maintained and all minutes relating to functioning of water harvesting structure has to be recorded in the register.

5.12 Suggestions and Recommendation on Social Security Schemes

Social Security system in the State has been introduced to provide help, medical treatment and food security to the old persons, poor and destitute. The Indira Gandhi Old Age Pension Scheme is a 100 per cent Central Scheme supported under National Social Assistance Programme. The rate of pension under the scheme has been enhanced to Rs. 300 per beneficiary per month up to the age of 79 and Rs. 500 for 80 years and above. Similarly, National Family Benefit Scheme, Madhu Babu Pension Yojana and Home for the Aged are functioning in the State.

These programmes are catering to the welfare of old age, BPL category and destitute. However, there are certain lacuna in the implementation of the programme. Hence, the following suggestions have been made to improve the system.

1. In order to manage with the present market rate, the pension amount should be enhanced from Rs. 300 to Rs. 1000 per beneficiary per month.
2. Needy beneficiaries are to be carefully selected by the implementing agencies.
3. Influential and non-eligible beneficiaries are to be discouraged.
4. Age criteria of beneficiaries are to be properly assessed before sanction of the pension.
5. Beneficiaries should be selected in the Palli Sabha meeting in presence of all adult members of the village and all eligible beneficiaries to be selected in a fair and impartial manner.
6. Annual verification by the implementing agency should be conducted every year and delete the name of the migrated and expired beneficiaries from the acquaintance register.
7. Awareness among the people has to be created on the benefits of the National Family Benefit Schemes and the rate of amount should be enhanced from Rs. 10000 to Rs. 100000 (Rupees One lakh) only for rehabilitation of the deceased family.

5.13 Suggestions and Recommendation on Non-Bankable IGS (Plantation Programme)

The non-bankable income generating schemes implemented for the poverty elevation programme has better impact on the tribal beneficiaries. Permanent assets have been created with handsome income sources. During the field investigation some lapses have been identified for smooth implementation of the plantation programme. Therefore, the following suggestions have been recommended for the better implementation of the non-bankable schemes and more profitable for tribal beneficiaries:

1. Plantation programme may be completed within the month of August so that the survival possibility of plants will be high. In this regard, the beneficiaries selection process should be completed before rainfall.
2. Knowledge about plantation is highly required for the beneficiaries. Adequate training is highly essential before the commencement of plantation.
3. Proper treatment of the pits are necessary to kill the insects in the pit and application of compost is required.
4. Market facility has to be created for selling the products at a fair price.

5. Awareness has to be created among the beneficiaries to maintain the plantation, so that they apply the compost, hormone and fertilizer in time and get more products from their fruit garden.
6. Beneficiaries should be encouraged for intercropping within the plantation area to provide.
7. Beneficiaries need to be selected after joint verification with the line department officers, financeal institutions and implementing agency.

In spite of the efforts made to highlight all the programmes and schemes introduced from the 1st Five Year Plan, only important programmes could be discussed in this study. However, adequate care has been taken to highlight the programmes and schemes.

MAPS

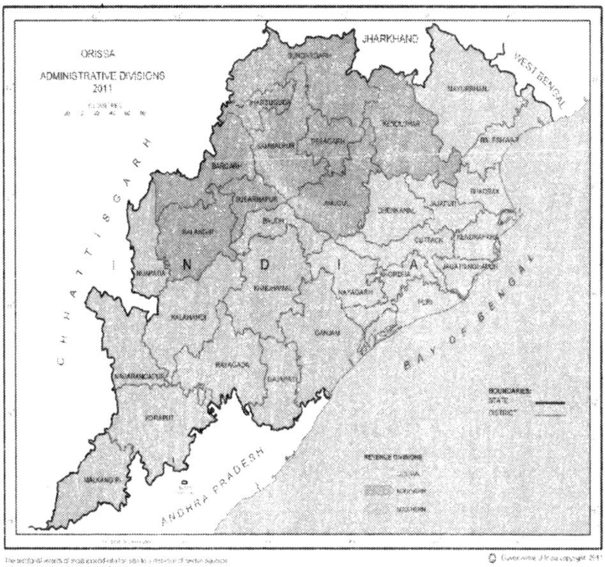

Map of Odisha

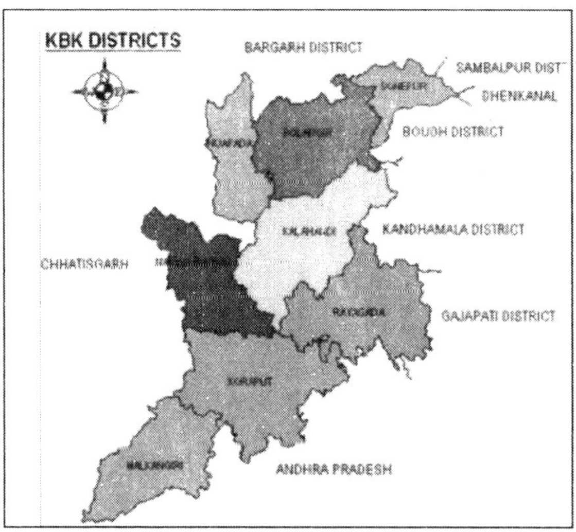

Undivided Koraput Rigion Map

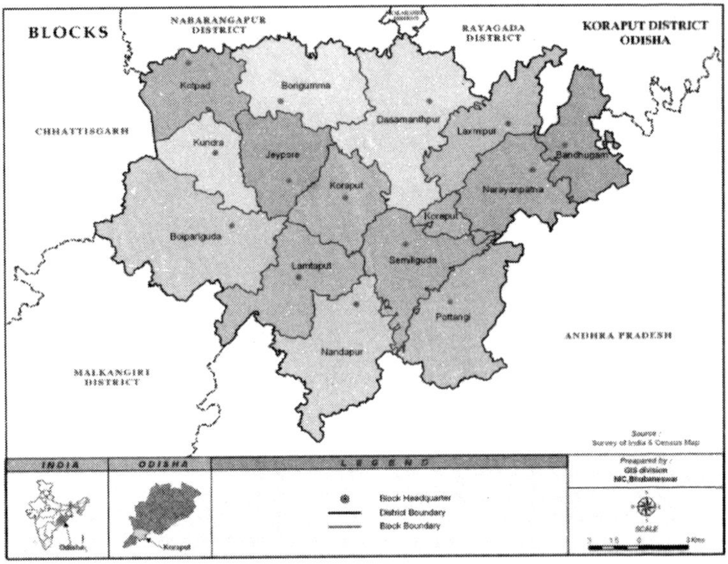

Koraput District Map

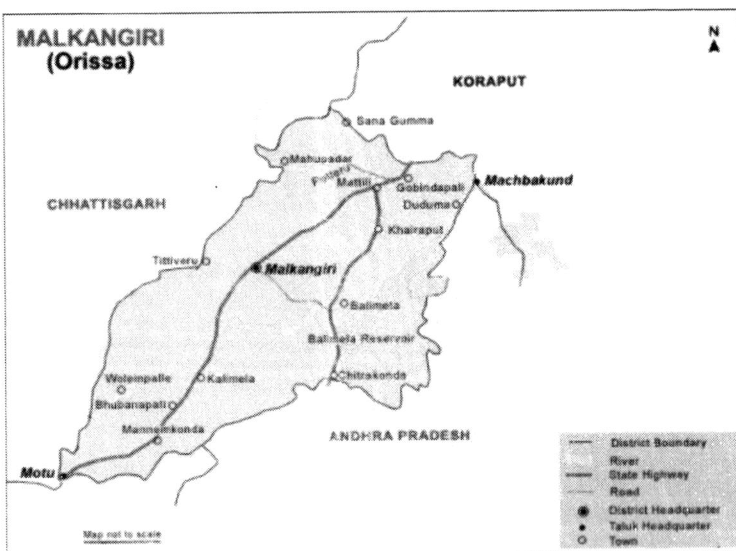

Malkangiri District Map

Kundra Block of Koraput District Map

Boipariguda Block of Koraput District Map

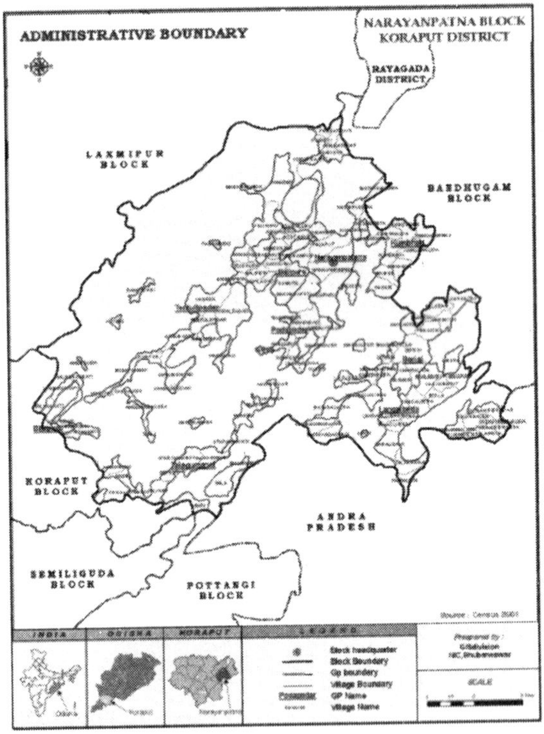

Narayanpatna Block of Koraput District Map

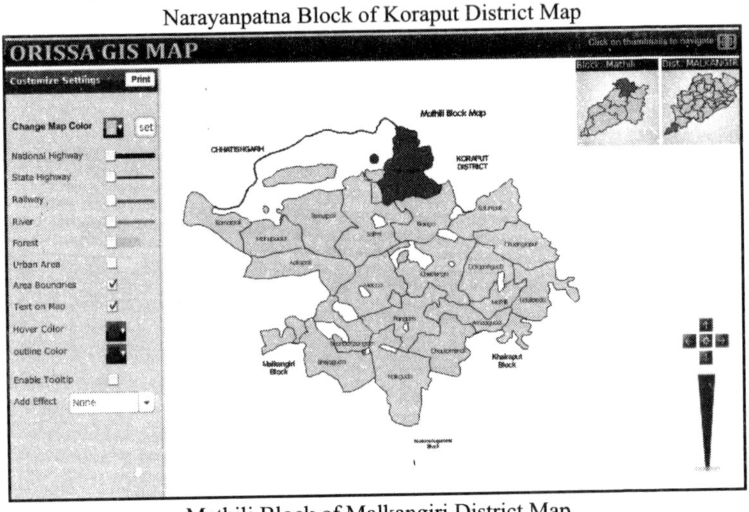

Mathili Block of Malkangiri District Map

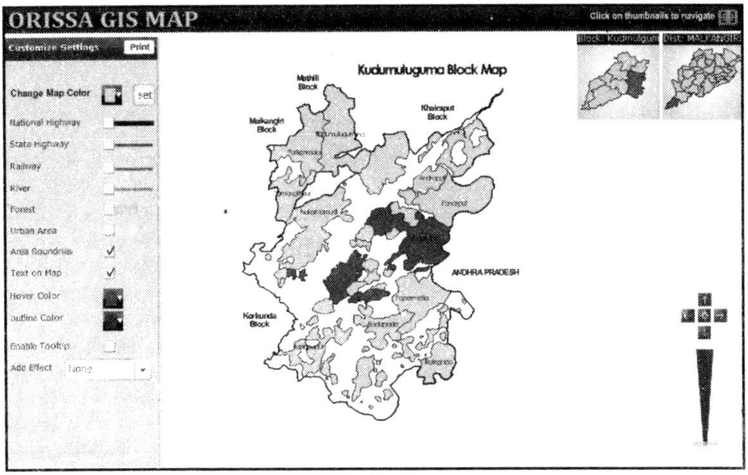

Kudumulugumma Block of Malkangiri District Map

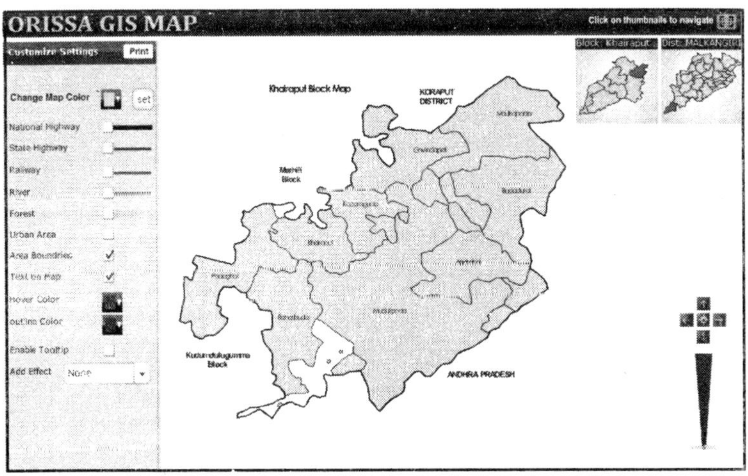

Khairput Block of Malkangiri District Map

Bibliography

Abdul Kalam, APJ. 2005. "For Dignity of Human Life", *Yojana*, September, Vol. 49.

Acharya, Sunita. 2013. "Education as an Instrument of Empowering SC/ST Youth", *TEEKA: A Journal of Education for Teachers Empowerment in the Era of Knowledge Application*, June-December, Vol. 2, No. 1 & 2.

Behera, P.K. 2011. *Traditional Panchayat System of Koyas and Parajas*, Kunal Books, New Delhi.

Bhatnagar, Arun. 2001. *Guideline for Watershed Development Department of Land Resources*, Ministry of Rural Development, Government of India.

Bhurik, S.D. 2001. National Commission of Scheduled Castes & Scheduled Tribes, A Report 1998-99, Vol. I.

Census of India. 1991. *Orissa State District Profile*, Government of India, Text Book Press, Bhubaneswar.

Census of India. 1999. *Orissa State District Profile*, 1991.

Cernea Michel. *Involuntary Displacement in Dam Project.*

Chandra Maculi, E. 2013. *Census of India, 2011, Scheduled Tribes in India*, Ministry of Home Affairs, New Delhi, India.

Das, H.H. 1993. *Introduction to Panchayati Raj and Community Development in India*, Kalyani Publishers, Delhi.

Das, N. 1967. "Panchayats in Tribal Areas", *Adivasi*, Vol.III, Tribal Research Bureau, Cuttack, 1966-67.

Depgenkar, S.G. *Tribal Administration & Development.*

Dhebar, U.N.1960-61. *Report of the Scheduled Areas and Scheduled Tribes Commission*, Government of India Press, 26.10.61.

Dileep Singh Bhurta.1998-99. *National Commission for Scheduled Castes and Scheduled Tribes*, Fifth Report 1998-99, Vol. I.

Fernandes, Walter. 1992. *National Development and Tribal Deprivation.*

Fernandes, Walter & Anthony Raj, S.A. 1992. *Development, Displacement and Rehabilitation in the Tribal Area, Orissa.*

Gomango, Giridhar.1992. *Constitutional Provisions for the Scheduled Castes and Scheduled Tribes*, Himalaya Publishing House, Bombay.

Government of India. 1991. *Manual for IRDP and Allied Programmes of Trysem & DWCRA.*

Government of India. 1994. *Manual on Jawahar Rozgar Yojana*, Government of India, Ministry of Rural Development.

Government of India. 2005. National Rural Employment Guarantee Act, 2005.

Government of India. 2005. *A Guideline on National Food for Work Programme,* Government of India, Ministry of Rural Development (Department of Rural Development), Krishi Bhavan, New Delhi.

Government of Orissa. 2010. *Annual Report on the Administration of Scheduled Areas in Odisha for 2004-05,* ST and SC Development Department.

Government of Orissa. 2012. *Annual Report, 2011-12,* ST and SC Development, Minorities and Backward Classes Welfare Department.

Government of Orissa. 2003-2004. Annual Report 2003-2004, Panchayati Raj Department.

Government of Orissa. 1966. *Tribal and Rural Welfare Manual*, OGP.

Government of Orissa. 1999. *Report on Annual Administration of Scheduled Area in Orissa for 1995-96,* Welfare Department.

Government of Orissa. 2000. *Annual Report of the Administration of Scheduled Area in Orissa for 1997-98,* ST & SC Development Department.

Government of Orissa. 2003-04. *Economic Survey 2003-04*, Directorate of Economic and Co-ordination Department, Government of Odisha.

Government of Orissa. 1991-92. *Report on the Annual Administration of Scheduled Area in Orissa for 1991-92*, Government of Orissa, Tribal Welfare Department.

Government of Orissa. 1990-91. *Report on the Annual Administration of Scheduled Area in Orissa for 1990-91*, Government of Orissa, Tribal Welfare Department.

Government of Orissa. 2006-07. *Report on the Annual Administration of Scheduled Area in Orissa for 2006-07*, Government of Orissa, Tribal Welfare Department.

Government of Orissa. 1987-88. *Report on the Annual Administration of Scheduled Area in Orissa for 1987-88*, Government of Orissa, Tribal Welfare Department.

Government of Orissa. 1997-98. *Report on the Annual Administration of Scheduled Area in Orissa for 1997-98*, Government of Orissa, Tribal Welfare Department.

Government of Orissa. 1979-81. *Report of the Commission for Scheduled Areas in Orissa for 1997-98*, ST & SC Development Department, Welfare Department, Orissa.

H & T.W. Department Orissa. 1996. *Tribal and Rural Welfare Manual*, Vol. II, Government of Orissa, OGP, 9-12: 1966.

Kurup, A.M. 2000. "Indigenous Knowledge and Intellectual Property Rights of Tribals: A Case Study", *Yojana*, No. 44, April.

M. Shankar Rao, Communication. 1976. *Report of the Communication for Scheduled Caste & Scheduled Tribe 1973-74* (Twenty Second Report), Controller of Publication, Delhi, 1976, pp. 248-49.

Mahapatra, P.C. *Key-note Paper on the Problems of Tribal Development in Orissa.*

Mahapatra, P.C. 1987. *Economic Development of Tribal India.*

Mahapatra, P.C., Samal, J., Pradhan, N.N. *A Pilot Study on Integrated Early Childhood Development Programme in Koraput District of Orissa.*

Malaviya, H.D. 1956. *Village Panchayat in India*, AICC, New Delhi.

Mohaptro, P.C. & P.M. Mahapatra. 1997. *Forest Management in Tribal Area: Forest Policy and People Participation*, Concept Publishing Company, New Delhi

Mohapatro, P.C. 2001. *An Investigation to Identify the Factors Contributing towards Dropping Out of Scheduled Tribe Boys in Borigumma Block of Koraput District*, COATS, Koraput.

Mohapatro, P.C. 1982. "Problems of Tribal Education in Koraput District", *Vision*, July-December, 1982, pp. 85-96.

Mohapatro, P.C. 2013. "Political Empowerment of Scheduled Tribes and the provisions of the Panchayats (Extension to Scheduled Areas) Act (PESA), 1996", *Tribal Studies :* A Journal of COATS, June, 2013.

Mohapatro, P.C. 1987. *Economic Development of Tribal India*, Ashish Publishing House, New Delhi.

National Council of Applied Economic Research, New Delhi. 1961. *An Appraisal Report on Tribal Areas* (Techno Economic Survey of Orissa)-September 1961 (Mimiographed pp. 44-45).

Ota, A.B. & Anita Agnihotri. 1996. *Involuntary Displacement in Dam Project*, Prachi Prakashan, New Delhi.

Patnaik, Nityananda. *Primitive Tribes of Orissa and their Development Strategies.*

Pitroda, Sam. 2006. *National Knowledge Commission*, Government of India.

Planning Commission, Government of India, New Delhi. 2003. *Tenth Five Year Plan 2002-2007*, Volume-II, Sectoral Politics and Programme.

Planning Commission, Government of India, New Delhi. 2003. *Tenth Five Year Plan 2002-2007*, Volume II, Sectoral Policies and Programme.

Pradhan, Gopinath. 2009. *Didayi : The Primitive Tribe Livelihood and Participation in Panchayati Raj Institutions*, COATS, Hindusthan Offset Press, Jeypore.

Pradhan, N. & J.K. Pattanaik. 2011. "Challenges of Education of Scheduled Caste and Scheduled Tribe Children : A Case Study of an Ashram School". *The Revenshaw Journal of Education Studies*, Vol. I, Issue I.

Pradhan, N. 2001. "Factors Contributing to Dropouts amongst the Tribal Girls in Nandapur Block, Odisha – A DPEP, SSA, Sponsored Study", PG Department of Education, Koraput.

ST & SC Development Department. 2006. *Annual Report on the Administration of Scheduled Areas in Orissa for 2002-03*, Government of Orissa.

ST & SC Development Department. 2011-12. *Annual Report*, Government of Orissa.

ST & SC Development Department. 2013-14. *Annual Report*, Government of Orissa.

T & RW Department Orissa. 1976. Report of the Review Committee on the Working of the OSTDCS Ltd., Government of Orissa, 1976, p. 5.

Tribal Research Bureau. 1972. "Evaluation of Ashram Schools", *Adivasi*, Vol. XIII, Nos. 3 & 4.

Tribal Research Bureau, Orissa. 1971-72. "Evaluation of the Grain gola of the T & R.W. Department", *Adivasi*, Vol. XIII, 1971-72, Orissa, Government Press, 1972, pp. 11 to 18.

Tripathy, B. 1973. A Portrait of Population of Orissa, Census of India, 1971, Controller of Publication, Delhi.

V. Elwin. 1960. Report of the Committee on Special Multipurpose Tribal Development Blocks, Government of India, Delhi.

Verma, R.C. 2000. *Indian Tribes Through the Ages*, Publication Division, Ministry of Information and Broadcasting, Government of India.

Vidyarthi, L.P. & Rai, B.K. 1976. *The Tribal Culture of India*, Concept Publishing Co., New Delhi.

Index